SELF-LOVE AND CODEPENDENCY

4 Books in 1: Self-Love Workbook for Women, Resilience to Cure Codependency, Narcissistic Abuse, Anxiety in Relationship

Beverly Reyes

liable for any hardship or damages that may befall them after undertaking information described herein.

Additionally, the information in the following pages is intended only for informational purposes and should thus be thought of as universal. As befitting its nature, it is presented without assurance regarding its prolonged validity or interim quality. Trademarks that are mentioned are done without written consent and can in no way be considered an endorsement from the trademark holder.

Table of Contents

RESILIENCE TO CURE CODEPENDENCY

NARCISSISTIC ABUSE

ANXIETY IN RELATIONSHIP

SELF-LOVE WORKBOOK FOR WOMEN

A Life-Changing Guide to Learn how to Say No, Take Care of your Body, and Change your Mind. Discover the Powerful Methods Used by Successful, Famous Women

Introduction

We all feel down in our lives every once in a while. We do everything we can to make ourselves feel happy and comfortable with our lives. But even with all that, it is still a challenge to try and make our lives as great as they could be.

It is a necessity for all of us to think about the things we can for improving our lives and making them feel stronger and better. This guide is all about helping you to understand what you can do to give your life a greater sense of purpose.

It is especially critical for you to look into what you can do to restore your life and give your self-esteem the boost it needs. When you feel better about yourself, your life becomes a little easier. You will not try and make things all the more challenging than they have to be. You will certainly feel confident about who you are without dragging yourself down any paths that might be harmful or dangerous.

Your emotions will also be easier to control when you have the self-esteem you require. You will not feel as though you are letting yourself or other people down.

It will be easier for you to have better relationships with other people as well. The general public prefers individuals who feel positive about themselves. They want those who are ready to do anything and are not afraid of themselves.

More importantly, you will feel happier about yourself when you have enough self-esteem in your life. There is no reason why you should feel upset with your life. As you are improving upon your attitude for life, you will find that it is not all that hard for you to get the most out of your everyday experience.

Avoiding Comparisons

One of the greatest reasons why so many people struggle with their lives is because they are constantly trying to compare themselves with others. Some like to compare themselves because they want to think that they are as good as others.

It is natural for all of us to compare ourselves to other people. We all have our own heroes or idols that we love to follow. But sometimes we get far too caught up in those things. We start to think far too much about people and what they are like.

We all like to compare ourselves with all of these people because we think they are all better than us and appealing in some way.

But when we do this, we struggle to look at the big picture.

It only takes a few thoughts or observations of other people to start getting the wrong idea over what can be done in life to make it stand out.

But the truth is that you cannot compare yourself to other people all the time. Think about it for a moment. Let us say that you like to play baseball. You want to try and build your skills up to where you can be the next big-name baseball player.

But no matter what you do, you might struggle to be a big star. You might try and work yourself to death just to try and make it onto a particular team.

It can be difficult to think about how you are not as good as baseball as other people are. That does not mean that you should be comparing yourself all the time.

Not everyone who plays baseball can hit a ball as hard as Aaron Judge. Most certainly cannot throw a ball as fast as Max Scherzer can. They might not be able to make the smartest managerial decisions like Mike Matheny or Joe Madden could.

More importantly, you will feel as though you are not willing to let yourself be who you truly are if you compare yourself to others all the time.

You will not feel all that comfortable with who you are in general when you keep on comparing yourself with others in some way.

Simply put, you have to stop comparing yourself to other people all the time. Everyone has their strengths. You just need to think about yours.

Look at Your Strengths

When you work to improve your life, you have to think about your strengths. Look at what you do for a living and think about how you might excel in certain things.

Everyone has skills that make them great at something. Some people might be talented writers who have a way with words. Others can fix up all sorts of vehicles.

Look at the strengths you have and see what you can do to build upon them or to use them to your advantage. If you are good with cars, then maybe you could consider working at a vehicle repair shop. Maybe you could go to a technical education program to learn how to work with commercial vehicles or high-end vehicles from Maserati or Ferrari, among others. The potential for you to go far with your skills is endless when you know what you are great at or when you build upon those abilities.

Think about those strengths that you have in your life and see what you can do to move forward with them. You might be surprised when you think about what you are good at and work on those things in particular.

As you look at those strengths, you will be free to be who you truly are. You will not be limited to trying to be like someone you are not. Instead, you are blazing your trail as you stick with those positives. It makes your life all the more worthwhile when considered right.

Focus on Being Good Enough

You should not assume that you have to be perfect in everything you do in your life. Perfection is something that no one can ever truly accomplish.

Rather, you should think about being good enough for whatever it is you are doing. Look at how you are working on your goals and how you are moving closer to completing them.

For instance, you might have a desire to be a car technician. You could study at a vocational school and complete your tests to be certified. After this, you would find a great job with a quality repair shop or another place that could use your services.

Do not think that you have to be perfect in every aspect of your work. Instead, think more about what you can do to pass your exams. Look at how you are going to work on different vehicles at the start of your career.

You have to think less about perfection and more about what is coming in the here and now. When you complete your exams and find a job, you will see that you truly are good enough to be where you want to be.

Of course, you can use this as a steppingstone to a much greater objective like working for a distinct group or taking care of unique cars that might be a little fancier. But whatever the case is, everything you do must be done gradually without forcing yourself into situations that might be too tough to get into.

Keeping your life organized and in check can truly be helpful. Be certain when looking at your life that you think carefully about how well you are not likely to lose control of it all.

Avoid thinking that everything has to work as well as possible. Focus more on being positive with your life while looking at what you could do to move forward in any manner.

More importantly, avoiding perfection is critical in that reality can get in the way of this concept. You might think you have to do things in a certain way, but in reality, you would end up having problems happen that cause you to think bad things.

As you stick with a better mindset, you will find that your life is indeed worthwhile. You will not be a slave to your own mind as you start to get on your way to happiness. More importantly, you will not feel as though you cannot go anywhere in your life.

Be ready to think for yourself. It makes a world of difference when you see what makes your life stand out and powerful.

Chapter 1: How Famous Women Who Have Had Disadvantages in Their Lives Have Managed to Overcome Obstacles! What Principles Did They Use?

According to Emma Watson, self-care is all about self-love. Most of us find it very hard to love and accept our own self. I want you to understand that you can never truly love and accept another person without loving and accepting yourself first.

If you do not agree with this, then think about it again. Is there someone in your life whom you love immensely? How do you feel about them? Do you like everything about them or do you feel that they would be perfect if only some things would change? Most likely, you want to change some things about them even though you know that they will most likely never change (at least, not until they decide to change which is something you have very little control over).

The sun does not compare itself with the moon, a rose does not compare itself with a marigold, a skylark does not compare itself with a nightingale. There is room enough for all of us to be amazing without stepping on each other's shoes.

Let the inner love flow towards your own heart. After that, you will have ample compassion to offer to others. Your example will inspire others to love and accept their own self. You will be a beacon of love and beauty in this world. Hence, be gentle and compassionate towards yourself. You are your own greatest responsibility.

Deepen Your Relationship with Yourself

Which is the most important relationship in the world?

Whether you currently realize this or not – the most important relationship in the world is the one that you have with your own Self. How you relate with your own Self sets the ground for how others relate to you.

The outer world is only a mirror to your inner reality. The relationships you have with other people are, in some way, a reflection of the relationship you have with yourself.

Do you like yourself? Do you love yourself unconditionally? Do you see the good in yourself? Or do you constantly beat yourself up for the flaws that you think you possess?

I have said it before, and I will say it again. Accepting and loving yourself unconditionally is the very foundation of a life of self-care.

Even if no one has said this to you yet – I am going to say this to you today, and you better start believing it! You are beautiful, you are amazing, you are gorgeous – you deserve the best that life has to offer. There never was, never has been, and never will be another one exactly like you in this world or in any other. You must reclaim your power and your gifts from the Universe by acknowledging the limitlessness of your soul and the inherent beauty of your individuality.

Get past the scarcity mindset by ceasing to compare yourself with others. You can only be the protagonist of your own story and your story is just as unique as you are. When you compare yourself with others you fail to realize that your only competition is with your own self. As long as you are striving to constantly grow and become a better person than who you were yesterday, you are living the true potential of your soul.

There is room enough for all of us to be gorgeous, amazing, and superbly brilliant. Which flower ever craves to be like another one? Yet, each flower is so incredibly beautiful in its own unique way. If you go to any natural place, you will realize that nature is all about harmony and co-existence. The wind is not competing with the water. The sun is not competing with the moon. The forest is not competing with the desert.

Nature has so many varieties, yet every element present in it is unique and beautiful in its own way. There is no competition. Human beings are also meant to be the same way. Each of us is a diamond shining with its own distinctive luster and brightness.

From now on, put a full stop on all comparisons, and start relishing your own individuality. There just cannot be another you.

Never forget that the secret to stop comparing yourself with others is to love and accept yourself unconditionally. The more you are in love with yourself, the less chances there will be of you wanting to compare yourself with anyone else.

We are usually very hard on ourselves. If only we could see ourselves from the eyes of those who love and admire us, it would not be so difficult to accept our own inherent perfection.

No matter what you believe about yourself, trust me you are a far more amazing person than you think you are.

Spend Time with Yourself & Reward Yourself

How easy or hard has been for you to love and accept yourself unconditionally so far? If you are like most people, then this has likely not been an easy journey for you. You might be struggling with crippling self-doubt, constant self-abnegation, and instant self-criticism.

I just want to tell you that no matter where you are in your journey right now, things ARE GOING TO START LOOKING UP if you only persist with this course and continue doing what you must do to get to your goal of effortless self-care and boundless self-love.

Now, let me ask you something: What do you do when you are in love with someone?

You give them all your attention and spend as much time as you possibly can with them. Isn't it?

Have you been spending any time with yourself without constantly looking for distractions so that you do not have to face the voice within your own head? Today I want to urge you to spend time with yourself. Dare to be alone with no one but your own self for company. No matter how uncomfortable this makes you, I want you to do it and I want you to start from today. Also remember that growth starts at the end of our comfort zone. Greatness is not achieved by living a comfortable life – it is achieved by constantly moving out of our comfort zone to face new challenges that compel us to raise our standards and hold up our own self to a new much higher one.

Celebrate Yourself

You become the person that you believe you are. If you believe you are smart and beautiful, that is what you will eventually become. If you believe you are a loser who cannot do anything right, then that is the reality you will create for yourself. And by believing, I do not mean what you think of yourself or try to think of yourself in your conscious mind. I mean what you truly believe to be true for yourself within your subconscious mind.

The people around you simply mirror your own beliefs about yourself. You are constantly emitting thought vibrations about what you believe to be true for yourself. Any person who comes in contact with your aura picks up these vibrations and starts treating you the way you think you deserve to be treated.

Have you ever noticed how on those days when you look in the mirror and say, "I'm looking very good today," you end up receiving a lot of compliments? Then, there are those days when you look in the mirror and say, "I look awful. I'm a total

14

mess." On that day, it seems like every other person is reaffirming this idea to you.

Eliminate Clutter and Create an Inspiring Space

Clutter not only affects the aesthetics of your outer environment but also the beauty of your inner space. Just try meditating in a room that has dirty laundry strewn around and you will know what I mean. It will not be too far-fetched to say that your environment is your mind. You just cannot think clearly enough as long as you have untidiness surrounding you.

This week, I would like you to eliminate clutter from your life. Eventually, I want you to work on both your inner and your outer environment. To get started, we will focus on the outer clutter.

I would suggest that you start identifying what is truly important to you. Begin the decluttering process by removing everything that you do not use anymore or that is broken and non-functional.

Say YES to Life!

We all have these things that we keep putting off for 'someday.' Someday we would wear our favorite dress, join the ballet class, learn piano, take out that fine China for dinner and what not. Yet the only time we have is this present moment.

A lot of people reach the end of their earthly life feeling like they never got a chance to be truly alive. There is nothing worse than regret. Tomorrow you will regret everything you did not do today. Also, when you constantly put off living until tomorrow, you never end up fully appreciating all the gifts that you have today.

In order to completely embrace life and make the most of it in the here and now, you must show up at your best. Wear your best clothes, use your fine china for meals, do what you really want to do on a daily basis as if today was the last day of your life (because one day you are going to be right about it). When death comes, most people do not regret the mistakes they made as much as they regret the time that they lost which they could have spent in being truly alive.

Learning to Say NO

Just like saying 'Yes' to life is important, saying 'NO' at the right time and place is equally important. A lot of times we say 'yes' to the wrong things for the wrong reasons. Usually, this happens when we do not want to disappoint the other person. We make a compromise with our own wishes and say yes to something that does not feel good to our heart.

The problem with this is that even though you end up looking good to the other person, you are letting your own self down. You are bound to feel resentful and also angry (most likely) towards yourself and towards that person.

It is very important to know who you are as a person, what your values are, what you are okay with, and what you are not okay with. This will help you set powerful boundaries. Not having boundaries will constantly make you feel as if you are being pushed in different directions by other people. Taking a firm stand for yourself is necessary for living a happy and fulfilling life.

Chapter 2: The Equation of Self-Love. What Are the Principles That Make Us Love Ourselves?

Self-Compassion & Your Emotions

Why We Feel What We Feel

EMOTIONS ARE UNIVERSAL. We are all born equipped to feel a range of emotional experiences, from the elation of joy to the hopelessness of despair. Emotions bring color and intensity to our everyday experiences, and if we pay attention, they can provide us with important information on how we are experiencing things moment to moment. Our strongest emotions—like love—can give our lives meaning and purpose. However, emotions can also be challenging and, at times, quite painful. All too often we fall into the habit of judging ourselves for having certain feelings, such as fear or vulnerability. It is also common to try to avoid unpleasant feelings, and in so doing, we cause ourselves even more pain.

Emotions serve an important purpose in that they help us interpret our experiences and successfully navigate the world. Anxiety, happiness, and excitement can highlight and guide us toward what matters and also let us know if a given situation or interaction is going well or not. Do we feel confident? Threatened? Bored? Anxious? When we tune in to our emotions, we find a wealth of crucial information.

We have many different types of emotions that function to help us in different ways. For example, we experience:

→Emotions that signal threat or danger: anger, fear, or disgust.

→Emotions that alert us to losses or disappointments: sadness, remorse, or grief.

→Emotions that show us things we like, or want to achieve or acquire excitement, desire, anticipation, and joy.

→Emotions that help us feel soothed, safe, and connected: contentment and calm.

We also can and often do experience more than one emotion in any given moment. A single event or experience can bring up a range of emotions, which sometimes makes understanding and responding to our emotions challenging. For instance, going on a first date might cause a mixture of happiness and anxiety, while making a mistake at work might evoke anxiety, anger, and possibly even sadness. Each evoked emotion comes with different sensations, thoughts, and motivations. When we experience a mix of emotions, it can sometimes feel like they are pulling us in different directions.

If we can learn to approach our emotions with self-compassionate awareness and understanding, we are more likely to be able to experience our emotions without being ruled by them. Self-compassionate approaches to emotions allow us to accept, understand, and respond to our emotional experiences in a helpful way. This can prevent our feelings from randomly taking over our actions and essentially running our lives.

Getting Centered

To prepare for engaging with your emotions, you will begin with a primary practice that lays the foundation for much mind-body work: centering rhythmic breathing. Variations of this practice are used in many forms of compassion training, from ancient yogic meditations, to Tibetan Buddhist visualizations, to modern psychotherapy techniques. In fact, rhythmic breathing exercise is a foundational practice in Compassion Focused Therapy, a type of therapy developed by Paul Gilbert. This initial exercise in training the mind in compassion is directly related to cultivating self-compassionate awareness and attention and will be the first step on your path to self-compassion. The aim here is to learn to center your awareness, slowing down your mind and body. This frees you to focus your attention on accessing compassionate awareness. From this grounding in mindful compassion, you can truly pay attention to what is going on here and now.

CENTERING RHYTHMIC BREATHING

Find a comfortable and quiet place to sit. Sit upright, with a straight but relaxed spine, so you can breathe comfortably and deeply. Feel free to adjust your posture at any time to remain in a comfortable and open position throughout this practice.

Allow your eyes to close and bring your awareness to your breath. Let your attention gently rest on each inhalation and exhalation. Notice the gentle rise of your chest or belly when breathing in. Notice the gentle fall of your chest or belly as you breathe out. Feel yourself letting go. Simply allow yourself to notice the sensations of breathing.

Your mind will wander. It is what minds do. When you notice this happening, gently bring your awareness back to your experience of breathing.

With your next inhalation, see if you can allow your breath to gradually slow, extending the in-breath and allowing it to be slower, deeper, and longer. As much as you can, breathe slowly, smoothly, and evenly. Feel the in-breath for a count of four to five seconds, hold for a moment, and release the out-breath for four to five seconds. Take a few moments to experiment to find a pace that feels right.

Stay with the even, slow rhythm. Focusing on the full experience of the slow, even in-breath and slow, even out-breath, rest your awareness in the act of breathing, holding yourself in kindness, for a few moments longer.

Before you open your eyes, give yourself some credit for taking time to practice caring for yourself in this way. Next, expand your awareness, feeling your feet on the floor, your weight supported by the chair or ground, your open posture. When you are ready, at your own pace, open your eyes, exhaling and letting go of this practice.

Self-Compassion & Your Body

OUR EXPERIENCES OF THE WORLD AROUND US and the way our bodies feel are closely connected. However, because we are not always consciously aware of how we feel physically, we can easily overlook how much the state of our bodies influences things like our mood, motivation level, and the lens through which we perceive what is happening to us. Too often, instead of being nurtured, our bodies are ignored, neglected, or wind up being the focus of self-criticism. Increasing self-compassion also involves learning to cultivate awareness and paying better attention to our physical selves. Compassionate understanding of the impact your physical experience has on your life can lead to a new appreciation of your body, its rhythms, and its needs. Self-compassionate motivation and action can help you find ways to be more helpful and kind to the body that works so hard for you every day.

Noticing Your Bodily Experiences

Awareness and attention are the first steps in bringing self-compassion to your body. A good way to begin is by paying attention to how your body is feeling here and now, and how you might be responding to those feelings. Just like you practiced with your emotions, you will learn to notice and attend to how your body is functioning, your posture, your physical feelings, and the experiences of your senses. With this next exercise, I invite you to take a few moments to check in with how your body is feeling right now.

NOTICING PHYSICAL SENSATIONS & EXPERIENCES

Close your eyes and take a few slow, even breaths, or engage in centering rhythmic breathing. After you have centered your attention with your breath, bring your focus to your body. Take a brief inventory. What do you notice about your body temperature? What do you notice about your muscle tension? Do you notice any sensations of touch? Hearing? Smell? Simply allow yourself to note any and all felt experiences of your body, here and now.

When you are ready, open your eyes and get your notebook. It is time to write down some of your observations and reflections, using the following questions to guide you:

→Body temperature: Are you warm, hot, cold, or cool? If so, where do you notice this?

→Muscles: Are you tense or tight? Are you relaxed? If so, where do you notice this?

→Other sensations: What else are you feeling in your body? Is there any tingling? Numbness? Something else?

→Additional senses: Do you hear anything? Smell anything? What about taste?

In this exercise, you may have noticed some judgmental thoughts or criticisms of your body. The new self-compassion skills you are learning are not easy, but they are even more challenging if you are judging yourself. Self-compassion helps us become more aware of our physical experiences without judging them. Once we are more able to tune in to how our bodies are feeling with compassionate awareness and attention, we can determine how to take good care of ourselves. Next, we will look at the different ways you might be judging your body and find alternative responses to your bodily experiences.

How Are You Judging Your Body?

Many of us treat our bodies as rivals rather than allies. We view the physical sensations and bodily functioning as a source of constant dissatisfaction or disappointment, and the subject of our criticism and judgment. Struggling against unwanted sensations or focusing on how our bodies do not look or perform the way we want them to, leads to unnecessary distress.

Taking a judgmental approach toward our bodies can lead to shame and self-criticism, as well as problematic behaviors like avoidance, denial, or attempts to control our bodies in unhelpful ways like excessive dieting. While we cannot—and should not—avoid or deny the fact that we will not always like our bodily experiences, we can learn to respond in kinder ways. As you cultivate compassion for your body, you will be better equipped to respond more effectively to discomfort or distress.

Chapter 3: Why Be Inspired by Women Who Have Achieved Success with A Touch of Selfishness?

According to Emma Watson being selfish with your time and effort does not make you a bad person. Sometimes these actions protect us from the danger that is out there and for people that could use us for their own benefit.

We have to learn to say no when we actually want to say no, compromising is sometimes not needed because it makes us slaves for other people, and we forget that we need to take care of ourselves too.

When we become selfish with our time most people feel like we are anti-social but actually we are doing that to take care of ourselves. We have to learn not to be always there when wanted. Learn to be unavailable and try not to please everyone because you cannot.

How about you please yourself? How about you become selfish with your time because you also need to spend time with yourself?

It is just like effort, we keep doing stuff for people, but they do not return the favor, how about you start being selfish with your effort? How about you start pulling back and fading in the background with your efforts? Some will look at that in a bad way, remember you are doing this for yourself and not for anyone out there.

Learn to say I cannot make it when you actually cannot make it. Do not force yourself to be in environments that are not conducive for you or where you do not feel welcome. Sometimes you will be forcing yourself to fit in. It will take a lot from you; you will feel like you are disappointing everyone else, but the end results will be great. You will be happy because you are taking time to teach people that you are not always going to be there, we also need to be there for ourselves.

When people miss having you around, they start questioning if they did anything wrong sometimes, they evaluate your friendships or your relationships and they start treating you differently, it is ok the phase will pass. You will have to be ready for it and know you do not need excuses. You can be honest and tell people that you are working on yourself. Those who will pull out of the relationship you have with them were always going to go because true friends support each other. Always

Gratitude

At the end of it all we have to be thankful and show appreciation. Gratitude can change your life completely and you realize you have been so uptight, and you need to loosen up and gratitude will help you do that.

Gratitude on its own can build a person because a lot is learnt. Being nice and you look at things in a totally different way.

Start a habit of starting your mornings with words of gratitude, if you have a book or a journal every morning jot down what you're grateful for, if it's something that was done by someone, or you're just grateful for Life. You can be grateful for the family that you have or grateful for the job that you have, just write it down so that it can be a reminder that you have always said thank you when it matters.

Gratitude makes us appreciate even little things we never paid attention to and we should know that gratitude carries so much power because our emotions relate to feeling thankful and being appreciated. You are becoming a very nice person because of gratitude; you look at the things you have and be grateful that someone out there does not have them, but you are there with everything that is around you.

Even when you wake up in the morning, being grateful that you saw another dawn, a new day and someone out they did not wake up and the family is mourning. Gratitude is important but we forget it a lot during our lifetime until we go through something and it is not supposed to be like that.

Gratitude should become part of your personality trait, mood, and emotions because that is going to be a beautiful radiance of love connection with the world because gratitude can change your mentally.

Most people are not aware that being thankful can actually make one a happy person like I said it changes a person completely. Things that did not matter start being important. Those times of waking up and having little complaints than usual go away and that is what gratitude does.

Benefits of gratitude are a lot but, in this book, I just want to focus much on self-introspection like asking yourself if you have been more thankful and grateful or you have been focusing more on the negativity of life. That is when we lose it, when negativity takes over, we lose a lot of thankfulness. We start seeing everything in a negative way even when people smile at us.

Gratitude can change that, clearly you can be happy that at least in a day someone smiled at you, with so many people walking around with serious faces someone smiled at you. Gratitude encourages development of patience and humility and wisdom to the fact that now you start being positive and you are doing things differently. You start appreciating life, you become patient because impatience is one of the most negative things that you can keep around with you. Impatience can make you miss opportunities by a minute.

Humility is underrated but as much as we express it in the world and also appreciate things, people start looking at us differently when we express such humility, we carry a lot of greatness. It covers us with greatness because people start looking at us in a different way and they start seeing a different person who appreciates life and humility is also brought by being grateful.

Gratitude has been used as guidance for some people who have gone through stuff. Sometimes they are asked questions that have to do with gratitude so that they realize that even when they are going through troubles there are things, they can be grateful for.

 Right now, you have access to a book like this one that can help you, someone out there is going through a lot fighting demons by themselves and they have no one not even a material to read but here you are, reading this guide.

It is one of the things to be thankful for, you have access to tools that can help you be a better person.

Gratitude carries value that is meant to connect people with each other in a nicer way, gratitude makes you become light and life lightens up the burdens that you have carried.

You offload most of the things because you become optimistic, you are thankful for what you have, and you know tomorrow you will be thankful for beating the demos that you are fighting.

You can make gratitude a tendency because it changes things, when you make it a tendency it becomes easy, it does not become forced or you don't seek it you don't even have to remind yourself that you have to be grateful. It comes naturally even when you do your morning prayers or devotions you realize that when you start with a gratitude everything flows easily.

Even people that have done things for us and we show the sign of gratitude and we are thankful we can still go back to them and ask for help and they will always help us not because we gave them anything but because we were thankful and grateful.

So now this is the great weapon that you carry, gratitude makes you happier to be honest. Being thankful makes everyone happier, I believe so because you carry so much happiness that comes with humility. With things that are happening in your life like being late at work, sometimes when you get there you realize that no one has come but all the way you were angry with yourself because the bus left you but again you have to be grateful that you made it to work.

Chapter 4: Why in Some Circumstances Do We Have to Put Ourselves Before Everything Else First?

LOVE YOURSELF, BEFORE YOU LOVE ANOTHER

Self-love is a source of goodwill and respect. If these feelings are not enough, the relationship becomes authoritarian or is built on the type of "victim - persecutor".

Psychologists agree on one thing: self-love is an essential thing necessary in order to love other people too, and the whole world, and generally feel comfortable.

First of all, it is good for your health. Self-love is the most reliable vaccine against all sorts of psychosomatic diseases and stress prevention. One who does not love himself first uses, and then destroys the confidence of the partner. "The supplier of love" becomes embarrassed, he begins to doubt and eventually gets tired of proving his feelings. The mission is impossible: one cannot give to another that which he can give himself only, love of himself. One who does not love himself often unconsciously calls into question the feelings of another: So, he's worse than me!" The lack of self-love can also take the form of almost manic devotion, obsession with love.

Importance of self-love

Still, to see, understand, and love another, you need to understand and love yourself: Who Am I? What am I? How do I? If you learn to respond to your pain, joy, your desires, then you can respond to the feelings of another person close to you.

How to understand that it is time to transform your attitude

Consider yourself a failure? Do you think that there is nothing attractive about the opposite sex in you? All these thoughts are reflected not only on your face but also in your behavior, in your daily communication with friends, colleagues, relatives.

If a person suffers for some time in contact with others and suffers, if he does not like his own life, then it is worth thinking. But it is hardly worth it to "change yourself," but opening up yourself to the present and falling in love over again with yourself is real.

This understanding comes to different people in diverse ways. And it is all hinge on the person himself. If he thinks about why he is not valued, respected, or why someone is constantly manipulating him, then these are visible signs of dislike for himself. And you may have to do something about it.

It is time to care for ourselves, as a rule, reminds us of a state of depression when your own "I" is in the shadow of the "object" in a passive position. When there is no faith in ourselves, when we think that something good can only be thanks to the efforts of other people, and not our own. Also, the criterion that you require to heed to self-love is the absence of close and emotionally warm, stable love relationships. A person who loves himself, and not suffering from selfishness, always find a steady and fulfilling relationship, where he is loved.

Learning to love yourself

What to do, how to go about caring yourself with all the shortcomings?" - we asked psychologists. And how practically, successfully should our love for ourselves be revealed?

You can assume that you are a moms and dad to yourself. And study how to love yourself from this position - discover to feel your requirements and desires, accept errors as an experience, give yourself support, and so on. But better than dealing with a psychologist, it is not likely that you or anybody alone can do it yourself. I feel, authorize, offer myself support, look after myself, cultivate myself, do not permit the usage, and so on" - she recommends taking this mindset as a basis.

Self-love techniques

Set objectives, albeit little ones, but be sure to attain them! And whenever you reach, applaud yourself and value you for your determination, for your work, for your efforts. Appreciation influences. Avoid popular slogans like "well done."

Bear in mind that even effective business owners and acknowledged beauties-models are not without complexes. Take a little book or a paper and split it into two columns or sides. Compose your strengths on the right, on the left - what you wish to alter in yourself. If you attempt to be objective,

You will comprehend that really, there are no fewer positive qualities in you than reasons for dissatisfaction with yourself and cultivating complexes.

Self-love should, to start with, be revealed in caring for yourself. About his health, about his appearance, about the complete satisfaction of his own, and not somebody else's desires. In the necessary observance of details health - you needless to fill your brains with all sorts of negativity. Self-love is the capability to develop convenience around you - both psychological and physical.

There are individuals for whom looking after kids, family, and other individuals comprises the meaning of life. Do they have to find out to enjoy themselves more?

And it cannot truly successfully care for other people who forget about themselves. And therefore, he teaches his close ones how not to enjoy oneself. When an individual with super care takes children into a life, he is left without meaning.

Excessive care for other acts as a desire to affirm one's value, not to feel in requirement of care, but to feel strong and positive. I cannot care for myself, due to the fact that I feel shame, guilt, vulnerability ... Then I put my "child" part in another person and care for him as myself, while I can likewise permit myself to feel crucial, necessary, and almighty.

How self-love differs from selfishness

How to comprehend where the border lies, does not self-love mean common egoism? Psychologists plainly share these concepts. Selfishness is behavior that is totally determined by the idea of one's own advantage, advantage when a private puts his interests above the well-beings of others. A man who loves himself will never ever consider himself superior to others. He understands his value, respectively, understands that everyone is as important as he is. He will treat others around him with respect and love.

Preferably, when an individual really loves himself, he generously provides it to others from the excess of love inside himself.

And if one is selfish, then his love for himself will be selfish. Strictly speaking, it is more correct to talk here not about love for oneself, but about falling for oneself. The charm of oneself, self-absorption, exaggeration of one's virtues are signs of falling for oneself, and such a love is really quite selfish. If a person thinks about others and cares about them, then his love for himself is not connected with egoism in any way, it is easy and natural for him to love both himself and others. The forces for this are quite enough. Anyone who loves himself for a while and naturally does not devote too much time to this, just as a well-maintained gardener does not require too much trouble. It is easy to care of oneself to a healthy and vigorous person. Did you wake up? She raised herself sweetheart with pleasure, washed herself beautiful, was glad for herself peppy - and there is no longer much need for herself to do anything else. Everything is already great, I already want to do something or someone else: prepare a delicious breakfast for we and home, kiss everyone and help get together. The reality, however, is that those who have become preoccupied with self-love, at least initially become more selfish - just because the main focus, in this case, begins to be on their beloved. Supplementing self-love with attention and care for others is perhaps not difficult, but it is a completely separate area of work. Love for others in itself from love for itself does not follow and does not follow. One of the mysteries of self-love is in this inner joy and in its simple formula, namely: heat, light, and energy. It is fine! But sometimes it is cold in your soul, and when you feel cold in your soul, you do not have love. If a person describes a picture of his inner world as - grey, well, some winter, some evening, maybe the lights went out, and there is no joy or energy in his voice - such a person lives without love. But how to give birth and maintain light and warmth in your soul? What needs to be done for this?

People often think that self-love consists in satisfying their simplest needs with pleasure, forgetting about duties and other people. Allow yourself to explore and do what you want, allow yourself shopping, surround yourself with romance and give yourself gifts - an exciting program for a human child who does not intend to grow up. Can this be called love? It is possible, but the level of this love is the same as the love of a mother, in whom the child feeds mainly on candies and Coca-Cola, spending time mainly on computer games and other entertainments.

Strictly speaking, it is even hard to call needs. These are the desires and whims that spoiled children insist on. And the most essential thing is that they give joy, not for long, only while it is new and while others are jealous of it. After some time, everything becomes boring, the joy leaves. Sometimes a girl seemed to give herself everything: slept, watered, fed herself, and arranged for herself shopping - but inside everything is bad.

Sadly. The world is gray, and the girl is still nibbling herself for something. Does she love herself? No. It turns out that a woman is interested in shopping just because she is ill with herself. And if a woman is in some kind of insult to life, she can arrange a shopping for herself, and then she looks at these things, but there is no joy. In itself, satisfying needs is not self-love, and far from always, it ends with inner joy, light, and warmth. You will not fill yourself seriously with any purchases; this is just some trick. As a temporary measure, as a substitute for self-love - this is possible, but you should not believe the TV, this is not the joy of life, and this is not self-love. This is a low-quality life, this life is not serious, and an intelligent man with such a woman will not speak for so long now about something good, good, real.

Satisfying one's needs is not yet self-love. Someone after this begins to love themselves, and someone does not. Satisfying one's needs is sometimes only a substitute for self-love when a person seems to be buying off gifts from the fact that he does not love himself. Of course, needs are different. If you really desire to move forward, develop, need to care for other people, need to be needed, or need to master any business with dignity, quality, then satisfying such needs, you will have more reasons to love yourself. You will have one thing to be proud of. If all needs come down to eat and entertain yourself with shopping or TV, then such a love of self is unlikely to be long-lasting, and one who turns into a pig is no longer a human being.

Chapter 5: How Famous Women Take Care of Their Bodies: How They Take Care of Themselves and What Their Routines Are?

According to Emma Watson, stretching before exercise routines that last anywhere from 15 to 20 minutes will allow you to easily perform the routine if you are running short on time. It does not matter how you prefer to exercise. However, we recommend getting started by using an evaluation method, or what we would like to call "the preparation phase."

You can consider the preparation phase, or prep phase if you like, as a warm-up session. You should use the prep phase to check how active each part of your body is.

There are three sections that these exercises focus on: the upper, middle, and the lower sections.

If you have already been exercising every day in your life until recently, then you might not have to try out the prep phase. You can still go through the phase in order to check your body's stamina and capabilities. But for those who are getting back into workouts after a break, however long that break may have been, or those who are exercising for the first time, we highly recommend that you go through the prep phase in order to evaluate your physical capabilities.

We ideally recommend performing the below preps on a mat if you have one. In the absence of a mat, you can still use the floor, but make sure that you are not feeling any discomfort from exercising on the floor.

Lower Body Prep

Place your back against the wall without bending forward too much. Now slide down the wall until your thighs are almost parallel to the floor. If you cannot move down far enough to attain this position, then try to slide down as much as possible.

Start the timer and hold the position for as long as you can.

• if you can hold the position for 90 seconds or more, then you can give yourself an excellent score.

• if you can hold the position for at least 60 seconds, but no more than 90 seconds, then you can give yourself a good score.

- if you can hold the position for at least 30 seconds, but no more than 60 seconds, then you can give yourself an average score.

- if you can hold the position for at less than 30 seconds, then you can give yourself a below-average score.

Final Result

Your score lets you know how much stamina and physical prowess you have. For example, with an excellent score, then you are likely in peak physical form. But do note that this prep was just for your lower body.

Middle Body Prep

This prep is fairly simple. You are going to perform as many crunches as you can. To do a successful crunch, lie down with your back to the floor. Fold your legs until they are making a rough 'A' shape. Place your hands behind your head. All you have to do is lift your shoulders off the mat or floor. Ideally, your shoulders should incline at approximately a 30-degree angle.

You need to do as many reps, or repetitions, as possible.

Each repetition consists of the following:

- Lift your shoulders off the mat (to the 30-degree mark).

- Bring the shoulders back down.

When you are ready, begin counting the reps.

- If you can perform 50 reps, then you can give yourself an excellent score.

- If you can perform anywhere from 35 reps to 49 reps, then you can give yourself a good score.

- If you can perform anywhere from 20 reps to 34 reps, then you can give yourself an average score.

- If you can perform fewer than 20 reps, then you can give yourself a below-average score.

Final Result

Once again, the final score lets you know just how much stamina and physical capability you have in the middle section of your body.

Upper Body Prep

For your upper body, you are going to perform a half push-up. How does that work?

To begin with, one of the complaints that many people give is they are quite unsure how to get into the perfect push-up position. This is understandable. There are so many recommendations from fitness health instructors that, often, people are left wondering what advice they should follow.

Here is what you need to remember:

• You should own the plank position. Ideally, you should be balancing on your toes curled inwards. Make sure you practice this, so you do not injure your toes while doing the push-up.

• You should start in the upright position, where you have pushed yourself away from the floor as far back as possible.

• Keep your body straight. We have seen people bend at the hips or the buttocks area and that is not the right way to do a push-up.

• Your arms should be below your shoulders, slightly apart.

Image: Your arms should be below your shoulders and not

below your abdomen, as some people like to assume.

So, what is a half-push up?

In a typical push-up, your knees are lifted off the ground. However, in a half push-up position, your knees are placed on the floor.

When you are ready, perform as many reps as possible. For a successful rep, push yourself close to the floor until your chest is just a few centimeters away from the floor (or mat, if you are using one). Then push yourself back into an upright position, back to the initial position.

● If you can perform 20 reps, then you can give yourself an excellent score.

- If you can perform anywhere from 15 reps to 19 reps, then you can give yourself a good score.

- If you can perform anywhere from 10 reps to 14 reps, then you can give yourself an average score.

- If you can perform fewer than 10 reps, then you can give yourself a below-average score.

Understanding Scores (And Why You Should Not Feel Dismayed)

We understand what it means when you can barely lift yourself on the 9th rep of your half push-up preparation. There is this sense of defeat. You feel as though you are weak and are probably not physically capable of going through any of the exercises mentioned in this book. Others might imagine that it is far easier to just give up and spend time in front of their PlayStation. At least through their video games, they have some sense of accomplishment, right?

Firstly, we want you to understand why the aforementioned preps were necessary. Picture this; you step into a gym and you spot some with beefy arms and chest that looks like it could deflect bullets. In fact, if Thanes (from the Marvel movies) snapped his fingers in front of this muscular behemoth in your gym, then chances are that the snap's effects would be nullified simply because of the pure testosterone running through each vein in the muscle man's body. This particular muscle man is easily going through 30 reps of weightlifting, each weight on the bar looks like it could be heavier than the average man. Motivated, you feel like you should at least aim for 30 reps of your exercise.

But that is the wrong way to go. Remember this rule when you are exercising it is not about how much you do, but how well you do it.

When you go through the preparations mentioned above, you understand the limitations of your body. Knowing such limitations helps you structure your workout plans. Remember that doing 20 pushups a day is wonderful. But it is okay if you can only do 5 in the beginning. When you keep repeating those 5 pushups every day, they eventually turn to 10 pushups, which turn to 15, and then you finally reach your goal of 20 pushups. The key point to remember is that you have to maintain consistency in your exercises. Set a time every day for the following workout routines. If you like, you can do all of them or choose one that fits your requirements and perform it every day.

Let us Start with Stretches - Warmups

Stretches are a great way to get the blood flowing and make you flexible. If you find yourself unable to cram a long workout routine into your day, then consider going through some of the stretches mentioned in this section. You are likely going to take just 15 to 20 minutes to go through them. However, you might require more time if you are still getting used to some of the positions.

Stretching is a form of exercise that anyone can master, given enough time. They do not have the challenges that other forms of exercises, such as weight training, have. But that does not mean that you do not have to pay proper attention to how you do them.

An important point to be made here is that stretching also helps you align your posture. Our bodies are remarkable constructs. They are capable of getting used to practically any situation, molding themselves to seek comfort even in uncomfortable situations. When you are bent over your desk, your body in a stooping position, then your body is slowly trying to get used to it. Which is why, the problem is not the body attempting to get used to new positions – it usually does – but whether it actually becomes used to that position – in which case the position becomes a permanent fixture in your life.

Stretching helps your body to remove those fixtures and gain more fluidity in its movements.

Let us start with a simple warmup stretch.

The Knot

- Stand up with your back straight, your feet slightly apart and your arms by your side.

- Your feet should be at shoulder-width; ensure that the bottom of your feet have maximum contact with the floor.

- Tighten your leg muscles. This step might take a few tries to get used to, but it should feel as though your muscles have contracted inwards.

- Take a deep breath and when you exhale, raise your arms to the sides at shoulder height. Your palms should be facing forward.

- Inhale and as you take breath into your lungs, raise your hands above your head. Clasp your fingers and then exhale. Your hands should look like they are making an 'o' shape. You will not be able to make an exact 'o' shape, but that is okay. As long as you get the gist of the position right, where your arms have to be curved inwards and joined together on top of your head, then you are doing it right.

- Your elbows should be pointing in opposite directions. When they are, pull your hands. It will feel as though you are playing tug-of-war with your fingers.

- Inhale before you pull your hands, stretch as much as you can for about six seconds.

- Exhale and then relax your hands. Do this a couple of times.

Chapter 6: Do Famous Women Also Have Low Self-Esteem? How They Managed to Defeat Their Fears and Improve Their Self-Esteem?

What is the value of self-esteem?

According to Emma Watson: "Your self-esteem is probably the most important part of your character. This precedes and affects your success in almost everything you do. Your level of self-esteem is really your degree of mental fitness. You should be in a constant state of self-esteem if you want to succeed at the highest and feel great about yourself." Self-esteem should allow the individual to be more confident and more successful in achieving their goals. Individuals with low self-esteem usually feel inadequate and under different circumstances may not perform well. They formed inaccurate feelings that they are not welcomed or appreciated by anyone. Those with a healthy self-esteem, on the other side, will feel good about their life and then about themselves. They can and do things more efficiently; they can feel proud of their achievements and of themselves.

We will be able to enjoy life more and more by feeling good about ourselves. Feeling that we are welcomed, valued, and respected implies that we have a healthy self-esteem, and that feeling will be mirrored in our ties.

Low self-esteem is one of the main causes of broken relationships.

Developing self-esteem helps us in our lives to welcome joy. That sensation makes you believe you deserve happiness. This faith, the belief that you really ought to be happy and fulfilled, is very important to understand, because with this conviction you will treat people with respect and kindness, while preferring rich interpersonal relationships and preventing destructive ones. Too no self-consciousness may cause people to become unhappy, fall short of their ability, or accept abusive situations and relationships. Several findings indicate that low self-esteem contributes to stress, depression, and anxiety. Research shows a positive relationship between healthy self-esteem and many positive outcomes, including satisfaction, modesty, endurance, and confidence. In almost everything you do; self-esteem plays a role.

A healthy self-esteem helps you to embrace yourself as it is meant to be and appreciate life.

Could you create a healthy self-esteem? The fact is, there is hardly any positive self-esteem. According to a study published by the American Psychological Association, self-esteem is the lowest in young adults, but rises during puberty and peaks at age 60, just before decreasing again. Participants in the survey assessed 3,617 U.S. adults ' self-esteem. In average, during most adulthood, women had lower self-esteem than males, but self-esteem rates converged as men and women entered their 80s and 90s. During young adulthood and middle age, blacks and whites have equal levels of self-esteem. The lead author of the study, Ulrich Orth, PhD, said: "Self-esteem is linked to better health, reduced criminal behavior, lower levels of depression and, ultimately, greater life achievement. Thus, it is important to learn more about how the self-esteem of the average person changes over time." Your emotions are the main source of self-esteem, and these feelings are within your power. It will grow low self-esteem by dwelling on your failures and shortcomings. Through reflecting instead on the positive points and attributes, you can counteract this kind of thought.

Your self-esteem in the present is not just how you feel about yourself, but how you fundamentally assume yourself over the long term. If you have low self-esteem, day-to-day activities can have a big impact on how you think. A nice smile or a better day at work, for instance, could make you feel great for a couple of days. Or even a not that great day can make you feel extremely low. And let us face it most days are uneventful and dull, so staying high can be a struggle when you have low self-esteem! A good healthy self-esteem is focused on knowing what you are-know who you are and be happy, just like you are!

Argue with your "inner voice" to help improve self-esteem

We all have a voice inside our heads that is continuously chatting away. Commenting about everything we've done / have / want to do. And it reassures so rewards those with healthy self-esteem. The inner voice criticizes us with poor self-esteem, sets us down and stands in our path! Of starters, if you do anything-compete in sport or go for a job interview, and someone compliments you the inner voice might suggest something like "he was cheating, you were bad, don't bother next time." What you have to do is challenge the inner voice, then snap back with something like-" He congratulated me when I performed good, maybe I wasn't flawless, but win lose or draw I did my best and I'm proud of myself! "Arguing with your inner voice is going to improve your self-esteem, begin now! Remember, you are the manager, you are in charge, do not let the critic get you down inside!

Use Negative Affirmations to Boost Self-Esteem

A positive statement about yourself is a positive statement. Use them in a method for relaxation as well as by explaining them to yourself in your head every day. Ideally you would like to rest at least once a day and only make those positive statements to yourself softly playing some calming music at the same time is really good help!

Definitions for positive self-esteem affirmations: Who you are-I'm great I'm good I'm unique Who you're going to be-I can be a champion I can be powerful I will recover I will lose weight I'm going to do-I'm going to smile more I'm going to control my emotions by constantly repeating those stuff for yourself you have no option but to accept them profoundly! You are able to become those things, and the self-esteem increases.

Self-Nurturing to Improve Self-Esteem

For order to improve self-esteem, self-nurturing is important. Begin by physically taking care of yourself, eating healthy, staying in shape, and obtaining all the rest you want-not too much and not too little.

To improve your self-esteem, self-nurturing makes you feel worthwhile. Regularly reward yourself by doing pleasant and enjoyable activities-especially if something positive has been accomplished. You have to be praised for successes! Think about the things you love about yourself and note them all the time. Do not dwell or punish yourself for failure-reward yourself in the first place for trying. Try to focus on the good and learn to forgive what you feel is the poor. Days when you do not feel good or optimistic are important, you have to seek things that are good for yourself, no matter how small they may be! Those things will help to boost self-esteem. It can be a great help to receive encouragement from loved ones to boost self-esteem. Tell family and friends to show you what they like about you. Tell them to be your release valve when you are feeling low and upset-this can be a huge help to boosting self-esteem by just listening when you let off steam.

The community is essential for enhancing self-esteem and preserving it is a huge factor of self-esteem that is surrounded by moist, loving people. Already I realize for a bit that is not true, not everybody has a loving partner or community network. Nonetheless, you have to make sure you are respected by those you have in your life, and you have to respect them for who they are. A feeling of understanding will help you realize that people's variations are all wrong. It will be easier to build relationships with others by understanding this. Bond to those you see and connect with every day, just speak, contact, display love, listen, be helpful, and be honest. Understanding that those around you think the same about you is a huge boost to your self-esteem!

Criticism

You are not sorry for who you are! When and when you are questioned, make sure to "judge" what is being said to you before you react for whatever reason. Do not apologies immediately! If the critique is valid then take it into consideration and respond by agreeing with the critic. If unfair, then, as with your inner voice, stand up to it. A well-composed and self-possessed individual will uninterruptedly listen to feedback and then react. Make certain to critique at appropriate times, it is often more difficult for people with poor self-esteem to give than to accept. Before you "boil flat," do not let annoyances go, it is usually better to nip stuff in your bud. Be tactful and seek not to damage the self-esteem of others. Use the term "I" not "you," for instance-when that occurs, I have problems.

Environmental Factors Vs Self-esteem

Self-esteem is generally considered as a subjective self-evaluation. Self-esteem is generally believed to be nothing but your own image of yourself. It is not outside of you; it is an internal thing. Self-esteem is about how we think inside and how we respond outside will be influenced by this emotion. Our self-esteem tends to define our personalities, defining our behavior, determining how we react to the stresses and challenges we face in our lives, and definitely influencing our interaction with other people as well. Particularly residing in a healthy environment for a relatively long time, positive thinking, productive actions, and feel-good experiences not only improve our motivation and growth, but also provide us with a strong foundation for our future goals and accomplishments. Thus, one can tackle challenges comfortably with the requisite confidence and maintain a high level of self-esteem. As a consequence, the level of satisfaction and confidence would be so high that ambitious aspirations such as self-actualization, self-improvement, and the standard of' ideal' identity could be reached.

Self-esteem is not an individual concept; it is combined with other important concepts such as self-respect, self-pride, self-confidence, self-dignity, and so on. It was never possible to separate all these ideas from self-esteem. As when we can compose alphabets, interpret alphabets, enter them in a coherent word that we can understand what it means, we can finally say we can read and write in English to some degree or to some point. Likewise, if we are able to make decisions, if we accomplish those goals based on our faith and commitment, if we are respected by the people, we consider important, we obtain a good position in our community, we believe that we are respectable human beings. Eventually, these emotions drive us to high self-esteem. In other terms, they have a lower level of self-esteem.

In this post, we concentrate on the environmental factors that have a tremendous impact on self-esteem. Although it is practically impossible to change one's climate, it is a reality that if we go into a different situation and momentarily switch our condition, we feel different. We feel scared / composed when we are in the company of outsiders, so when we are in the company of friends, we feel safe and happy. We could easily choose a better company.

Chapter 7: How the Lack of Love for Oneself Affects the People Around Us: Children, Husband, Friends?

Low self-esteem can be drilled into a child when either the parents ignore him or her, or take notice of their achievements, while harshly criticizing them for any mistakes they may make. The child feels there is no point in trying, and even if they do good, nothing will ever come out of it, so it is futile to excel.

Of course, it is not just the parents who are able to develop this most unwelcome function. Families are always, and often wrongly, an easy target.

One of the worst crimes of all when I was a child was conceit. That is why the contributions seemed to be downplayed so often.

But it is not self-esteem, nor is it self-love. It is neither pride nor envy. The Scriptures tell us that pride and vanity are deadly sins, and the apparent reason is that we and God cannot love ourselves. You do not leave room for other people or things if you are full of yourself.

On the other end of the scale, for example, if you are really a talented artist and somebody is staring at one of your works. Let us assume this guy, when it comes to art, knows what they are talking about and they are saying how good they think it is. You, with your complete lack of self-esteem, turn around and say,' Well, that's kind of you, but it's not really very good.' It is not just an angry response; it is insulting as well. You tell this person, in truth, that he or she has no clue what they are talking about!

"That's kind of you doing that. Yeah, I am pleased with how it worked out," it's perfectly acceptable. You do not sound your own horn; however, you appreciate your own ability as well as the expertise of the other guy.

Lack of self-esteem holds us in Do Nothing's lonely place. It can keep us from doing things that others love, so our hopes and goals can be ruined. So, is caring with self-esteem? Yes. So, what is it exactly? Here are five points of self-esteem.

An honest appreciation of what we can do.

Realizing our own values and abilities honestly.

Comprehension about our weaknesses.

Not being too concerned about what other people might think of us.

I guess this last is the most important thing. Not only can we be held back by ignorance of the viewpoints of other men, but these beliefs are generally unspoken. That is why I thought I wrote. Just look at how our imagination, in so many other ways, can keep us from achieving Healing Trauma and Stress Starts with Self-Love Your heart, mind, body, and spirit all need security and compassion. Therefore, in the cycle of healing depression and reducing stress, self-love is so necessary.

Your spiritual development and recovery will be hindered without healthy and caring support and guidance and self-love.

Your nervous system needs security to unlock trapped survival energy so you can enjoy life's pleasures with a cool, vigilant mind and stress-free body at last.

When you begin with some degree of self-love and self-acceptance, you are in a better place to allow someone else to support you overcome your pain and reduce your life stress.

Here is an important truth when it comes to true inner healing: true inner healing takes a lot of courage from you, because with the emotional wounds you will have to trust someone else.

For the strength you have built to try and overcome the pain and tension in life, please applaud yourself right now. You are on the way to a lot of happiness and joy. You deserve a life free of fear and anxiety.

Is it time for you to restore the nervous system entirely, because in many cases you are now guilty of over-reacting or shutting down fully, and you do not want to function like this any longer?

If so, just plan to respect yourself right now.

When looking in the mirror every morning when you brush your teeth, you can begin to increase your self-love and say to yourself, "I esteem you." You can also make the decision to stop criticizing yourself. I realize it is easy for me to say that and it is difficult to do that, but at least it is my intention to start putting yourself down now. Harmful attitudes create negative feelings, which in the nervous system causes anxiety. Give yourself some freedom from your practiced conditioning, most definitely as a teenager, and learn new healthy habits of self-acceptance and self-love.

On the road to trauma healing and stress reduction, your self-love will accelerate your recovery and ensure a life full of joy and love that is your birthright. These feelings are supposed to go away while fear and anxiety are part of life. Such emotions do not go anywhere for you, so they sometimes get worse over time. The depression is not good either for you.

Anxiety disorders are the most common mental illness in the US, and you can now, once and for all, resolve this epidemic with all the modern stress recovery methods. Trauma is no doubt a lifetime prison sentence. It is time to celebrate and encourage yourself to through your self-love and recover 100% of your trauma. When you offer yourself this wonderful gift, the stress level will drop to a healthy level.

From Pain (Suicidal) To Self-love

Suicide is a permanent solution to a temporary problem, and this is what helps us to grow and become stronger people. Nothing is worth taking a lifetime, particularly another man or women. If someone has that influence on you, you do not have to continue with them in your life. Only suck it up, walk away, take care of you and be the person you can be!

I was in that position too. I looked like I was sick from a divorce. The gut-wrenching I already know, I-want to-crawl-in - a-hole-and-die agony! It was nearly paralyzing at times. It was not until some years had gone by and I could take a step back, that I started to see more distinctly how I played an enormous part in the split. Why? Because I saw someone who did not take care of themselves the way they should have been, and I took a good hard look at myself.

There was definitely a lack of self-love in my life at the time. So self-inflicted damage is not perceived to be self-love! It was difficult to see anything lovable about myself through the haze of pain. But I knew I had to learn to love myself if I ever had a healthy relationship. I will continue to draw unhealthy people into my existence if I were sick. All I wanted to do was get smarter and more self-confident, because a strong person is much more desirable than a weak person. So, it has to continue with me, otherwise I do not have anything to do with a new relationship.

Love yourself, be true to yourself, and prioritize your well-being. Spiritual, physical, social, and intellectual focus on yourself. Set goals and carry through at all times. Make positive comments for yourself. Surround yourself with people positive and uplifting. Do for yourself something good. For someone else, do something nice. The list continues and begins. There are so many ways to learn how to love and be content with yourself, and a healthy relationship is important.

After all, if we cannot even recognize ourselves, how can we consider someone else? When we cannot even respect ourselves, how can we expect others to accept us? In establishing a stable, loving relationship, self-love and self-acceptance are crucial first moves.

Note, love starts internally, and only when you achieve self-acceptance and self-love can you really express it with someone else.

Chapter 8: The Techniques That Famous Women Use to Overcome Anxiety About the Obstacles They Have to Overcome

Anxiety can impair the normal functioning of a person as an unknown fear stays with the victim forever. Uncertainty becomes a part of life, and people start shying away from unbridled public exposure.

Most things that lead to anxiety are not real threats. It is the mind trying to put you into a protective cocoon. There are several ways to counter stress and anxiety effectively.

Ways to Deal with Anxiety

Mindfulness

Mindfulness is the phenomenal concept to help one remain grounded in the present. We all like to believe that we live in the present, but that is not correct. We live in a world identified with several things and memories to back that up.

For instance, if you are a successful person, you may expect people to greet you when they meet you. It is because you are identified with your position and feel that it commands that respect. When someone whom you expect does not greet, it kickstarts the thought process about the significance of that event. Normally, the greeting might not have meant anything to you. But because you feel so identified with your position that the absence of greeting might begin to look like a question to your authority. Thoughts and memories also have a profound role to play in this whole mash-up.

This event would keep running in your mind long after you have left that place. It does not remain a simple question of not greeting you anymore. It may also start creating self-doubt, and you may begin questioning your relevance and standing.

5 Basic Principles of Mindfulness

Detachment: It is a way of living that helps you in remaining detached. To live in this world and enjoy it, you do not need to feel identified with it. There is no need to categorize things as good and bad. The way we look at things can change the way they behave for us.

Non-judgmental Attitude

The biggest reason for our unhappiness is our judgmental attitude. We judge everything on the basis of our past experiences. We label everything and then make firm beliefs about things that can make us happy and sad. These classifications have little to do with the way that things really turn out to be. Mindfulness is all about experiencing things as they are without judging them on the basis of old ideas.

Living in the Present

Most people never let the past go. They hold on to the past very strongly. Due to this, they are never able to enjoy their present. They keep working hard to make their future like their past, even better than it. However, they miss the present.

Acceptance

We have become very rigid in our beliefs. We resent any kind of deviation. Most people are never even able to accept themselves as they are. They are always in a constant pursuit to change themselves for an image that looks better. This attitude only brings unhappiness and discontentment. When you try to go against nature without reason, the results are never very pleasant. Mindfulness helps you in accepting everything as it is. Working for betterment is something entirely different but loathing something cannot be a part of the plan as it would lead to stress and anxiety.

Openness

Mindfulness is the idea of letting go of rigid ideas and opening up to new things and experiences. You do not stick to certain belief systems because you have been taught about it or have seen people follow them. You remain open to new experiences.

Visualization

Visualization is a great way to lower stress and anxiety. The main cause of anxiety is excessive focus on some negative emotions. It simply remains hooked on to negativity and does not allow you to come out of it. One major problem here is that there are so many negative emotions that they do not allow positive thoughts to come to your mind.

Visualization can be a big asset in such scenarios. It is a simple practice of visualizing something sweet and pleasant that you have always wished for but do not relate to it strongly. It detaches you from the negative emotions and gives your mind the required diversion.

You get a chance to visualize the things you really like, and they bring positive emotions to your mind.

It is a very easy practice, and there are several tools that can help you. You can listen to guided visualizations whenever you feel anxious, and that would help you in taking your mind off the negative triggers.

When you visualize pleasant scenarios, you are actually able to see them from the eyes of your mind. Seeing is believing, and your mind is able to switch tracks easily. Always remember that positivity is the only thing that can help you in the hopeless darkness of negativity.

Simple emotions of love, beauty, nature, and compassion can help your mind in thinking positively.

The scope of visualization is very wide, and it can become a powerful tool in fending off stress and anxiety.

Emotional Freedom Technique

Most people do not realize, but the cause of most of their physical and mental lies in the imbalance of energy inside them. We are more than just the body. Our emotions, life energy, and physicality work in unique sync. Whenever any part of this system goes out of balance, we suffer as a whole. This is the reason most eastern medicine practices also heavily rely on energy healing. Healing practices like acupuncture and reiki can have a profound impact on correcting such imbalances.

Emotional Freedom Technique (ETF) tapping also works on similar principles. It is a technique that has been used to treat soldiers suffering from post-traumatic stress disorders, and it has proven to be very effective.

While for acupuncture and reiki, you will need to go to an expert, you can do ETF tapping yourself anywhere and bring down your levels of anxiety. Even in case a person is going to have a full-blown panic attack. This tapping can help in lowering the level of stress and anxiety and prevent the panic attack.

ETF is very effective, and it is very easy to perform. You can customize the whole process as per your need and feel your level of anxiety going down as you practice it in times of need.

ETF is performed in cycles. With every cycle, you will have to assess the level of anxiety you are feeling, and you can continue repeating the cycles until you start feeling comfortable.

Through this process, you address the negative emotions that may be contributing to stress and anxiety. By tapping on various meridian points in the body, you allow the energy in your body to flow more freely. This helps in restoring the smooth flow of emotions, and your mood also starts improving.

1 Single Out the Issue Causing Anxiety

There can be several things that may be driving you towards anxiety. However, if you will try to address all the things that are making you anxious at the same time, it would not be that effective.

It is important that you identify the strongest emotion that is making you feel anxious at the moment. If there are other stronger issues, too, you can address them separately.

You can enhance the outcome of the process if you address each issue in its own time.

2 Identify the Intensity of Anxiety

Before you begin ETF tapping, it is important that you close your eyes briefly and try to assess the level of anxiety you are feeling at that moment. Rate your level of anxiety on a scale of 0-10. It is important that you know the level of anxiety before you begin so that you can see the calming effect you are having and know the number of cycles; you will have to perform tapping. If you begin without scaling the level of anxiety you are feeling, you will face difficulty in assessing your progress.

3 The Setup

ETF tapping follows a two-pronged approach. While the tapping helps in unblocking the neural pathways, the positive and reassuring statements help in making you emotionally balanced.

In the third step, you will have to establish a setup phrase that will help you in addressing the problem, causing stress and anxiety.

This setup phrase should simply have two main portions:

1. It must directly acknowledge the issue you are facing

2. In this statement, you must accept and encourage yourself despite all the problems

For instance, if you are feeling really frightened due to anything, acknowledge your fear in the first part of the statement. In the second part, accept yourself despite your fears and flaws and reassure your mind that you will come out of it.

Your setup statement can be something like this:

Even though I am feeling scared and anxious, I completely accept myself, and I will come out of it.

I want to run away from all this, I understand I am scared, but I will come out of it, I accept myself.

I am feeling lost at the moment, but I will find my way. I love myself and accept the feelings I am having at the moment.

As an individual, you can have your own setup statement that addresses the most important issue you are facing at the moment. Try to keep the statement simple and more focused. Also, remember that your setup statement should only have your problem as the center argument. Including the problems faced by others does not work here. It is not a prayer; it is a way to heal your mind.

4 The ETF Tapping Sequence

In this part, you will have to tap the meridian point explained below. You can tap the points from your index fingers or your middle finger or both if you like. Even if you want to use more fingers, feel free to do that. The tapping does not need to be very hard; remember some parts are sensitive, and it can hurt if you tap too hard. You simply need to stimulate those parts through the tapping so that the neural pathways open up.

There are 9 meridian points that you will be tapping in this step are:

Hand (Karate Chop)

This is the side of your palm below your pinky finger. The part of the hand used for giving karate chops. This is the reason it is called karate chop. Using the fingers of the opposite hand, tap on this surface.

The inner edge of the eyebrows

You will need to tap at the center of your eyebrows just above the bridge of the nose.

Side of the eyes

This is the outer edge of the eyes where the eyebrows end. This will be the part between your eyebrows and the temple.

Under the eyes

This is the area under the eyes where the hard part of the cheekbone is.

Under the nose

This is the area just below the nose and center of your upper lip.

Chin

This is the area at the center just below your lower lip and above your chin

Beginning of the collarbone

This is the area where the collarbones begin

Underarms

This area is approximately 4 inches below the armpits.

Top of the head

This is the crown of your head. The topmost part.

Chapter 9: How to Improve Your Love Life by Starting to Love Yourself More?

Be firm but gracious when communicating your limits with men. The key to expressing your boundaries or rebuffing a man's premature sexual advances in an attractive way is to allude to your desire for him while setting your standard.

Never be afraid to enforce your personal boundaries or express your limitations with a man. Being able to do so with poise and decorum will subconsciously communicate to him that you are a high-value woman, one who has standards and reasonable expectations. Women who can confidently tell a man what they want and do not want are rare and therefore VERY sought after.

Unfortunately, many women are terrified to set boundaries with a man they are highly attracted to because they fear that he will lose interest, withdraw, or become completely turned off. These women believe that telling a man "No" or shutting down his premature sexual advances might drive away a potential boyfriend. If you struggle to set boundaries with men due to a deep fear of potential loss, you can stop worrying about it. Your fear of loss is groundless, and here is why: The men who will not be turned off by your limits are the ones who will cherish you the most.

Of course, if you are worried about coming across as being "too demanding" or "not interested enough", try to use the "firm but enticing" technique. When you must express your limitations or outright reject a man's advances, simply state how you feel but use a hint of seduction to keep him intrigued. Here is a simple yet powerful step-by-step communication method for accomplishing this:

Compliment him by telling him how he makes you feel. The best way to do this is to say something genuine about him that singles him out as being "better" than other men in some way.

Communicate your boundaries and tell him "No" in a clear but courteous way.

Express to him why the boundary is important to you.

For example, if a man is trying to be too sexually forward with you, it's one thing to tell him, "No, I'm not ready," and another thing to tell him, "Listen, Mike, I like you. A lot. I mean...you make me feel things I have never felt for any man before. But I am not ready for this yet. I want to give myself to the man who wants me for a lifetime. I hope you understand."

Did you see the difference there?

The first boundary setting is perfectly fine, but it will not make his mind burn with anticipation and curiosity like the second one. And if "Mike" considers himself to be a potential "lifetime lover" candidate, he will do whatever he can to prove to you that he is the man for job, no matter how long it takes.

By using the firm but enticing technique you will communicate your limits and make the right man desperate to see you again all at the same time. Men do not mind being rejected once it is done with grace and respect for their ego. A man is less likely to see your rejection as a sign of your "lack of interest" if you can communicate your boundaries with a sincere expression of desire.

Never make yourself a fool for flaky male behavior. If you allow a man to flake on you once, he will most assuredly do it again...and again...and again.

In the event you are not familiar with the term, a "flake" is basically someone who does not follow through. They are major procrastinators, highly unreliable, and nearly incapable of keeping their word. The major factor in determining whether or not a flake will actually follow through is based on his or her mood at the time or the urgency of the need to act. In short, flakes make terrible friends and disastrous partners (both in love and in business) to those unfortunate enough to rely on them.

But what are the telling behaviors of the flaky male specimen in a dating situation? Below I have listed a few of the most common examples of flaky behavior a man might unknowingly display when interacting with a woman:

He becomes wishy-washy with his attention and might even break off contact with you as soon as you begin showing a serious interest in him.

He disappears from time to time or does not respond in a reasonable amount of time when communicating with you and does not give a valid explanation for doing so.

He cancels dates on short notice without suggesting a future date to make up for it.

He arrives unreasonably late and gives off an attitude of indifference towards his tardiness.

He defends his flakiness with the belief that he "doesn't owe you anything" and that he can "do as he pleases", in spite of the fact you have already made significant investments of love and loyalty towards him.

He does not follow through on his word and usually gives a dishonest excuse for doing so. That is, if he actually cares enough to provide an excuse at all.

Simply put, a man who flakes on you does not hold you in high regard. If he does not hold you in high regard, he does not deserve your attention. It does not really matter "why" he flaked, as men flake on women for a myriad of reasons that could span a book of its own (most of those reasons have nothing to do with you by the way). All you need to concern yourself with is how you respond to Flaky Frank moving forward. Once you realize that a guy is not respectful of your time and attention, you must cease to entertain him and turn your attention to more persistent admirers.

The high-value woman does not accept unreasonable tardiness without a reasonable excuse

Let us say a handsome gentleman (we will call him Mr. Handsome Face) you met through a friend of a friend has finally asked you out on a date. Let us also say that he tells you he is going to pick you up on Friday night at eight o'clock sharp. Excitedly, you prepare for the date well in advance with some long over-due personal beautification and you even borrow a gorgeous outfit from one of your close friends (you know, the one who has ALL the clothes you like).

Friday evening arrives and you eagerly wait for Mr. Handsome Face to show up. Seven thirty rolls by and you are almost done getting ready. Seven fifty rolls by, and you are done-up proper and waiting patiently on your couch trying to read a novel to distract yourself. Eight o'clock rolls by and you are expecting him to knock on your door at any moment. Eight fifteen rolls by and naturally, you are getting a little over-anxious. Eight thirty rolls by and now you are getting a little concerned.

Ignore his tardiness and go on the date anyway.

Graciously ask for an explanation for his tardiness and then politely refuse the date if he does not have one.

Throw a drink in his face right before you slam the door on him.

As a self-possessed woman of class, I'm going to assume you went with B, as B is truly the only option if you want to communicate to a man that your attention is valuable and that your good-graces are not cheap commodities. Accepting a man's extreme tardiness without a reasonable excuse will go beyond him thinking that you are "easy-going", he'll simply think you're "easy." Not having standards or setting boundaries when it comes to your attention forces a man to make a value judgment about you that tells him: She is not worth my best wooing efforts.

Let us be real here. Being unreasonably late to meet someone or do something is basically bad manners no matter the situation, and thus it is not the kind of behavior anyone should encourage. If you consistently entertain such behavior you will find that people will not respect your time, which ultimately means that they do not respect you. The same applies when it comes to a fresh romance. If you begin making allowances for a guy early on without some sort of polite penalty or gracious reprimand, he will not value the attention you give him and thus, he will not respect you. And if you do not know by now, a man will not commit his all to a woman if he does not respect her.

Do not tolerate men who show indifference towards your tender display of emotions. Use your emotional vulnerabilities to test a man's compassion, esteem, and earnestness of affection for you. Only the man with a kindred soul will be drawn to you even more when you share your soul with him.

One of the most effective things you can do to determine if a man is genuinely interested in you is to share your vulnerable side with him, then observe how he responds to you (assuming he responds at all). Of course, you do not have to confess your deepest darkest secrets to him, but instead, share private little intimacies with him that you would not share with the average person. Such private merriments and concerns may include but are not limited to:

Cherished childhood memories.

Painful memories from your past, such as a friend's betrayal.

Present-day struggles, such as your fear of switching careers or the issues you are having with a co-worker.

Quirky interests that you are passionate (or obsessed) about.

Things that make you deeply emotional in any way, such as mistreated pets, domestic violence, your church's ministry, or your sister's rehab journey.

If you open up about such things and Mr. Tall-Dark-and-Handsome does not appear even remotely interested, moved, or engaged with what you're saying, he's probably not as into you as you would have hoped. When a man has a sincere romantic interest in a woman, he will not be able to hide his sympathies and enthusiasms whenever she shares the beautiful varieties of her emotions with him.

Truth is, getting emotional with the man you are dating will either frighten him away (Mr. Wrong) or draw him closer to you (Mr. Right), so you cannot lose with this strategy. Becoming vulnerable with a guy allows him to catch glimpses of your soul. And if he is Mr. Right he will become even more curious and infatuated with you over time. He will see you as a "kindred soul" so to speak and will feel even more emotionally drawn to you in the process.

Now, my only caveat with this approach is to be sure that you are only showing 'glimpses' into your soul. Things can easily backfire if you spew out the contents of your heart all in one go. Doing so can potentially frighten guys away if you are not discerning with your approach. You want to reveal just enough of your heart to see if he can engage with you on an emotional level, but not so much that he feels overwhelmed all at once.

Chapter 10: How to Become More Seductive by Loving Yourself More

All of these factors combined make up what I believe to be self-love and if you want to learn to love yourself, you will need to learn and develop each of these components to healthy levels. Since my aim in this book is to try to teach you how to love yourself correctly, I want you to understand what you need to have in order to be able to completely love yourself.

Self-Esteem

In the simplest of terms, self-esteem is generally what you think of yourself. It can be said that confident people have a high degree of self-esteem while those lacking in confidence have low self-esteem. It usually develops through a combination of upbringing and personal experiences that shapes the way we view ourselves.

Most kids who grow up with loving parents initially develop a high level of self-esteem because parents would always tend to complement their child regardless of their actual abilities. It is the same with society in general. Normal adults always praise children and are generally encouraging. No reasonable person would think to give a child negative criticism.

As a result, we as children have a high-level of self-esteem because most of the feedback, we get is positive and adults try to be as kind to us as they can. As we grow up, the feedback we are given becomes more honest and our view of ourselves start to shift into a more realistic one.

Self-Esteem is dynamic. It changes depending on a person's status and perception of themselves. During times of failure, self-esteem normally goes down because we generally also receive negative feedback while in periods of success, self-esteem goes up because the feedback we get is also positive. It is your evaluation of yourself, based on the feedback you get.

It is not always grounded in reality, and it can be subject to changes in a person's condition or social environment. It is also a result of the accumulation of the experiences and affirmations that we have had since childhood which builds an image in our minds about who and what we are and where we ideally should stand in the social order.

Self-confidence

Self-confidence generally refers to your faith in your abilities. It develops from awareness or at least a perception of what you are capable of. For example, if you believe that you are terrible at math, then your confidence in tackling mathematical problems will naturally be low. If you think that you are a terrible dancer, then you would tend to avoid dancing-related activities.

Like I said earlier, it is about your faith in your abilities and is not always tied to reality. You can be confident about your singing abilities because you believe that you have a golden voice while in reality other people who hear you sing think the opposite. Because of your misguided confidence in your singing abilities, you might be inclined to actively promote yourself as a singer regardless of what your actual voice quality really is.

If you ever watch talent shows on TV, you will see a lot of people who have a high level of confidence in their abilities. They view themselves as extremely talented and try to impress the judges and audience only to be disappointed when they do not win or even get angry if they receive a fair criticism from the judges.

It is because self-confidence does not necessarily reflect your actual abilities but instead reflects what you think of your abilities. It is similar to self-esteem in that it usually comes from your upbringing and personal experiences, but it differs from it by being more specific. You usually develop your confidence in particular abilities because of the feedback you have received whenever you display these abilities.

When I was little, I used to like singing in public. I used to sing at school presentations and I really thought I had a great voice because my parents would always compliment me whenever I sang. During school presentations, the audience would clap after I sing and of course they did, what kind of adult would tell a child that their voice was terrible? This made me confident about my singing abilities.

When I grew up and started hanging out with people other than my parents, I started getting feedback that was not always positive whenever I sing. Unfortunately, people become more honest in their feedback when you are no longer a child, so I lost confidence in my singing. While I still love to sing, I am no longer that confident about it that I would never sing on stage with an audience unless I was really forced to do it.

Self-Acceptance

Self-Acceptance, on the other hand, is when you learn to accept yourself for what you are. It is when you forgive yourself for all your faults and failures. It is when you appreciate your individuality regardless of how others perceive you. It is close to self-love as having self-acceptance means recognizing your flaws and knowing all your negative traits but still appreciate yourself.

Unlike self-esteem and self-confidence which are generally affected by other people's feedback, self-acceptance is something you attain despite the feedback you get. It is internal and more of a conscious choice rather than something that easily changes depending on what other people think.

When you learn to accept yourself, you do not judge yourself, and you do not compare yourself to others. It is being aware that you have specific weaknesses, but you do not let the awareness of these weaknesses bring down your opinion of yourself.

It is accepting your limitations as a human being. It is recognizing that you are not perfect, you make mistakes and you are not good at everything but still be okay with it. In other words, it is being content with yourself.

Self-Awareness

Self-awareness is similar to self-acceptance in the sense that it is the acknowledgment of your traits. It is about recognizing the changes in your emotions as they happen and exerting a degree of control of your actions following these emotional changes. It is understanding how these emotions affect your thought processes and knowing how you act in response to these emotions.

Having self-awareness is also similar to self-acceptance in that it is also about having an accurate assessment of your own weaknesses and limitations, but unlike self-acceptance, it is more about knowing how these weaknesses and limitations affect the world around you. Basically, it is about knowing how to control your own behavior despite your emotions instead of letting your emotions control how you behave.

It is like the idea of professionalism. You act according to how you are supposed to in order to get the job done correctly, regardless of how you feel about your boss or your coworkers. You treat your boss and your coworkers with respect despite feeling intense dislike for them because you understand that you need to cooperate with them in order to get the job done.

Having self-awareness means understanding that your emotional state can affect your performance and behavior. It is knowing how to interact with your environment and other people in a morally acceptable manner despite your emotional state. Having self-awareness means that you know how to control yourself.

Self-Respect

In simple terms, having self-respect means having pride in yourself and as a result, you behave in such a way that upholds your sense of honor and dignity. It is sometimes easy to confuse having a high degree of self-esteem or confidence with a high level of self-respect, but unlike self-esteem, having self-respect does not mean simply having a high opinion of yourself.

It is knowing what you are worth. It is having reasonable standards for yourself and behaving according to those standards. You do not settle for less because you know how much your worth and you do not hesitate to ask for what you deserve.

You are probably familiar with the phrase "Don't sink to their level" right? Having self-respect means exactly that. It means not compromising your own standards for anyone, even if they do not have any standards. It is about valuing yourself and because you value yourself, you do not let other people treat you any less no matter who they are.

Having self-respect also means that you have integrity. Your standards apply regardless of the situation. You do not bend your own rules or lower your standards just because it is easier to do so in certain situations.

If you have self-respect, you do not feel the need to beg for anyone's approval because for you, just knowing your own worth is all the approval you need. Basically, self-respect combines the elements of self-esteem, self-acceptance, and self-awareness in that you have a reasonable opinion of yourself, you are aware of your weaknesses and limitations, and you keep your actions within an acceptable moral standard.

It means knowing who and what you are and taking responsibility for your actions. It means that you feel worthy of being loved and accepted by others. It is acting with honor and dignity because you know that you deserve to be treated with respect.

It also means knowing how to properly ask for what you deserve and standing up for yourself if you are not treated with respect. You do not allow other people to give you less than what you ask for and you do not let other people disrespect you.

As a result, having self-respect means you also treat others with the same level of respect because you know that treating other people poorly demeans you. Having self-respect also tends to make other people treat you with respect because they see that you have standards and that you behave according to your own standards.

Personal Empowerment

Personal empowerment is taking control of your life in a positive way. It is taking all the above factors in order to determine your own worth and then using everything you know about yourself to set realistic goals and using your abilities to achieve them. It is knowing your weaknesses and aiming to improve on them, and it is knowing your strengths and using them to advance yourself.

Having personal empowerment means knowing how to take control of your circumstances in order to achieve your personal goals. It is also about understanding your own strengths and weaknesses well, making you better equipped in dealing with any problems that you encounter. You know how to recognize opportunities and know how to take advantage of them appropriately in order to succeed.

It does not simply mean having the power to make things happen. It also means knowing how to set realistic goals and having the freedom and the ability to make conscious decisions and taking the appropriate actions in order to achieve these goals.

Chapter 11: What Is Narcissism?

There is more to narcissism than having an inflated sense of self and being conceited and egotistical. Yes, these are all unattractive qualities when they are in the extreme; however, true narcissism involves a maniacal pursuit of praise, ambition, and gratification. Those who suffer from the slightest degree of NPD can be arrogant, smug, and vain and have an unusually high level of self-esteem. This is their outward appearance, but deep down they are extremely insecure and feel as if they have little self-worth. They thrive off admiration from others, which is how they feed their belief that they are more important than anyone else. Psychologists refer to this as "narcissistic supply," and it is almost like a drug for the narcissist. They are addicted to receiving confirmation that they are indeed superior beings. Typically, narcissists do not have an empathetic bone in their body, which basically means that they do not have a care in the world for anyone apart from themselves.

There are different degrees of narcissism; in fact, psychologists believe that we are all slightly narcissistic. It is even possible that narcissism is required as a method of survival in the world today. Being a little egotistical can be beneficial; however, the behavior of a fully narcissistic individual is very destructive.

According to the Diagnostic and Statistical Manual of Mental Disorders, to be considered narcissistic, a person's behavior must fall into the following categories:

- They blow situations out of proportion and are incapable of putting things into perspective.

- The narcissist is unable to empathize with the feelings or thoughts of others.

- The narcissist is only concerned with their own issues.

- The narcissist has no respect for authority.

- Deep down the narcissist feels inferior and will compensate by doing everything they can to be seen as superior.

- The narcissist is incapable of receiving constructive criticism.

- The narcissist needs sexual admiration and is often an exhibitionist.

- The narcissist is vain, exploitative, and dependent on others.

To a certain degree, all people who have been diagnosed with NPD exhibit these traits. However, there are also other types of narcissistic behaviors. Since the 1950s, there has been a dramatic increase in the number of people who suffer from narcissism. During this time, therapists have noticed that there are variations in the condition, which have been divided into several categories. Narcissism in children is typically a result of learned behavior from their primary caregivers and can be unlearned. Therefore, psychologists are reluctant to diagnose children with NPD. Fully-fledged NPD only exists in adults and is treated differently; other types of narcissism include the following.

- The Phallic Narcissist: These are typically males who have a great love for themselves and their physical bodies. They strut like roosters and are very aggressive and athletic. They are exhibitionists who enjoy putting their bodies on display.

- The Manipulative Narcissist: They enjoy manipulating and influencing others. The manipulative narcissist feeds their need for power by manipulating, bullying, lying, and intimidating others.

- The Paranoid Narcissist: The paranoid narcissist suffers from a deep self-hatred; they project this onto others with extreme jealous behavior, and they are overly sensitive to criticism.

- The Craving Narcissist: Although narcissists are extremely egotistical, craving narcissists are very needy, demanding of love, emotionally clingy, and attention-seeking.

The most significant personality trait of a narcissist is grandiosity. This is not the same as boasting or pitifulness, it is an unrealistic inflated sense of self. If a person will not stop going on about how they were the MVP of their college basketball team at a dinner party, it might show that that individual is boastful, conceited, or even a little ill-mannered. This can be extremely annoying; however, it is not narcissistic if it is true. But if the person did not even play on the team but sat on the bench all season, that is being grandiose.

What Causes Narcissism?

Babies are born selfish—it is natural. Their number one concern is getting their immediate needs met and that is it. They have zero understanding of other people's desires and needs. As they transition into their teenage years, this self-centeredness is still very much a part of their nature as they go through the battle to attain independence.

In order to care and protect themselves, children need to

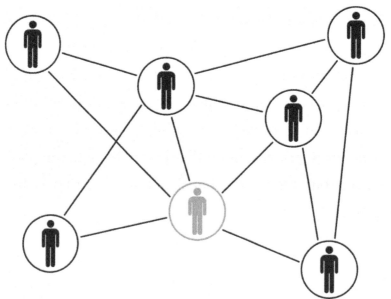

develop a healthy level of self-esteem, at the same time as being able to care about others to stay connected to society and family and avoid dangerous influences. When a child has a healthy level of self-esteem, it is an indication that a child feels that they are worthy and loved within their family and valuable to society. The essence of healthy self-esteem is not feelings of self-centeredness because the individual does not feel as if they need to trample on others to get their needs met.

There must be a transformation in childish self-centered behavior in order to experience sound mental health in adulthood. The ability to function effectively in a family, and in society is dependent upon the child's ability to gradually see other people's points of view and to experience empathy. So, an emotionally healthy child should eventually become sincere about the well-being of others. The inability to develop empathy as a child is a red flag that they may be at risk of developing a personality disorder in adulthood, and this includes narcissism.

Preteens do not have the mental capability to be manipulative, which is why mental health professionals are reluctant to diagnose NPD any earlier than the age of 18. However, there are certain behaviors in teenagers that indicate that they might be on their way to developing the condition in adulthood.

- Continuous bullying behaviors such as degrading, threatening, making fun of, or scapegoating people, including their parents and other adults

- The desire to win regardless of who gets hurt

- Constant lying, they will lie about the lies they tell, blame others for their lies, refuse to accept accountability by attacking those that report them to their parents

- A high and unnatural sense of self-worth

- Determined to get their needs met over others

- An attitude of extreme entitlement that leads them to act as if they should be treated differently than anyone else, and that regardless of the circumstances, they should get what they want

- Aggressive responses to being wronged, criticized, or upset

- Constantly blaming others when things do not work out the way they want

- Less cooperative and more competitive

The bottom line is that NPD is a result of the family environment that a child was raised in. All children want the attention and the approval of their parents, and they adapt to their surroundings. However, there are some home environments that are so destructive that the only way a child is capable of adapting is to become narcissistic. Here are a few scenarios to illustrate this.

Unconditional Versus Conditional Love – The Effects

Everyone wants to be loved unconditionally for who they are. If children feel that their parents only love and value them because they are special, this can lead to insecurity. It is impossible to win all the time, there is always going to be someone else out there who is better than you in some way. Children whose parents idealize them end up believing that they are only worthy when they are being idealized, if not they feel as if they have failed at life.

How They Perceive Flaws and Shame: Children who are idealized become ashamed when they realize that they are not the perfect people their parents raised them to believe they were. They cannot handle the fact that they have flaws like everyone else and so strive to be perfect in every area of their lives.

Unable to Identify Who They Really Are: These children are unable to get in touch with who they really are. They only focus on doing the things that will appease their parents and win their approval. They never spend any time exploring their true identity and discovering what their interests are and where their talents lie.

Occasionally, the golden child may resist their role and avoid becoming narcissistic. They actually feel embarrassed by the over the top praise they receive. The role that has been ascribed to them becomes somewhat of a burden. For example, one child of an overbearing excessive parent told his mother that he no longer wished to be a part of the circus and that he would like to live his life without having to live up to the expectations of his overachieving parents.

The Exhibitionist Admirer

The exhibitionist narcissist parent will reward their children with attention and praise as long as they remain subservient to and admire the parent. These children are trained how to be narcissistic, but at the same time, they are prohibited from being in the limelight. The role they play within the family is to worship the awesomeness of the narcissistic parent without ever being critical of them or trying to surpass them in greatness.

This is how closet or covert narcissists come about, the children learn that they are provided with the narcissistic supplies of praise and attention if they refrain from competing with their narcissistic parents. If they ever attempt to be openly acknowledged as special, these supplies are withheld. The value they are given is based on their ability to act as a crutch to the egotistical nature of the exhibitionist parent.

As adults, children who were raised in these families feel too vulnerable, exposed, and uncomfortable to be in the spotlight, so their self-esteem and narcissism issues are not as obvious to anyone who is not close to them. Some take on the role and play it very well, ending up in a job supporting an overachieving exhibitionist narcissist that they have nothing but admiration for.

The Bottom Line

If you are ever concerned that the person you have met may have narcissistic tendencies, ask about their childhood and what their parents were like. Once you get a clear picture of their home environment it will not be difficult to work out whether they have narcissistic tendencies or not.

Chapter 12: Practical Exercises For 21 Days to Change Your Mind, Improve Self-Esteem, And Achieve Your Successes in Life

When you apply the exercises and steps you find in this 21-day self-love exercises, you will be able to discover both your outer and inner beauty and see what is truly magnificent about you like you never have in the past. You will become passionate about things in your life and when you are in love with the person you are today, you will find that your life is better in many, many ways.

When you have completed this 21-day challenge, take some time to look back on where you began just 21 days in the past. Chances are you are going to be amazed about how far you have come.

Day 1 Activity

Today's activity is simple, use your journal and write about why you feel as though you do not love yourself the way you deserve. Make a list if you need to, just be sure to put everything down that you do not like about yourself and things that you wish you could change.

Day 2 Activity

When you look in the mirror, go further than just saying "I Love You." Point out a great feature and say why you love it – for example, I love you (your name) because (reason). Do this each morning for the entirety of the 30-day challenge, and do not forget to jot your feelings down in your journal.

Day 3 Activity

During your shower, imagine it is Love, not water, pouring all over you. While this may feel uncomfortable or sound ridiculous, it is a way to begin to feel that love that you have been missing. Write down your honest thoughts on this in your journal and describe how you felt afterwards.

Day 4 Activity

Make two lists – one for physical and one for inner things you love about yourself in your journal. Review and add to these things regularly.

Day 5 Activity

Today, you will learn to forgive yourself. Use the steps above to go through each thing you dislike about yourself and write them down in your journal.

Day 6 Activity

Simply do something good for yourself. Do something that is going to make you feel good about yourself that you normally do not do. Get your nails done, buy a new outfit, or simply take the day to turn your phone off and curl up with a good book. Whatever you choose to do, make it something that makes you feel good and something that you normally would not do. Write about your feelings afterwards in your journal. Describe how you felt when you were finished, if you feel better about yourself, emotionally or physically.

Day 7 Activity

Put yourself before others. Let the universe know that you are important too. When you are writing in your journal about this activity, make sure to note your feelings. Did you feel guilty, liberated, and important?

Day 8 Activity

Write down memories when you really "rocked" something and the amazing way you felt. Add to these as you remember more memories, by unlocking these memories, you will begin to remember things that happened long ago that you may have forgotten about.

Day 9 Activity

Write as much as you can in your journal about who you are today and why you love who and where you are in life.

Day 10 Activity

Write down where you would like to be in the future and what you can change now to achieve this goal. You can also elaborate and add as much detail as you would like on how you are going to reach those goals and steps you need to take to get there. Make sure to add you fears, doubts and concerns and come up with ways to turns those into something positive.

Day 11 Activity

Make it a point to do one random act of kindness for someone by paying it forward. When you are done, take a moment and write down your reflections on it. How did you feel? Were they appreciative? Were you uncomfortable approaching them to help?

Day 12 Activity

Choose one place in your home, or even your vehicle, and declutter it. Pick one drawer, one closet, one cupboard, or the trunk of your car and get rid of the items that you do not use or are no longer needed. If you are choosing a closet, donate your old clothing to a Goodwill or Salvation Army store.

Day 13 Activity

For this activity, you are going to have to have some tough skin. Recruit your closest friends and family members. You can do this over the phone or in person. Tell them how you feel about yourself and the challenge you are doing. Ask them to give their opinions on things that you may be able to change about yourself that could make you feel better about yourself. Be prepared, they may notice things about you that you never realized and some of the things may not be wonderful and complimentary. Just remember, they love you unconditionally and would never intentionally do anything to hurt you. They are trying to help you and you are asking for their thoughts.

Day 14 Activity

Try something new as a hobby. It does not have to be something that you have to stick with, just give something new a try. You may find that even if it wasn't something that you absolutely loved in the beginning, at the completion of it, you might have found something that you are incredibly good at and makes you love yourself even more. Make sure to keep a list of hobbies you try and explain the project you did and how you felt when you were completed.

Day 15 Activity

Reach out to old friends. Reminisce about happy times and things you did together. By getting reacquainted with them, you can see where you started and how far you have come in life. Make sure to document in your journal about the experiences from your past, the fun times you had, as well as how you felt after meeting up with them. Are you proud of your achievements? Did you remember how you felt about yourself all those years ago when life was easy and fun? Write down anything that is positive.

Day 16 Activity

Relax and pull out your journal. Start at the beginning of your challenge from two weeks ago and read through all of your journal entries. As you do, reflect on how things have changed from the beginning. Jot down any additional items you want to add to the various lists you have made or make notes on how you feel that you have changed over the course of this challenge so far.

Day 17 Activity

Spend today smiling. When you pass a random stranger or are standing in the checkout line at a store, smile. If you are at work, and a coworker approaches you, instead of just looking at them and saying hello, smile while saying it. You will notice a change in how people respond.

Day 18 Activity

Graciously accept compliments today. Throughout your day today, whenever someone gives you a compliment, accept it. Do not let that feeling of doubt take over. Remember that you are worthy of the compliments. In your journal keep track of the compliments you receive today and write down how you felt when you received them.

Day 19 Activity

Spend 10 minutes meditating. Take the time for yourself to focus on your own wellbeing and to reflect on your good qualities that make you the wonderful person you are.

Day 20 Activity

When getting ready for your day, take the extra few minutes to put on makeup, do your hair, or wear that nice outfit that has been hanging in your closet. Throughout the day notice how differently people approach you and how you feel better about yourself overall.

Day 21 Activity

Love who you are. Spend 15 minutes telling yourself that you love who you are and that you are glad that you are unique. Highlight the personality traits that you have that set you apart from everyone else. Think back to things that people have told you in the past that they love about you. It could be your witty personality, your attention to detail, your ability to really listen to other, or even something small like the way you laugh, or how dependable you are. Write these down in your journal.

The first thing to understand is that emotions come and go. One moment you feel happy, the next you feel sad. While you do have some control over your emotions, you must also recognize their unpredictable nature. If you expect to be happy all the time, you set yourself up for failure. You then risk blaming yourself when you 'fail' to be happy, or even worse, beat yourself up for it.

To start taking control of your emotions you must accept they are transient. You must learn to let them pass without feeling the need to identify strongly with them. You must allow yourself to feel sad without adding commentaries such as, "I shouldn't be sad," or "What's wrong with me?" Instead, you must allow reality to just be.

No matter how mentally tough you are, you will still experience sadness, grief, or depression in your life— hopefully not at the same time, and not continually. At times, you will feel disappointed, betrayed, insecure, resentful, or ashamed. You will doubt yourself and doubt your ability to be the person you want to be. But that's okay because emotions come, but, more importantly, they go.

Chapter 13: The Nature of Emotions

Your negative emotions are not bad or useless.

You may blame yourself for experiencing negative emotions or, perhaps, you see yourself as mentally weak. You may even believe something is wrong with you. However, despite what your inner voice may say, your emotions are not bad. Emotions are simply emotions. Nothing more.

As such, being depressed does not make you less of a person than you were three weeks ago when you were happy. Feeling sad now does not mean you will never be able to laugh again.

Remember this: the way you interpret emotions, as well as the blame game you engage in, creates suffering, not the emotions themselves.

The positive role of negative emotions

Your emotions are not here to make your life harder, but to tell you something. Without them, you would not grow.

Think of your negative emotions as the emotional equivalent of physical pain. While you hate being in pain, if you did not have pain, chances are you would be dead by now. Physical pain sends a powerful signal that something is wrong, nudging you to act of some kind. It could be to consult your doctor, which may lead you to undergo surgery, change your diet, or increase exercise. Without physical pain, you would not do any of these things and your situation would worsen, potentially leading to a premature death.

Emotions work the same way. They signal you to do something about your current situation. Perhaps, you need to let go of some people, quit your job, or remove a disempowering story that creates suffering in your life.

The fleeting nature of emotions

No matter how depressed you are, how much grief you are experiencing, or how horrible you feel at a given point in time, this shall pass.

Look at some of the negative emotions you experienced in the past. Remember the worse times in your life. During these most difficult periods, you were probably so caught up in your emotions you imagined never being able to escape them. You could not imagine being happy again. But even these episodes ended. Eventually, the clouds dissipated and the real you shone again.

Your emotions come and they go. Your depression will go, your sadness will vanish, and your anger will fade away.

Bear in mind, if you experience the same emotions repeatedly, it probably means you hold disempowering beliefs and need to change something in your life.

If you suffer from severe, chronic depression, it might be a good idea to consult a specialist.

The trickiness of emotions

Have you ever felt you will never be happy again? Have you ever been so attached to your emotions you thought they will never go away?

Do not worry, it is a common feeling.

Negative emotions act as a filter that taints the quality of your experiences. During a negative episode, every experience is perceived through this filter. While the world outside may remain the same, you will experience it in a completely different way based on how you feel.

For instance, when you are depressed, you do not enjoy the food you eat, the movie you see, or the activities in which you engage. You only see the negative side of things, feeling trapped and powerless. On the other hand, when you are in a positive mood, everything in life appears better. Food tastes great, you are naturally friendlier, and you enjoy all the activities you partake in.

You may now believe that, armed with the knowledge you have gained from this book, you will never be depressed again. Wrong! You will keep experiencing sadness, frustration, depression, or resentment, but hopefully, each time these occur, you will become wiser and wiser, remembering that this too, shall pass.

I have to admit, I can easily be fooled by my emotions. While I know I am not my emotions, I still give them too much credit and fail to realize they are just temporary visitors. More importantly, I fail to remember they are not me. Emotions always come and go, but I remain. Once, the emotional storm has passed, I generally feel like an idiot for having taken my emotions so seriously. Do you?

Interestingly, external factors might not be—and often are not—the direct cause of a sudden change in your emotional state. You can be in the exact same situation, with the same job, the same amount of money in your bank account, and have the same problems as always, but experience radically different emotional states. In fact, if you look at your past, this is often what happens. You are mildly depressed for a couple of hours or a few days, before bouncing back to your 'default' emotional state. During this period of emotional stress, your environment does not change at all. The only thing that changes is your internal dialogue.

I encourage you to make a conscious effort to notice whenever such events happen and start seeing through your emotions' trickery. You might want to go one step further and record these events in a journal. By doing so, you will gain a deeper understanding of how emotions work and, as a result, you will be better equipped to manage them.

Eckhart Tolle, the Power of Now.

Negative emotions are like a spell. While you are under their influence, breaking free from them seems impossible. You may know dwelling on the same thoughts is pointless, yet you cannot help but go along with the flow. Feeling an intense pull, you keep identifying with your thoughts and, as a result, feel worse and worse. When this happens, no rational argument seems to work.

The more these emotions fit your personal story, the stronger the pull becomes. For instance, if you believe you are not good enough, you may experience negative emotions such as guilt or shame each time you judge what you do is 'not good enough.' Because you have experienced these emotions so many times before, they have become an automatic response.

The filtering power of emotions

Your emotional state can drastically affect your outlook on life, leading you to act and behave differently.

When you are in a positive state, you have more energy available. This gives you:

- More confidence in everything you do

- An openness to consider new actions that could improve your life

- The ability to leave or break out of your comfort zone

- More emotional room to persevere during tough times

- Better ideas and enhanced creativity, and

- Easy access to positive emotions within the same emotional range.

When you are in a negative state of mind, you have less energy available, giving you:

- A lack of confidence that affects everything you do

- A lack of motivation that reduces the scope of actions you are willing to take

- A reluctance to take on new challenges and leave your comfort zone

- A reduced ability to persevere in face of setbacks, and

- A propensity to attract negative thoughts within the same emotional range.

Let us have a look at a real example.

Real life example:

Let me share with you a real example from my own life. Both cases happened under the same external conditions. The only difference was my emotional state at the time.

Case 1 - Feeling excited about my online business:

- An openness to consider new courses of action: I am open to new ideas or to work on a new project. I can think of ways to collaborate with other authors and start building a new coaching program to offer my audience.

- The ability to get out of my comfort zone: It becomes easier for me to push myself beyond my comfort zone. I may contact people I don't know or run 'Facebook Lives' for instance.

- More emotional room to persevere I stick to my projects even when I lack motivation.

- Better ideas and enhanced creativity. I am open to new ideas. I might come up with new ideas for books, articles, or other creative projects.

- Easy access to more positive emotions: I attract more positive emotions. At the same time, my mind rejects negative thoughts more easily, by refusing to identify with them.

Case 2 - Feeling mildly depressed due to my lack of results:

- A lack of confidence: I start doubting myself and all the projects I am currently working on. Suddenly, everything I do becomes useless or 'not good enough.' Thoughts like, "What's the point?", "I'm not going to make it," or "I'm stupid," cross my mind. Needless to say, promoting myself becomes a major challenge.

- A lack of motivation: I do not feel like doing anything. I am attacked by, and am unable to escape, negative thoughts. I have the same negative thoughts again and again, which repeat like a broken record. They seem so real and taint all my experiences.

- A difficulty to take on new challenges: I have little energy left over to leave my comfort and undertake challenging projects.

Chapter 14: How to Build Self-Confidence

If you want to be seen as confident, and reap the benefits that come along with self-confidence, you want to make sure that you are able to walk the walk that goes along with the talk. This means that you need to start building up the traits of a self-confident individual. As you develop these traits, you will find that you are far more likely to succeed in your interactions with other people. People tend to love those who are self-confident, and if you can manage to make yourself as self-confident as you reasonably can, you will find that your own positivity will attract more positivity into your life.

Believing in Yourself

Perhaps the most important step to becoming self-confident is beginning to believe in yourself. This is a tough one, as most people find that they struggle, at least in some capacity, with believing in themselves from time to time. Do not worry—you do not have to be able to believe in yourself all of the time. In fact, you should absolutely know how to tell what your weaknesses are as they arise, allowing you to tell whether you are actually capable of doing something or not.

Remember, a major portion of being self-confident is knowing your own abilities, good and bad. Even knowing your weaknesses and having a realistic idea of when it is best to completely reject the idea of being able to do something can be considered self-confident. For example, if you are being asked to go get something out of the deep water, but you do not know how to swim, no one is going to think twice about you politely declining and saying that you cannot— because you truly cannot. This does not mean that you lack self-confidence—in fact, it solidifies the self-confidence you do have because you recognize that your inability would prevent you from safely completing the request.

When you can do whatever is being requested, however, it is important that you believe in yourself. It is okay to be afraid of failing, but actually allowing yourself to fail due to inaction is far worse. Take the time to remind yourself that you can, and should, be able to do what you are being asked, spend a moment to walk yourself through the steps, and go for it. If you feel like you are entirely incapable of everything, then start branching out. Trust yourself enough to learn. Respect yourself enough to give it a legitimate try. Love yourself enough to not quit needlessly when you could have legitimately finished the project with a bit of extra effort.

Remember, you are more capable than you know. You just have to give yourself the chance to succeed. The bird trusted itself when it leaped from the nest for the first time to fly. The baby trusted himself enough to let go of the edge of the sofa he was holding onto in order to attempt to walk. You can push yourself over the edge and try to do things, too. Just believe that you can and give it your best shot. The worst that could happen is failure, and failing is rarely as bad as people think it will be.

Persuading Yourself

When you find that you cannot believe in yourself for some reason, it is time to persuade yourself to do so. Your self-confidence is based upon your own self-reflection and your ability to acknowledge your own strengths and weaknesses. This means that you need to be willing to convince yourself sometimes that what you are asking of yourself is not something that is impossible. It is not something that is even scary—all you need to do is give it a shot, and if you fail, you just try again.

This can be a scary one for many people—it is tough trying to look at yourself as someone that is capable after a lifetime of self-doubt. However, life on the other side is much more pleasant. Instead of being afraid of failing and letting that fear cripple and stunt you, you are using it as a launching pad. Everything was new to you at some point, and that is okay. Everything was new to everyone at some point—even the people next to you that you are comparing yourself to were new in the beginning for them—they started this life with exactly what you did: A blank slate. It is up to you what you do with that blank slate.

When you are trying to convince yourself to try something or to feel a bit more confident, try to stop and think about what you are good at. Everyone is good at something—you just need to figure out what that is for you. If you cannot think of something that you are good at, try some new things. Find a few new hobbies and attempt them. You will find something that you can take pride in—and you should. That pride will help boost you up into self-confidence that you can take with you and use better other aspects of your life.

When you do find those things that you are good at, latch onto them. Remind yourself that you have permission to not be good at everything that you attempt, but that you are also skilled at several different things as well, such as your ability to engage in whatever that newfound hobby is.

If you still fail to come up with anything that you are good at, try asking other people that you trust. If you were to go up to a loved one or a trusted one and say that you are working on your self-confidence, but really struggling to identify something that you are good at, you can probably get a few suggestions from those that see you when you are not paying attention. You may find out that you are actually significantly better at plenty of different things than you ever really expected, and that alone can help boost up some confidence.

Letting Go of Negative Thoughts

Negative thoughts tend to be at the root of all struggles with self-confidence. If you struggle to be self-confident, it is probably because you have all sorts of negative thoughts swirling around in your mind, and those can be dangerous if you let them continue to grow unchecked. When they grow and fester, you will find that more and more of your thinking and ability to rationalize your own abilities will become negative as well. Negativity is contagious, after all.

Think about the last time that you bought berries and left them in your fridge for too long. One berry begins to mold, and soon, that mold spreads and takes over all of the berries that were nearby, even though several of those berries may have been perfectly ripe still. Your negativity is like the mold on the berry—it will spread. It will begin to infect other areas of your life. Your one negative thought can slowly become two, then three, and eventually, using a negative thought

132

process has become your natural state of being. You stopped trying to avoid negativity and instead unintentionally embraced it. In embracing that negativity, you discovered the dangers of negativity, and any confidence that you may have had will pay for it.

Ignoring Other People's Opinions

When you lack self-confidence, much of your life is spent worrying and wondering how other people feel about you. Instead of focusing on how you feel in your skin, you start to put your value in the feelings of other people on the subject. You want to make sure that you are popular, or that you are taking the road that most people would agree is best. You stop thinking about what you want or who you want to be and instead begin to focus on becoming who you think others want you to be.

Remember, the only person whose opinions of you matters is yourself. Ultimately, if no one else likes who you are or what you choose to do with yourself, that is their own loss. You do not need to live your life trying to prove yourself for other people that do not matter. You need to assign your own self-worth and look at that through your own eyes.

When you are willing to ignore the opinions of other people, you learn to be truer to yourself. You learn to embrace what you love, no matter what the consequence of doing so, maybe. You no longer see situations as ways that you could be embarrassed. An accident is no longer a mortifying event. All that matters to you is how you are feeling about yourself because, ultimately, the only one who has to live with you is yourself.

Focusing on Positivity

Finally, when you want to build self-confidence, you need to not only leave behind the negativity but also to focus on the positivity. Stop worrying about what went wrong—accidents happen. People are not perfect. Not everything is going to work out according to plan. However, you should be capable of dealing with the instances in which things do not go as expected. This means that you should be capable of recognizing positivity when you see it.

There is almost always something positive to be found, even in the worst of situations. For example, is a car accident that kills someone who becomes an organ donor and saves five other lives really all bad? Yes, the fact that the one person died is terrible, but there are five positives right there as well.

That does not mean that you cannot grieve if someone dies, or that you cannot be upset about something going wrong. However, instead of letting that grief or upset consume you, try to find the positives that you can see. Do not cry that you lost someone—be glad that you had them to begin with. Not everyone is lucky enough to have the friend, family member, parent, or child that you had, and you should think about how lucky you were that you had them in your life, no matter how long.

Conclusion

Possessing low self-esteem may result in people being discouraged, falling short of their ability, or tolerating abusive relationships and circumstances. It can also be a symptom of pathological narcissism in which individuals can act in a self-centered, narcissistic, and dishonest manner.

Including academic and professional achievement in friendships and mental health, self-esteem will affect life in many ways. Nevertheless, self-esteem is not an immutable characteristic; both personal and professional achievements and failures will cause variations in self-worth feelings. Self-esteem has been shown to influence not only current physical and mental wellbeing and health-related attitudes, but also long-term health and wellbeing-related habits in adulthood. Self-esteem is an extremely useful tool for health professionals during their encounters with clients, staff, other members of the health-care team, hospital, and medical students.

Women with low self-esteem consider many flaws in themselves, whether it is real or not. They are too eager to please and win the affections of other people and not to offend them. They are also jealous of other women with characteristics and possessions that they want to have. They have an aura of animosity around them and have no excuse to be irritable. They focus on the thoughts and compliments of other people to draw an image of their worth.

Women with low self-esteem may establish an attitude of the survivor, which may find it increasingly difficult to see the future favorably and express themselves. The more a woman deals with chronic low self-esteem, the more vulnerable and depressed, she may feel when it comes to changing her thoughts and behaviors. She may be searching for people in her life that strengthen her negative view of herself and those around her without being conscious of it. It is a process to change how women perceive themselves, and some women may need a professional's support to do so.

All women have the ability to make changes in their lives and be productive. Little experiences may give great lessons for women. She should take the spackle and do it herself instead of asking for her husband or a handyman to patch the ding in the wall behind the bathroom door. Small successes make a woman feel good about herself and accomplished. That emotion will drive her to take more risks and grow higher self-confidence and esteem. Through behaving with control, people can begin to feel it. Women can also pay attention to other women in their lives who take risks and have a strong sense of self-esteem and recruit one or more of them as their mentor.

If a woman is ambitious and has a habit of contrasting herself to others, she may feel inadequate if she does not reach her expectations. This can have an effect on her self-esteem. If at her last work-related conference, she gave a less impressive message, her therapist can help her develop a plan to cope successfully with failures such as these in a manner that is not conflicting with her self-worth. A woman sees hundreds, if not thousands, of other women who do not look like her every day of a woman's life, on the internet, on television, in magazines, and on posters going to work. These images affect how she feels about herself and directly correlate with the faith of that woman, chipping away all day long at her happiness.

Taking Better Care of Your Diet

Better health overall always starts in the gut. Your gut health is directly responsible for nearly every else in your body, from balanced hormones to proper organ function. When you are taking good care of your gut health, taking care of everything else becomes significantly easier. So how do you do that?

Proper gut health starts with a nutritious diet that is rich in everything you need to not only survive but also thrive.

Eating a diet rich in color and with adequate proteins, fatty acids, and other important nutrients can support you in having stronger health in general. This means that you will begin to experience greater self-worth and greater self-esteem!

While supplements can be a beneficial way of getting important nutrients into your body, the best way to go about it is to eat a diet that is rich in what your body needs. Supplements do not tend to be broken down and absorbed by the body as easily, resulting in you simply passing many of the nutrients via urine or stool. If you do choose to use supplements in addition to a healthier diet, it is important to choose organic, high-quality supplements that will deliver the best impact on your body. You should also adjust your diet to increase your levels of healthy nutrients and vitamins.

Some things that you should begin adding to your diet to improve your overall health, specifically your mental health, include things like chia seeds, salmon, spinach, and eggs which are all rich in omega fatty acids. These acids are excellent for your brain health. Other foods include berries, nuts (especially Brazil nuts), oysters, yogurt, liver, and broccoli. These all contain high levels of vitamins like vitamins C, D, and B, protein, calcium, and other minerals.

You can further increase your nutrient intake by choosing organic, pesticide-free food.

Exercising More Frequently

Exercising is an important part of our lives that many of us tend to overlook. When we do not exercise adequately, we begin to experience the side effects of this behavior both physically and mentally. Physically, we struggle to do things that may have been easy for us at one point. Perhaps we may feel like we are not on par with our peers. It can be more of a challenge to carry things, enjoy doing activities with loved ones, or otherwise stay active and involved in others' lives when we are struggling from ill health due to lack of exercise. Low stamina and increased instances of chronic pain are just two of the many things that people with a poor exercise routine face.

Increasing your daily exercise and staying on track with a routine are great ways to increase your physical and mental health. Physically, it relieves stress from your body and helps you get back in shape. As a result, your hormone levels balance out and you begin to feel better. Your body and brain function optimally, your stress levels drop, your strong emotions dissipate in a positive way, and your capacity to face things in your day to day life increases.

Receiving Adequate Rest

In addition to eating right and getting enough exercise, you also need to make sure that you are getting a consistent, high-quality sleep. Rest is a highly underrated part of our daily lives, and it is typically the first to be impacted when we are feeling stressed out or unwell. We begin to find ourselves sleeping less, feeling more restless when we sleep, or otherwise not feeling fully rested when we wake. As a result, we are exhausted, and our ability to function effectively throughout the day is further impacted. Soon, we skip exercising because we are too tired. Then, we begin to continue skipping it because skipping becomes a habit. Before we know it, we are also skipping eating or eating healthy meals because we are feeling too tired to prepare them. The spiral continues until we are in a rut, feeling as though we are at our worst with a poor exercise habit, an unhealthy diet, and an even worse sleeping pattern.

Instead of letting yourself get caught in this spiral that is all too familiar for most, you can choose to pay attention to your rest and ensure that you are getting adequate sleep. Whenever you sense that you are not feeling rested enough or you are feeling too tired to do things, instead of breaking your daily routine, seek to add some extra opportunities to catch up on rest throughout the day. Take it easy by letting go of unnecessary tasks temporarily as you catch up on sleep. Go to bed a bit earlier and ensure that you practice a positive bedtime routine that will support you in having a positive sleep. Using things like chamomile, lavender, and other natural sleep aids can help you resume a restful sleep. You can also lower the lights in your house about an hour before bedtime, turn off screens, and prepare yourself for a good night's rest.

RESILIENCE TO CURE CODEPENDENCY

The Strategic Guide to Learn the Art of Detachment and Improve Self-Esteem. Find out how to Overcome Jealousy and be Codependent no More

Introduction

"Codependency" is one of those words that sound more harmless than it is.

On the face of it, it sounds normal and healthy to be mutually "dependent" with other people, doesn't it? This might explain why people frequently use this term incorrectly, putting the label on any relationship that looks enmeshed, unbalanced or unhappy.

But what does codependency really mean?

This concept comes from the field of addictions counseling. Very early on, psychologists and social workers realized that it was not enough to merely treat a substance problem by treating the person who happened to end up in rehab. Rather, when you look closely, you begin to understand that addiction is a problem that affects all the relationships in an addict's life. Even though the addict's friends or family or romantic interests don't themselves have a problem with the substance, their behavior is nevertheless warped and changed by the presence of addiction anyway. In other words, the addict is dependent, and the people in the addict's life are "codependent". While an individual is under the control of a substance, the people closest to him are in turn controlled and manipulated by the addict.

Imagine a man with a gambling addiction. He is a little "rough around the edges", and has always attracted supremely feminine, kind and long-suffering women into his life. His wife is his counterfoil. Although she hates gambling, she is as much a part of the problem as he is. Because she enjoys playing savior, and secretly relishes moments where people wonder aloud how such a lovely woman could end up with such a troubled man, she keeps re-enacting moments when she has to "save" him or play the martyr. Because she enjoys feeling needed by her husband, she unconsciously avoids anything that would end his addiction. The husband in turn is caught in a never-ending cycle of crime and forgiveness, unwilling to break his addiction since in all honesty, it forms the basis of his connection with his wife. If they never argued about gambling, what would they even talk about?

The term "codependent" has come to loosely describe any relationship that forms around a dysfunction, where one partner is unhealthily preoccupied with the needs of the other instead of their own. A codependent relationship is one where the boundaries between individuals are blurred, constantly violated or non-existent. Such people may be trapped in cycles and patterns of destructive behavior that both can't seem to break out of. Connections are tumultuous, conflict frequent. These are the couples that everyone quietly wonders, why are they even together?

Chapter 1 : Core of Co-Dependency

We all are born as unique individuals. We have an innate quality to feel and respond to our internal awareness as well as our external environment. This is how we are able to learn, plan, create and relate to others using our personal experiences. Co-dependency hinders the development of this unique sense of individuality thus restricting our engagement with the outside world in general.

It is very difficult to define the term self and should be simply understood as the coalescence of all your unique individuality, your essential being. Co-dependents adapt and react to other's individuality and the sense of self, totally negating their own unique being in order to cope up with life. This leads them to feel like a fraud and that they are cheating the world all the time. Co-dependents remain in an unhappy temperament owing to these facts.

147

Are you addicted? Are you ill?

Psychiatrist Timmen Cermak suggested that Co-dependency is a disease back in the year 1988. While it may sound morbid to term it as a disease, co-dependency should be seen as a condition with discernible, progressive symptoms that impair the regular or normative functioning of the individual. Like all other diseases or medical conditions, this can be treated and its symptoms are reversed. Alcoholism became an illness in 1956 and the American Medical Association (AMA) clubbed alcoholism with drug dependency in 1991. The 1960 publication of The Disease Concept of Alcoholism by E. Morton Jellinick removed most of the shame revolving around alcoholism, branding it as a disease and not a behavioral issue. Ever since then, many medical and psychiatric practitioners have applied the medical model of treatment to various addictions such as gambling, sex, drugs etc. The same medical model has also been applied to the treatment of Co-dependency by medical practitioners and psychiatrists. However, some practitioners and counselors object to the classification of co-dependency as a disease and argue that doing so stigmatizes, discourages and disempowers the person who is trying to recover. They believe that by labeling it as a disease, they make the patients see the futility of giving up on their addiction. People start believing that they do not have any power to put a stop to their addictive behavior.

The practitioners and psychiatrists on the other camp argue that, on the contrary, labeling co-dependency as a disease, it removes shame and the punitive treatment of any addiction. This makes it possible for the disease to be treated in a way similar to any other physical ailment such as diabetes, hypertension or blood pressure.

It has been intensively argued whether any biological component of addiction and co-dependency is required for it to be termed as a physical disease. Today by brain scans of addicts and co-dependents it has been revealed that there are defects in the patient's brain, primarily in the brain's pleasure center that process dopamine. It is still contestable whether the dopamine dysfunction predates the patient's addiction or it is the other way around. Investigations into this area are happening as we speak, all over the world as they try and examine how a person's genes play an important part in the addiction. Researchers have also found out that environmental factors that include parenting and trauma play a part in the development of an individual's addiction later in their lives. Trauma and depression have a negative impact on the chemistry of the brain and they induce negative thoughts leading to depression. It is important to understand that label or no label, it is totally up to you to recover from co-dependency. You can call it a disease, or an addiction, only your efforts can bring you out of the trap of co-dependency.

Cross-Addiction

All addicts are dependent by default. They depend and rely heavily upon the object of their addictions. They end up spending most of their time and resources in and around their addictions. When these addicts choose to abstain, they may develop cross-addictions. Sober alcoholics take to smoking cigarettes, overreacting; develop sex addiction and so on. Food addicts who undergo bariatric surgeries become alcoholics or shopaholics.

This cross-addiction can result from a variety of factors. Neuroscience claims that when addicts stop practicing their addictions, they adopt other secondary addictions. This is at the same level as their primary addiction and can be just as harmful to the recovering patient. For an instance, it is quite possible for an abstaining gambler to resort to drinking alcohol or chain-smoking cigarettes. The abstinence from gambling is of no use because the addict resorts to other addictions with as much passion as his previous addictions. This happens because the patient does not recover from their addiction at an emotional level bringing in co-dependent traits in their behavior.

Cross addictions are easy to pick up when an addict starts abstaining from his or her addictions. Many new abstainers try and rush into relationships. This has become to be sometimes jokingly called as the thirteenth step of the twelve-step program! They are confronted with the relationship issues they have faced in the past. They have to address these issues of emotional insecurity, a problem that they have avoided or tried avoiding for long. There are some who resort to a newcomer in their life, which could be their newborn child and even 'obsess' about it. This again brings us back to the initial problem of co-dependency from where it all started. Sometimes it takes up years before a person addresses his or her co-dependency issues, contributing to frequent relapses into addictions. The mental obsessions through which most recovering addicts skim though redirect their means of controlling anxiety and addressing repressed feelings. This book is an attempt to bridge the gap between the surfing addicts and their lost sense of self. That plays a big part in the addict's recovery and in preventing relapses.

Feminine aspect of Co-dependency

Women comprise a large part of the co-dependents today.

Biological Factor

Women are wired for relationships naturally. Their limbic systems complement their ability to bond with others. Under pressure, the male hormones prepare for action while the female hormones prepare them to tend for children or form relationships with others.

Development of a gender(ed) identity

Generally, girls grow up depending more on their parents than the average male child. They are emotionally bonded to their family and are more accepting of the parental values. The rupture of their relationship with the parents is a constant source of anxiety for them. Autonomy is the biggest challenge for most girls and the lack of the same promotes co-dependent characteristics in their behavior. For the male child, intimacy is a challenge.

Political reasons

Women have been subjugated politically and socially over the large part of the modern and pre modern history. They have been placed subordinate to the male on various levels and had to fend for the most basic of the rights such as the right to education and universal suffrage rights. Generations of oppression have made the women compliant and lower their self-esteem. They begin to seek identity from the established status quo and end up depressed and anxious.

Cultural Factors

In most cultures across the world, girls have had far lesser autonomy than boys. This autonomy has been restricted to girls in all walks of life from dressing choices to education choice and even matrimonial choice. They are seldom allowed to choose for themselves and thus do not have any sort of autonomy over their own bodies.

RELIGION

Almost all of the major religions of this world have placed women in subservient roles to men. They are expected to comply with the male figures in their families for all their lives. Women have had lesser authority over household matters and even matters concerning their own life.

SOCIAL

A greater number of women suffer from personal insecurities and a low self-esteem, which leads to depression and anxiety troubles. It has not been established whether this is a direct cause, a byproduct or a concurrence of co-dependency. According to a Dove study, over 40 percent women are dissatisfied or unhappy with their appearance and about two thirds suffer from insecurities regarding their bodies. The airbrushed ideal models of how the feminine should look are to be blamed for promoting the severe anxiety in people regarding their appearances and bodies.

Chapter 2 : Signs of Codependency

One of the most difficult roadblocks in combatting codependency is denial. Oftentimes, one or both parties involved in a codependent relationship will have difficulty recognizing, and then admitting, the fact that the relationship has become unhealthy. Sometimes, an outside party or an intervention is required in order for codependents to recognize the issue. Moreover, there are instances in which codependents are fully aware of the unhealthiness in the relationship, but he or she is reluctant to outwardly acknowledge the issue or take action.

Luckily, there are ways in which we can identify codependency, which is the first step towards overcoming it and achieving a healthy relationship.

Firstly, it's important to separate codependency from interdependence. Within interdependence, individuals involved in a relationship are only dependent on one another to a degree. For instance, in a family environment, one parent might rely on the other spouse to help pay bills or carry out routines to help with the children. Likewise, the other spouse contributes in other, meaningful ways. This

155

does not mean that they are codependent, or that they are relying on one another to establish a sense of self-worth; in reality, they are individualistic yet can still approach the responsibilities of a family in a shared, healthy manner.

Here's one way to determine whether or not you might be in a codependent relationship: ask yourself whether or not you are frequently second-guessing your behaviors and actions. Or, you might simply be experiencing an ever-present, high level of anxiety. Individuals in a codependent relationship are frequently judging themselves, reflecting on what they should have done or said differently.

In essence, one of the most common effects of living in a codependent relationship is low self-esteem. Oftentimes, low self-esteem isn't as easy to identify as one may think. Individuals who strive for perfectionism may actually be suffering from low self-esteem; likewise, they may outwardly appear to be confident, but it could be a façade. Inwardly, people who are experiencing low self-esteem may be ridden with guilt and shame.

Also, codependents are often people-pleasers. They feel compelled, and perhaps even responsible, for contributing to another's happiness. Typically, these individuals are fearful of saying "no" and may even experience anxiety when presented with a situation or invitation they'd prefer to decline. In many instances, people-pleasers will say "yes" to something that they may not have wanted to agree to, but felt compelled and will instead put another's desires and needs in front of their own.

Furthermore, codependents may have difficulty establishing boundaries. They often internalize others' issues, feelings, thoughts, or needs, and establish an unhealthy sense of responsibility for their partner's sense of wellbeing. Nonetheless, some codependents may become withdrawn and actively draw up their boundaries, making it difficult for others to become close to them. In other instances, codependents might vary the behaviors in which they establish boundaries; sometimes they'll let their walls down, whereas other times they might be completely withdrawn.

Caretaking is another common behavior found in codependent relationships. Oftentimes, the caretaker puts the other party in front of his or her own needs. The caretaker feels obligated to help the other individual, and might even experience feelings of rejection if the other refuses help. Moreover, the caretaker might become obsessed with the notion that he or she can "fix" the other person in the relationship, even if that individual isn't trying to overcome whatever obstacles he or she is suffering from.

Another behavior that might indicate codependency is overreaction. While most individuals do react to others' thoughts and feelings, codependents might feel threatened by adverse opinions. Instead of brushing off differing views, the codependent might absorb the sentiment and start to believer it; or, he or she might react oppositely and become extremely defensive. Either way, too strong a reaction to what should be an insignificant comment might be a sign of codependency.

Codependents also typically seek a strong sense of control. They might seek control over the other individual in the relationship, or they might seek extreme control over one aspect of their own lives. For example, codependents might become addicts in one way or another; sometimes, they'll even become workaholics to take control over one aspect of their lives in totality. Caretakers and people-pleasers might even use these behaviors in order to take the aspect of control to the extreme, using their influence over others to manipulate them.

Furthermore, codependents may try to control the other person in the relationship by restricting his or her actions. The codependent may try to give orders to his or her partner. Conversely, codependents sometimes won't let their partners participate in certain activities or behaviors that make them feel threatened.

While codependents often intrude on others' space, this can also become a physical phenomenon as well. Observe your behavior, or that of those around you: does it seem as if you're always spilling, tripping, or just generally accident-prone? Perhaps you're infringing on someone else's personal space, or vice versa. Establishing personal boundaries, both physically and emotionally, is essential to having a healthy relationship.

In many instances, codependents rely on dysfunctional means of communication. They may not be able to present their thoughts or feelings in a healthy, clear manner. Moreover, a codependent may have difficulty determining what he or she is thinking in the first place. If you notice this behavior pattern in yourself, it might be an indication that something is wrong in your relationship. Or, if you notice that you're unwilling or afraid to be honest with your partner, this could be a sign of dysfunctional communication. For example, if your partner asks your opinion on something and you're afraid to be truthful, it could mean that the communication has become dishonest, which is most likely a result of the other party's manipulation.

This is often referred to as the "doormat" side of codependents. The codependent becomes literally unable to determine how he or she actually feels about a given subject, because he or she is so used to simply agreeing with others to appease them. Nonetheless, it's important to establish your own opinions and formulate thoughts on based on how *you* feel. Codependents become chameleons, as their views begin to blend in with everyone else's.

In addition, at least one codependent (or both) in a relationship is usually given very few opportunities to get a word in, especially during arguments. One person may exhibit cues indicating that he or she is impatient, and simply waiting for his or her turn to speak instead of actually listening. That person has already determined what he or she is going to say, regardless of what *your* point is. Thus, the conversation will most likely become an unhealthy, one-sided argument in which one person's opinions or views will get squashed by the other's, instead of both parties trying to reach some level of understanding or compromise.

Finally, if you're concerned that you or someone you know could be involved in a codependent situation, assess the general emotions of the potential codependent: Are there signs of shame or rejection present? If you're suspecting codependency within your own relationship, have you sunken into a state of depression, resentment, or hopelessness? Usually, one party may develop a sense of failure: you might begin to feel as though no matter what you do, it's never enough to make the other party satisfied. Eventually, you could become numb and withdrawn.

You or your loved one may not exhibit all of the signs listed above, but chances are that if you've noticed at least some of these indicators frequently enough to become concerned, you may be part of a codependent relationship. Next, we'll discuss how you can move forward and work towards achieving a healthier relationship.

Chapter 3 : Advantages and Disadvantages of Co-Dependency

When we look closely at the co-dependent, we are often quick to judge and only see that dysfunction in their relationship. However, it is quickly forgotten that while this dysfunction is visible to us at its worst was most often rooted in the very foundation of one's love for their spouse, parent, or child. The question then becomes, when does one's love for their partner, parent or child turn from something wonderful to be cherished and becomes something dysfunctional?

Love for another and feelings of charity towards them are not often viewed as a disorder. However, the truth is that when the attachment towards another surpasses the norm to the point that we deny our own needs in order to provide for the selfish needs of our loved one, our feelings of self-worth and self-esteem are greatly diminished as a result. At times like these, it is right to conclude that there is something missing in our lives, am emptiness that we are looking to fill either one that we have had since childhood or one that has developed as a result of our past relationships. Either way once an individual has taken a turn down this path the emotional toll is vast.

Advantages of Co-dependency are certain uneven traits displayed towards the partner, like:

1) **Love**

2) **Responsibility**

3) **Caring**

4) **Peace**

5) **Assurance**

6) **Faith**

7) **Safety**

8) **Security**

9) **Support**

10) **Finance**

11) **Stability**

12) **Happiness**

13) **False Contentment**

The advantages of co-dependent relationships are often momentary, the results of certain events which give rise to a favorable set of circumstances. These advantages can be achieved even in a co-dependent relationship if there is at some point a healthy attachment to each other, one in which the needs of both partners in a relationship participate. However, this does not stand to say that love alone is a valid reason to become obsessively possessive of one another. Certain experiences together such as intimacy are capable of creating the illusion of everything in our lives becoming magical, miraculous or eternal. But in reality, the danger in not being able to recognize when the attachment has crossed from normalcy, to dysfunction!

If you find a virus in your computer and it fails to function properly you do not continue to operate that machine hoping that it will fix itself, instead you backup your computer and take it in for repair before more damage a can be done. Just like repairing your computer, it is possible to seek out help and repair the "virus" that is a co-dependent relationship in order to attain a healthy relationship. There are so many forms of help available to those who wish to find it, therapists, support groups, 12 step programs, counselors, treatment centers and self-help books. There is a tool to fit everyone's life and personal needs. All you need to do is take the first step and admit that you need help.

Disadvantages of Co-Dependency

Now to come to the obvious side of the issue, co-dependency is evidently a high dosage of negativity that can mentally damage or impair not only you but all of those around you. If you're the co-dependent or not, it is undeniable at least one addiction or negative emotional force has become the centre of your world. This is not only an unhealthy relationship, but has the potential to cause further disruption to your emotional state with feelings of depression, distress or hopelessness.

The first disadvantage of co-dependency is that if you are incapable of tolerating any disapproval, then you're setting yourself up to be exposed to manipulation. We are all individuals, no matter who else is in our life, parents, children, spouses, significant others, our failures and our successes are purely ours and not the result of what we can do for others. Each of us has a different perspective on life and a different perception of life than every other person alive. Once we are gone, no one else will ever have this same perception again, because it was purely ours alone. If people are unable to be content as an individual, their life is going to be one rough ride. It also means that at the advent of any a relationship, good or bad, the intensity and the toxicity of the bond shared has a chance of being misunderstood by the co-dependent. It is to everyone's benefit to be aware of the signs that you are slipping into these negative trends and prevent them from harming you and your relationships.

Some of the most toxic disadvantages of co-dependency are:

1) **Anger**

2) **Ownership**

3) **Commanding**

4) **Intolerance**

5) **Blame-game**

6) **Worthlessness**

7) **Strong Nihilism**

8) **Loneliness/ Abandonment**

9) **Undue pressure of responsibilities**

10) **Fear of everything**

11) **Recurrent panic attacks**

12) **Laziness**

13) **Exhaustion**

14) **Lethargy**

15) **Poverty**

16) **Contempt**

17) **Hatred towards people**

18) Social-awkwardness

19) Possessiveness

20) Confusion

21) Paranoia

22) Low-self-esteem

23) Pessimism

24) Instability

25) Indecisiveness

26) Guilt

27) Rigidity

28) Chronic lying

29) Poor communication skills

30) Poor personal space/ boundaries

31) Abnormal dependency

32) Obsession

33) Repression

34) *Lack of faith*

35) Intimacy issues

36) Control-freak

37) Perfectionism

38) Drug/Sex/ Substance abuse

39) Critically sensitive to personal criticism

40) Suicidal tendencies

Chapter 4 : Types of Codependent Behavior

One of the biggest problems with codependent behavior is the fact that many people don't recognize the various forms that it can take. Just because the term "codependent" is a single term doesn't mean that it only has one face. Instead, it's a bit like ice cream. Even though ice cream is one type of food it comes in many, many flavors. The very same thing can be said about codependency. Despite it being one condition, it can come in many, many forms. Therefore, it is vital that you learn the different faces of codependent behavior so that you can recognize the signs that you are in a codependent relationship.

This chapter will discuss many of the different forms of codependent behavior so that you can recognize it in those around you as well as within yourself. The most common behaviors have been divided into four distinct categories, making it easier to follow and understand how these behaviors relate to one another. Most people will exhibit behaviors from one or two categories, some of which may be subtle in nature, while others may be more obvious and extreme. By understanding the different types of behaviors, it will be easier to recognize what type of codependent relationship you may be living in. This will help you to know which recovery path is right for you.

Abusive behaviors

The most extreme type of codependent behavior is abusive behavior. This is the category most people are already familiar with, and so it is the one that they readily associate to codependent relationships. Of the different types of abuses, physical abuse is one of the most extreme, and fortunately, one of the least common. More often than not the types of relationships affected by physical abuse are parent/child relationships and husband/wife relationships. It is a very rare occasion that any type of friendship suffers physical abuse, especially to the degree of what is needed to constitute a codependent relationship.

In the case of the parent/child relationship physical abuse often comes in the form of punishment. A parent will hit their child as a form of reprimand for an act that is considered wrong and undesirable. Needless to say, many people have physically punished their children from time to time, especially when the child does something dangerous that causes the parent to react in an emotional way. However, slapping a child's hand or even giving them a whack on the backside does not constitute physical abuse as such. Instead, physical abuse is when the parent beats their child relentlessly. Furthermore, the use of implements such as leather belts, wooden spoons or the like also points to abuse. You don't need to use a belt to get the point across, therefore such an act is extreme, indicating a deeper, more sinister root cause. Beating a child is often done in order to gain control over their behavior, and this is where the codependent nature of the act comes into play. Any time a person tries to control the thoughts, feelings or actions of another person they are engaging in codependent behavior.

It is this need for control that induces people to physically abuse their spouse as well. Any time a person hits their spouse it is done as a means to subdue the other person, physically as well as emotionally and psychologically. Needless to say, a spouse doesn't require the same type of reprimand that a young child might need. Instead, any differences of opinion or mistakes can be sorted out through an adult conversation, in which both sides present their point of view. When one person beats the other in order to gain supremacy it is a clear sign of codependent behavior.

Abuse can come in many forms, not just the physical beatings that most people associate the term with. One such alternate form is emotional abuse. Any time a person acts in a way so as to make you feel guilty about something you said or did, they are demonstrating codependent behavior. The bottom line is that no one should ever strive to make a person feel guilty about anything. Even if the other person did something terribly wrong, to increase the guilt they feel for that act is nothing short of emotional abuse. In essence, emotional abuse is when a person causes another person to suffer from within. This can also take the form of inducing fear. Someone who engages in physical abuse may use the fear of a beating in order to gain control over a child or spouse. Therefore, any time a person tries to control the actions or mindset of another person by inducing negative emotions within them they are practicing codependent behavior.

Finally, there is the form of abuse that is psychological in nature. This is the most elaborate form as it requires a great deal of thought and planning to actually pull off. Therefore, even though psychological abuse may not be seen as being as harmful as physical abuse it is in fact just as devastating, and the person committing it is just as dangerous in nature. The most common form of psychological abuse is that of attacking a person's self-esteem. This can take the shape of attacking a person's looks, calling them fat, ugly, skinny or any other derogatory term that makes a person feel inferior to others. It can also take the shape of attacking a person's abilities, such as their intellect, their memory, or their ability to perform certain tasks. The overall goal is to undermine a person's self-esteem in order to gain and maintain control over them. Any time this happens it is a sure sign of codependent behavior.

Low self-esteem behaviors

Codependent behaviors can also come from the side of the victim of a codependent relationship. In these cases, the behaviors are not abusive in nature, instead they are subservient in both form and purpose. After all, codependency is a two-way street, requiring both a taker and a giver. Therefore, it is just as common for givers to practice codependent behaviors in all of their relationships as it is for takers to do the same. Although the behaviors practiced by givers are safer and even more beneficial in appearance they are nonetheless just as dysfunctional and need to be fixed just as much as the behaviors demonstrated by takers.

More often than not the behaviors demonstrated by givers come in the form of low self-esteem behaviors. One such example is the need to please other people. Again, this behavior unto itself is not necessarily a bad thing. After all, any good friend will want to make sure their friends are happy and cared for. However, it is the extreme nature of the behavior that points to codependency. Wanting to please people from time to time is fine, but needing to please everybody all of the time is something else altogether. Yet, this is the nature of codependent behavior as demonstrated by givers. Any time you see someone endlessly trying to please everyone around them you know they are a giver, and thus they need help. The very same thing applies if you find yourself feeling the need to always please everyone around you all of the time.

This behavior can be taken to the next level in more extreme cases where the giver feels the need not just to please everyone, but to fix the problems in everyone else's lives. The compulsive need to fix other people's problems is a classic sign of codependent behavior on the part of the giver. Again, any good friend will want to offer advice when someone is having issues in life, however a codependent person will not only provide advice, they will want to step in and literally save the day. This need to fix other people's lives is dangerous, as it not only creates undue stress on the giver, but it also creates undue stress on those whose lives they are trying to fix. More often than not the giver will try to step in and take charge, feeling as though their efforts are normal and the outcome will justify the means. This can result in them being overbearing in nature, something that can mask the identity of a giver as givers are usually subservient and passive in nature. Yet it is this servile tendency that can cause extreme givers to exert themselves in a bold and commanding way, one that is overbearing and intrusive to those they are trying to help.

Sometimes the giver can demonstrate behavior that is more self-serving, and thus less obvious in terms of being codependent in nature. An example of this is the codependent behavior of overachieving. Many people have a competitive streak, and thus will strive to be the best in whatever it is they are doing. However, such actions are usually quite harmless, reflecting a good-hearted competitive spirit and nothing more. Givers take this to another level, striving to be the best at all costs. One reason is to compensate for the low self-esteem they suffer as the result of being abused by one or more takers in their life. Another reason, however, is to be the best so that they can better serve others and make everyone else happy. Either way, the efforts of a giver when it comes to being the best will be extreme, unceasing and potentially destructive, both to them as well as to everyone else involved. Their need to be the best will consume them, thereby clouding their judgment and causing them to behave unpredictably. If you or someone close to you is driven to be the best at all costs it probably points to codependent tendencies.

Denial behavior

The third type of codependent behavior is what is known as denial behaviors. This is where the individual cannot accept the reality of a situation, and thus rewrites reality to suit their needs. Such behavior can be demonstrated by both the giver and taker in a codependent relationship. The main difference between the two is that the taker rewrites reality in order to make themselves look better, whereas the giver rewrites reality in order to make others look better. In either case, the core behavior is that of denying what is real and replacing it with something that the individual finds more desirable.

Perhaps the most common of denial behaviors is that of denial itself. In the case of the taker this comes in the form of denying their responsibility anytime something goes wrong. Even when all the facts are blatantly obvious and point to the taker being solely responsible for a situation, they will deny that they are to blame in any way, shape or form. This denial can often be seen when a taker loses their job. Even if they are fired for poor performance, breaking policy or some other reason that is their fault alone they will deny the facts and place the blame on something else altogether. They may choose to blame the economy, stating that their company was downsizing but chose to fire them in order to avoid paying unemployment. Even worse, they may accept that their performance was to blame, but they will blame their home life for their poor performance, thus shifting blame from them to someone else, such as a spouse or parent. In any event, they will never allow blame to fall squarely on their shoulders. Instead, they will deny their role in anything that goes wrong, no matter how obvious that role may be.

Denial on the part of the giver takes another form altogether. In this case it is when the giver denies the harm that the taker is causing. This is often seen when a giver is physically abused by their spouse who is the taker in the codependent relationship. Rather than calling a spade a spade and accusing their spouse of abuse the giver will rewrite reality, accepting blame for the abuse they suffered. They may go as far as to say they caused the taker to hit them with their words or actions, even though they may not have said or done anything at all to warrant any kind of negative response, let alone physical violence. Needless to say, no action or spoken word ever deserves a violent response. However, givers will feed into the narrative that they are to blame for everything that goes wrong, and thus they will accept responsibility for the actions of those who abuse them in any way whatsoever. Anyone who denies the true nature of an abusive friend, relative or spouse is demonstrating classic denial codependent behavior.

Humor is another denial behavior, albeit an unexpected one. This is when a person uses humor to mask the pain and suffering, they are experiencing due to their codependent relationship. Obviously, this is a behavior demonstrated by the giver as opposed to the taker. After all, it is the giver who experiences the pain and suffering more so than the taker, therefore they are the ones who need to use humor to soothe their pain. Again, using humor to compensate for an unhappy situation is not dysfunctional behavior unto itself. What makes the use of humor dangerous is when it is used regularly to mask constant sorrow and pain. While many people can be jovial in nature, cracking jokes and laughing often, codependent people are those who seem to always be laughing, and they tend to be the ones who laugh the loudest. Furthermore, they are the ones who are always looking for reasons to laugh, such as telling jokes, pulling pranks or the like. The bottom line is that humor can be a drug of sorts, just like alcohol or pain killers, and a codependent person can become addicted to humor just as easily as they can to any other substance that provides relief from pain and suffering.

Numerous stories have come to light over the years regarding famous comedians living lives of tragedy and sorrow. Many people are shocked to discover that the comic personalities who are considered always happy and full of life are in fact suffering from severe depression, pain and emotional turmoil. It turns out that they used humor to medicate their suffering, and those who were the funniest were often the ones who were suffering the most. This is the nature of a codependent use of humor. When a person needs to be laughing all the time, never seeming to take anything seriously, they are probably demonstrating codependent denial behavior.

Finally, there is the denial behavior of unrealistic hopes. This is when a person denies realistic hopes and expectations, choosing instead to believe in something completely based in fantasy and imagination. In the case of the taker this behavior takes the form of the belief that all the things that are wrong in life will somehow resolve themselves without any effort on the part of the individual. Thus, rather than taking responsibility for their role in events the taker will rely on a savior riding in and rescuing them from a life beneath their true worth. Alternatively, a giver will live in the delusion that their situation will improve when the takers in their life realize the error of their ways and begin to live normal, healthy lives. Unfortunately, this is never likely to happen, yet rather than accepting the inevitability of their situation givers will hold out hope for the proverbial miracle that will rescue them from their life of suffering. In short, any time a person holds on to impossible dreams or fantasies, especially those that will fix the problems they have, they are demonstrating codependent denial behavior.

Victim behavior

The final type of codependent behavior to consider is what is referred to as victim behavior. This is where the individual, both taker and giver alike, view themselves as the victim in the relationship and act out accordingly. In both cases this behavior is intended to engender sympathy and support, providing the individual with the boost they need to feel better about themselves. However, victim behavior only ever enables both parties to be at their worst, thereby perpetuating a codependent relationship in which all parties suffer.

In the case of the taker, one of the most common types of victim behavior practiced is hypochondria. This has its roots in hospital settings where victims of injury or disease became addicted to the care and support provided by those around them and thus chose to be in a constant state of pain or sickness in order to continue receiving that care and support. However, hypochondriac behavior extends into every environment, including work, home and anywhere that a codependent relationship can exist. The bottom line is that the taker will create some issue that justifies their inability to care for themselves, while also creating the need to be cared for by another. It can come in the form of actual physical illness or suffering, or it can come in the form of a general inability to be self-sufficient. Ignorance, fear of failure, insecurity and the like can be used as an excuse to shirk responsibilities and acquire extra care and attention from the giver. In short, a taker will use anything to create sympathy, which is what they crave most of all.

Another way that a taker will use the victim mentality is to create a mindset that is wholly self-centered. This means that everything in life affects them personally, even if it has nothing to do with them at all. One explanation for this behavior is that it causes the giver to redirect their attention and sympathies from the actual situation to the taker instead. For example, if there is a tragic plane crash on the news, rather than allowing the giver to feel sympathy for the victims and their families the taker will put themselves in the spotlight. They may say it reminds them of an experience they were in, thus bringing up traumatic memories and feelings, or they may simply feign depression from the bad news in order to get the sole attention and sympathy of the giver. In any event, takers will turn the focal point of any situation into how it affects them personally, thereby getting the support and sympathy they crave.

Finally, there is the victim behavior known as martyr mentality. This behavior can be practiced by both taker and giver alike. In the case of the taker the individual creates a narrative in which they sacrifice everything for the happiness and wellbeing of others. Ironically, this is them projecting the actual role of the giver onto themselves. Even more ironic, the giver usually feeds in to this narrative, thanking the taker for their sacrifices even though such sacrifices usually don't have any basis in reality. For example, a taker may claim that by marrying their giver-spouse they gave up many other dreams that they would have pursued otherwise. Thus, they gave up potential happiness in order to provide a life for their spouse. Needless to say, such statements are improvable as alternate history can never be demonstrated. Unfortunately, takers use the inability to disprove such statements as a way to give them validity.

Givers use the martyr mentality to justify their subservient lifestyle and the sacrifices they really do make on an almost daily basis. Rather than accepting that they are in a wholly dysfunctional relationship they give meaning to their suffering by painting themselves as the proverbial martyr. Sometimes they see this as punishment for past sins or perceived wrongdoing, whereas other times they see it as their calling, one that they will be rewarded for in a future life or afterlife. In short, the martyr mentality allows the giver to justify their situation, providing it with meaning and purpose rather than recognizing it as a purely dysfunctional relationship in which they are being abused and taken advantage of. Unfortunately, by finding meaning in this way the giver further commits themselves to their role in the codependent relationship, thereby ensuring that it continues to live on day after day, week after week and year after year.

Chapter 5 : Codependents and Their Personalities

Codependents have a lot to work on regarding their personalities. They are unique individuals on their own, but as codependents they have a lot within them and a lot to learn. They are a work in progress; they have such fragile personalities that hoping to change them will require patience and perseverance.

Codependents as Dependent Personalities

The irony about codependents is that as much as they feel responsible for others and attend to other people, they believe underneath that other people are actually responsible for them. They blame others for their problems and unhappiness, and for them, it's the fault of other people why they are unhappy.

Codependents find it hard to function independently; they must be involved in supportive relationships so they can manage their lives. To maintain their relationships, they will avoid getting angry. They'll become meek and docile; they tend to admire and love endlessly, and will be willing to offer all they can. They seem to be "perfect lovers" –

unquestioning, loyal and affectionate, and even considerate and tender on those people whom they rely on.

Unfortunately, these people aren't perfect after all: they feel inferior, and will meet even those unreasonable demands to avoid abandonment and isolation. They'll perhaps resort to abuse and intimidation because they fear they can't function by themselves. Unpleasant tasks are not a problem if it will mean having on hand the support and the care they need. Bonds are important to them, and if various sacrifices have to be made, then so be it.

Getting Better

Yes, you, as a codependent, can get better. How? This is by accepting that success and happiness can only be achieved by changing yourself and not the behavior of other people.

You have to detach yourself from other people and their problems. You have to learn how to stop reacting instinctively and impulsively as rescuers. Be in control of your own life. Getting involved with someone means that s/he will be an addition to your life – not someone who replaces it.

Detachment from Triggers

Detachment should be done emotionally, mentally, and – if necessary – physically from painful and unhealthy relationships. You have to learn how to let go of other people's lives and responsibilities, as well as those problems that you can't solve. By doing so, you'll become the person that you really are, and you'll grow. You'll understand that you can't change others, but you can make your life better.

Getting detached from other people doesn't always indicate that the relationship has to end. Sometimes all you need is *physical detachment*, and you simply have to be away for a while so these people won't provoke you and make you react. Yes, you react because these people are important to you, but you have to realize you can't control these people.

Once you realize that reality isn't all 'sunshine and roses', that's when everything will be clear. You have to admit that you can't fix everything. You can't mold someone into your ideals. You can't force someone to be a person s/he's not.

Going through the Grief Process

Without accepting reality, you can't take that first step to change. However, once you grasp the truth, though, that's when you make things better for yourself. It won't be easy; you'll undergo the grief process.

- Denial – Here you are still in the state of shock. You panic. You're numb. You refuse to acknowledge the situation you are currently in. You are anxious and repress your feelings.

- Anger – You're angry about everything. You're in a stage where you lash out and blame everything and everyone, regardless if justified or not.

- Bargaining – This is the "if... then" stage. You've calmed down by this time, and hope to stop or fix the current situation. You'll say, "If you do this, or I'll do that, then it will be okay."

- Depression – Bargaining and pleading won't work, hence you'll feel sadness and sorrow. You should be with people who'll support you when necessary.

- Acceptance – After you go through the first four steps, then you're on your way to acceptance. Reaching this point doesn't always mean that you're happy, this only means you are at peace with where you are. You understand that you can choose whether to stay or to go on, and you can make the necessary decisions. You have conceded, and are fine with your current situation. You realize that all is well and you've learned from your experiences.

Life is filled with mistakes, and this is inevitable as you learn to take care of yourself. You have to bear in mind that having done wrongs is okay, as long as you know that you were doing the best you could.

In getting better, focus on your goal rather than the recovery process. You have to make sure that the commitment is there to change yourself. Attainable goals are easier to fulfill. With these goals, you'll realize that you can still go on and make a complete recovery as self-reliant, independent and happier individuals.

Chapter 6 : The Habits of Codependent Individuals

- Please people at their own expense

Codependents are people-pleasers, that is, they try their best to satisfy the needs and wants of everybody around them. They are always the first to respond to calls for help. The "hero" chromosome in them always pushes them to the front queue of helpers and saviors whenever one is needed. They have an intense need to provide help, and they feed it upon the problems of their friends and family members. Often though, they provide help and care at their own expense. They go the extra lengths even if it means getting burned to make themselves indispensable to anybody that might require help

- Discomfort with receiving attention or help from others

Unfortunately, codependents do have scruples with asking for and receiving help. They have been conditioned to keep their emotions and needs close to their chest while growing up and cannot bring themselves to show what they see as weakness. Therefore, they suffer in silence. They don't ask for help and would rather brave the waters on their own. When they receive help such as cash gifts or an unsought for recommendation, they get discomfited and confused about how to react. Therefore, they keep themselves in positions where people don't even know they require help. They may even cover up their lack with an apparent projection of having in excess. Even from the same partner they are codependent upon, they find it hard to take anything apart from appreciation and more requests for help.

- See themselves from the eyes of other people

Codependents are some of the most self-critical individuals on earth. Their lack of self-esteem means they are forever insecure and wary of other people's opinions and perception of them. As such, they may out up a fake lifestyle to impress people while remaining essentially hollow inwards. They do not react to negative criticism well and may either respond aggressively or go out of their way to avoid criticism entirely. Most importantly to them though, they are obsessed with how their partner views them. Does he see them as totally indispensable? Are they the only port of call when he runs into trouble again? These are the most important questions that run through the minds of codependents.

- Conveniently ignore red flags

Especially in their relationships, codependent individuals always seem not to see the obvious signs. Largely inspired by their dependence on their partners and a reluctance to rock the boat or avoid conflict, they avoid fixing problems within their relationships until it is too late. They keep glossing over warning signs and refuse to heed warnings and obvious hints.

- Rationalize the mistakes of others

This is the crux of codependency after all. They are always there with a readymade excuse as to why their partner isn't up to social standards. Alcoholism? Well, he had a troubled childhood. Gambling addiction? He doesn't really gamble that much. Besides, he is rich. Their library of excuses never gets exhausted. Even when the partner obviously recognizes that he has a problem that needs to be solved, they would rather remind him they are there rather than join hands to find a lasting solution.

- Give more than they receive in relationships

It is constant in codependent relationships that one party gives out more care, attention and affection than the other. Individuals suffering from codependency constantly subdue the voice of their own needs, do not demand for much if anything at all and are too afraid to speak out their minds.

Therefore, it is not surprising to see them constantly giving out more than they receive. Anyways, most of the time, their partners may have "bigger problems" that cries out for their attention than taking stock of the attention they receive.

- Have loosely defined boundaries

Boundaries are important in every relationship. They are necessary to ensure that you don't get trampled upon. There has to be limits beyond which you won't go or tolerate. Your friends, family members and partners have to pay you some respect and not overstep their bounds. A boundary helps you mark a fine line to divide your finances, feelings, emotions and needs from that of your partner. Unfortunately, codependent relationships have undefined, poorly defined or blurred boundaries. Partners see themselves as an extension of the other half. There are no limits and invariably, emotions and desires get trampled upon. Codependents do not set boundaries because they want to remain open and be the first port of call for as many people as people when crises arise.

- Say yes, all the time

A codependent does not know or use the word "NO" to any request. He never opts out of giving a service if he can, no matter the lengths he has to go to provide it. This doesn't mean that he is totally comfortable with all tasks though. He has just been configured to make himself inconvenient before he thinks of disappointing any other person. Against the backdrop of a childhood most likely spent seeking the good graces and approval of difficult parents and probably unyielding siblings, it is easy to understand why the thoughts of turning down a request might be so foreign to a codependent individual.

- Feelings of guilt or responsibility for the suffering of others

The initial phase of codependency stems from a heightened sense of responsibility and duty to help other people overcome their sufferings. Especially for people who became codependent as a result of having to cater to the needs of an ill friend or relation, they become filled with the idea that they are the only ones in a unique position to help every other person around them. Therefore, they feel heavy guilt when they are unable to stem the tide of suffering that an associate is experiencing. They see it as a failure when they are not considered to help alleviate suffering or when their ministrations fail to yield positive results. They therefore relax their boundaries and limits lower to further cater for others. Their show of care is the only thing that gives them joy and satisfaction and when people suffer, it raises a sense of guilt in them.

- Reluctance to share true thoughts or feelings for fear of displeasing others

Children who grow up to be codependent are taught not to show emotions or admit weaknesses. They grow into adults incapable of intimacy. Intimacy in this instance does not refer to sexual activity although it has also been found to be affected. Intimacy in this context refers to the ability to share their feelings, emotions and desires with their partners and be capable of demanding for their rights as equal partners. Scared of displeasing people or thinking they may offend people by asking for help, they keep their true feelings within them and play to the gallery.

Chapter 7 : Codependency and Boundaries

Codependency actually comes from a lack of boundaries. All the scenarios and symptoms of a codependent relationship lead back to the lack of mental, psychological, emotional, and physical boundaries of an individual.

It comes from believing that there is a need for you to be connected to a dysfunctional person who mistreats you. It is also rooted in the premise that you cannot set a boundary because if you did, you can kiss your happiness goodbye.

You have to connect with your anger in order to get out of that codependent relationship. Why? Because anger is the universe's signal that a boundary has been violated. Listen to your anger and constructively work with it; then you can begin setting the boundaries so you can work on building healthy relationships.

A healthy relationship is one in which the two individuals have healthy personal boundaries. In the absence of personal boundaries, a codependent relationship exists. On the other hand, when there are strong and healthy boundaries, there exists an interdependent relationship.

However, defining boundaries and getting in touch with your anger are just the initial steps of overcoming a codependent relationship. Don't be surprised when the other person reacts to the boundaries you are setting. They aren't accustomed to you behaving in this way. They are used to a particular demeanor from you. They may push back, get angry or behave poorly as a result. None the less, don't waiver in setting your boundaries. Keep firm and continue being firm. Over time, they will learn that this is the new you and adjust themselves accordingly.

Setting Healthy Boundaries

Boundaries contribute to your growth as well as your sense of self. Taking risks and learning about true identities make your boundaries emerge, thus taking you to your higher being. Balance in life is good – it helps you develop a healthy being and understand how others should treat you.

There's nothing wrong with giving so long as you don't allow others to "invade your territory" and rob you. Healthy boundaries give you power, make you stronger, and provide you courage to stand manipulation.

How can you set boundaries?

Forget anger. Don't set boundaries when you are angry. When filled with anger, you tend to use lengthy arguments and are likely to attack the other person. It's best to communicate using a few words and by being specific. Sometimes anger is necessary when setting boundaries, but resentment should not be involved in setting one.

Your boundaries must match your behavior. Congruity is another vital prerequisite in establishing your boundaries. If your attitude does not match the boundaries you're trying to set, then your plans won't work. When setting boundaries, don't apologize and don't rationalize. Don't be neither scared nor ashamed, and listen to yourself.

Prepare for consequences... and enforce them if necessary. To set boundaries, you also have to have a particular type of readiness. You won't be able to enforce these boundaries if you're not ready for them. Your readiness is connected to your insight and personal growth; once you realize it's much needed – you can't tolerate others' attitude towards you anymore – that's when you can enforce it.

Take care of your needs. Ask yourself: what are those that you like and don't like? What brings you pleasure? Once you find the answers, you can get engaged in self-nurturing activities, and you won't get guilty in doing so. After all, you're simply taking care of yourself. You'll enjoy life more once you're able to set a healthy boundary.

To End or Not to End?

If you ever come to the conclusion that you need to end your codependent relationship, tread carefully. This is a decision not to be taken lightly. Ending a codependent relationship can be tricky. When you try to end it, you should make sure that you still break it off in a healthy way; otherwise, it could be the source of more problems. This is because you might end up setting the boundaries out of fear. You cannot stick around after you have set boundaries out of fear and expect the relationship to last. Most of the time, relationships based on fear are unhealthy and the dissolution of such relationships could come in just a matter of time.

Ending a relationship with a codependent using the wrong methods isn't healthy; doing so may commit more harm than good. If you won't do the process correctly, you end up setting a boundary that's fueled by fear. Fear-based decisions rarely end up as beneficial ones. Boundaries set because of fear won't work, and you shouldn't expect them to last. They're neither well-reasoned nor sensible as well, and won't emerge as constructive for you and your partner.

How Not to End a Codependent Relationship?

- Playing the blaming-game before ending the relationship

- Dumping the other person without giving a reason why

- Ending the relationship without warning

- Hurting them on purpose as you end it

- Sugar-coating the break-up piece so as not to hurt the other person

- Getting someone else to do it for you

- Abruptly running away

- Leading the person on – giving them the illusion that this is not the end and there is hope for a relationship in the future

Chapter 8 : Narcissist as A Co-Dependency Magnate

When a co-dependent personality and a narcissist come together, it is the perfect satisfied puzzle. In this case, a narcissist becomes a magnet for the co-dependent. A co-dependent person is deeply enthralled and excited to share the company of a narcissist because the narcissist makes the best partner for the co-dependent for follow. A narcissist is not diseased but a caregiver to the addicted. When the addict is addicted to his or her own self, then the role of a co-dependent partner seems to fuel all aspects of narcissism by diminishing the respect for the subject's self, confidence, respect and abilities.

A narcissist's love for himself is what attracts the co-dependent personality to relieve her or his own duties to make way for ways of worshipping the narcissist. This grows into such a setting that the subject even becomes the cause of the partner's self-destructive behavior. As co-dependents as endless givers, a narcissist drains all the passion and energy out of them, to make the other happy and content. They are stuck inside the pattern of perpetual giving rather than any receiving. In this moment, pessimism and discontent with the self-arises, to induce a feeling of constant feeling of jadedness and incapability in the co-dependent. As a narcissist never values other's feelings more than their own selfishness, a co-dependent compromise, adjusts and relies on making sacrifices to pleasures the narcissist, who does not regard any of this the slightest acknowledgement, lest appreciation.

A narcissist on the other hand is happy with this symbiotic relationship of them having the power to lead and command the co-dependent, who is more than happy to follow the narcissist. The attraction is strong at the start but highly diminishes with due time. The co-dependent easily buys the dysfunction being part of their own disability, incapability and flaws, by comparing themselves with the narcissists. In this case, the confidence and self-respect levels of both are immensely different as the former has extremely low self-respect while the other has the highest self-respect for the self.

Ultimately, the co-dependent reaches a point where his or her own desires are not voiced upon fearing heavy rejection and embarrassments of losing the narcissist if voiced. Additionally, another category of narcissists, also known as inverted narcissists to whom the profit or usefulness of the co-existence and co-dependency makes an impact only through a narcissistic exhilaration of the self.

Chapter 9 : Codependency in The Workplace

Have you ever felt put upon in the workplace? Yet you still volunteer to help out when there is something that needs doing in a hurry. The problem may be codependency but it may not be adding to your career prospects. No matter how hard you work and how much work you produce, if you are codependent upon a boss who uses you, the chances are that you also play a part in the situation. People who lack confidence and who seek approval for the work that they do are often codependent without realizing it. When they don't receive praise of any kind, they go out of their way to seek it. This doesn't make you a valuable member of staff, even though you may see yourself as being indispensable. You may even find that you are taken for granted so much that even when you take a vacation, you come back to all the work piled up ready for you.

In a situation such as this, you are being used because you allow yourself to be used. You may not see it that way and may crave the approval that you have. However, it's unlikely that you will be considered for promotion, because your needy nature means that you don't have what it takes to be management material. It may sound like a bit of a downer to you that you have worked so hard for little return, but you are placing yourself in a very vicious circle and need to break free of it. Not only that, you may also be someone who prefers to work alone and are not a particularly good team member. You don't know how to delegate and would rather be weighed down with work and feel needed than share what you have with others.

This is a situation that will eventually lead to burn out and although people may have warned you about that, your nature won't make you believe it. You do what you do because perhaps you don't get praise in any other area of your life. You need to appraise your life and decide upon the following:

- Do you have a good work life/home life balance?
- Do you enjoy the work that you do?
- Would you enjoy it as much without the praise that you seek?

To get out of the vicious circle that you have put yourself in for some reason or other, you need to look back into your past and find out at what stage of your life you first felt that you were not given recognition for something that you did, because often this type of codependence stems from childhood.

Linda knew that she had problems but she didn't know how serious they were. Every day she dutifully went to work and slaved although no one had ever expected that amount of devotion from an employee in a relatively junior position. The problem arose when she suddenly realized during the absence of her boss that no one else seemed to give her the kind of feedback she craved. She was lost. Then, looking through her past with a therapist, what she found was that during her childhood, her mother never recognized anything that she did as being worthwhile. Her mother would even leave the room rather than acknowledge that Linda could do something that her mother was incapable of. All the years of childhood, she had tried her best to impress her mother – not because she needed to – but because she felt displaced and even had doubts about whether her mother was really her mother. She couldn't understand why her mother could not acknowledge her. This followed her into adulthood and in her first job, she was surprised that people actually thought what she was doing was a worthwhile job. Then she questioned their sincerity in her own mind, believing herself not really to be worthy of the praise that she was getting. Thus, the cycle began and she craved that feedback that only her boss could give her.

The problem with this type of behavior is that she didn't actually need that acknowledgement and was quite capable of doing a good day's work but had slipped into the need for it feeling that it was the only thing that validated her. If you feel that you are falling into this trap at work, you need to find a new way forward because it is neither healthy nor productive to be so dependent upon someone else to validate who you are. A boss who wants more and more out of you may actually encourage weak people to do more and more work because usually people with low self-esteem don't ask much in return for their work. Often feeling validated is every bit as important as getting a fair pay for a good day's work.

Exercises related to work-based codependency

While it may not be the healthiest thing for you to give up your job, especially if you count on it to pay your bills, you need to take a different approach. Observe people around you and see how they cope with the workload that they have. If you don't ask for validation, the only validation you really need is from yourself. If you know that you did a great day's work, learn not to ask for validation. Instead of that, treat yourself to something and congratulate yourself for what you have done. In Linda's case, she learned to do things to please herself. You must do the same. Inside of you, you have something called motivation. Don't let it be controlled by someone else. Control it yourself and you become motivated without needing insincerity and wasting the time seeking it.

Most of the time, abusive bosses pile on more work when you seek this kind of validation and you end up feeling overwhelmed instead of pleased that you were able to manage your workload.

Don't do it for him or her. Do it for you. Set small goals for yourself that no one else knows about. People who always try come out as winners. Believe me, it takes a while for this to sink in but it really does work. For example, if you have a dozen tasks to do in a day, work out which ones take priority and set yourself little targets that are doable. Gain your confidence within yourself by keeping to your own timetable. Of course, priority jobs get done first, but you need to switch the motivation. It's not for the boss. It's for you. Make the competition inside yourself sufficiently motivating that when you succeed at something, only you know about it. What other people know about your skills and your goals is inconsequential at the end of the day.

By doing this, you build up confidence in yourself and don't need validation from anyone. In Linda's case, she was a brilliant artist, but because her mother had never acknowledged it, she had put away her paintbrushes and had given up on her passion in life. No one should ever let someone else dictate their success. When she finally built up her reputation as a brilliant painter, she did so on her own terms and people were quick to ask her to do drawings for them. In fact, she had no trouble making her passion into something quite substantial, although she also learned that she didn't have to please someone else as long as she was happy with the results. She also learned to say "no" which is a very hard lesson for someone who has self-esteem and codependency issues.

Exercise 2 – Setting yourself free

Give yourself some personal goals as well as work related goals and make them manageable. The reason you start simple is so that you can attain those goals. Then, little by little, as you gain confidence, you can make the goals a little harder. Remember that you are only creating them for yourself and for no one else. You are the only one that you are out to please. When you have made your goals for at home and you have kept them, look at your face in the mirror and see yourself as the success that you are. At the end of the day, the only person's opinion of you that matters are your own. When you can acknowledge your own successes, you don't need to be dependent upon your boss to validate you and you can go forward in your career because you are no longer a drain on people.

Chapter 10 : Improving Your Co-Dependent Life

The hardest but most fundamental responsibility that you will take on is facing your codependency and that of the people you are closest to. You will be taking a huge leap of faith, so you can become vulnerable with hopes of being a person who is more confident in the future. In order for this transformation to happen, you have to learn how to walk through your world with confidence and grace, set boundaries that are right for you, interact with people in a kind but direct manner, and be assertive when dealing with problems.

Learn to be a Better Family Member

Once you have learned your codependency patterns go back to your family, you may have discovered there are some skeletons in your closet. If you have been denying any shortcomings or abuse within your family, this might have been a rather painful revelation. You need to explore your family's origins, so you can understand your codependency. Remember that you aren't perfect and this means that your family isn't perfect either.

Origins of Family

You have to use your journal and really think about your family. Try to write down any patterns or behaviors that might have caused you to become codependent. Make a heading for all your family members and try answering all the following questions:

- What feelings do you feel the most when you are around this person?

- Was this person around when you needed them?

- From what you know now, are they really codependent?

- From what you know now, are they really narcissistic?

- Were the chronically physically or mentally ill?

- Did this person express their feeling easily?

- Did they yell or blow up at you when they got angry?

- Did they make you feel loved?

- Has this person broken any laws or engaged in dangerous or reckless activities?

- Were they ever physically, emotionally, or sexually abusive?

- Did this person push any mistaken beliefs onto you?

- How did they deal with anger or handle conflicts?

- Did this person ever get addicted to drugs, smoking, spending, alcohol, gambling, anger, etc.?

- Did the person ever model any codependent behaviors to you? If so, what were they?

Once you have written about all your family members and answered these questions, see if you can find out or affirm what you know about your family and how they may have unknowingly planted the seeds of your codependency.

Now, take some time to look at what you have discovered and see if there are unresolved issued within your family. It doesn't help to dig up pain and hurt and leave it unattended.

Find out if you can resolve these problems by yourself, or if you need to address them with a certain family member. Your goal is to stop being a victim. What could you do to stop these ghosts from haunting you?

There are some ways you can look at all the information you found out about your family. One way is to find out how these things might be affecting your relationships now, how they could change your behavior with them. The second way is to find out if you need to confront the problems you have with specific family members. Will this help lessen their power over you?

Some people like working with just their current family meaning their significant other and children. Some people want to talk to their family members and parents that they were around while growing up.

Connie remembered that she had been abused by her older sister while she was growing up during the time, she was writing in her journal being mindful and reading. Her sister would constantly jump out and scare her. Patricia would lock Connie in her bedroom, steal her things, choke her, turn out the lights, break her toys, beat her up, and try to smother her with a pillow. Connie constantly told other people that she had a good childhood except for some "sibling rivalry."

Once Connie decided to take a close look at her childhood, she experienced all the pain again. She realized that it was necessary to look at this relationship she had with Patricia. She also begins to wonder about her parents. Where were they during all this abuse? Why didn't they try to protect her? Why didn't Connie tell her parents, try to stop the abuse, or do anything? Connie decided to see a therapist to get help for her depression and anxiety that was triggered by all these memories.

During therapy, Connie realized that she really doesn't trust anyone. Since she can't really trust her husband, it makes her controlling suspicious. This causes many accusations and arguments that get very explosive. She also realized that she still feels like a victim most of the time. She is constantly on edge just waiting for somebody to hurt her. Connie decided to talk to her husband about this and asked for his help with her childhood abuse triggers. Connie was able to work on her trust problems with her husband's help. This, in turn, actually helped their relationship.

Connie hadn't been in touch with Patricia for a very long time and doesn't expect to see her again. She doesn't want to confront her about all the abuse. She decided to write Patricia a letter in her journal. She won't ever send it to her. While going to therapy, her sister gets sick and asks Connie to come for a visit. Connie panics. She talks about these thoughts and feelings with her therapist.

Quick Tip: You can give yourself messages that are called positive affirmations. These are small statements that you believe are true. You can tell yourself things like: "I'm a survivor." "I am good enough." "I've got this." "I am strong." "I am not perfect, but that is fine." The main reason behind these affirmations and saying them out loud is to continue saying them until you begin to believe them.

Connie decided it was time to speak with her parents and tell them everything she had experienced while growing up. She told them that she was scared every day of her life. She asked them why they hadn't ever stepped in and stopped the abuse. Her parents were genuinely shocked by this news. They apologized profusely and asked if there was anything, they could do now to help her. Connie decided to forgive them. This alliance with her parents made Connie feel better about meeting with her sister. Connie doesn't feel as if she is a victim to all of them. She feels affirmed because her parents understand and will help her be nice to Patricia.

Connie chose to deal with the origin of her problems where she felt the most pain. She devoted a lot of time in therapy working through her childhood abuse and this helped her talk to her parents. She felt like she has resolved the problems she had with her parents and decided she isn't going to confront Patricia.

There won't ever be a right or wrong decision when talking about family origin wounds. If they are still abusing you, you might need to decide to tell them to stop. You can stop spending time with them and put firm boundaries in place. You may decide to deal with any unwanted behaviors when they come up. It is totally up to you.

Being a Better Friend

Once you begin changing and moving toward a life without codependency, you will attract new friends. These friendships will be more interdependent and mutual. While working toward being an equal friend you are going to have two different aspects of friendship you will need to write about in your journal.

Getting to Know Your Friends Better

Just like you wrote about your family in your journal, you need to do the same thing with your friends. Don't worry about acquaintances, just the people you consider to be a real friend. Write their names at the top of the page. If you only have a few friends who are really close, this is totally normal. You could include friends that you think of as your second-tier friends. Now, you need to decide if your old friends still fit in with the new you. If these friendships are codependent, you can decide to move on, or you might decide to work on moving the friendship into a better place.

Answer these questions to help you figure it out:

- If you aren't available when your friend wants you, do they get mad?

- Are your friends very demanding?

- Do your friends ever cancel lunch dates or they just don't show up?

- Do your friends always ask for your advice?

- When you talk to your friend, do they talk more than 50 percent of the time?

- Is your friend unstable or fragile?

- Do you have to constantly walk on eggshells when you are around them?

- Are your friends not interested in what you are going through and don't realize you are struggling?

- Do your friends call and expect you to stop whatever you are doing and talk to them right then?

You may realize that some friends are making your life better. You are the only person who truly knows if the friendship is hopeless and you need to move on. If you decide to try to help them, these friendships might be helpful in giving you opportunities to consistently work on your codependency. Let's see what Paul did with his friends:

Paul Looks at His Friends

Paul has three close friends. Ed is his roommate; they work at the same place and see each other every day, but they don't have deep discussions. They ride to work together and their involvement is based on the apartment they share. Paul looks and his friendship with Ed and realized it is interdependent and they don't need to work on it.

Paul has another friend who is another work colleague. Aaron works in a different department than Paul but they are compatible. They have worked together on many projects and have had great results. They eat lunch together often. They normally talk about their hobbies, work, and video games. Aaron talks a bit more than Paul, but he likes to get Paul's opinion about things. If Paul were more withdrawn, he might be more of a listener and find himself in the role of a therapist. Aaron enjoys talking with Paul. Their relationship is an equal one.

According to his journal entries, Paul's third friend is the problem. Anthony also works at the same place but is needy and depends on Paul to help him on his projects. Lately, he has been asking for favors that don't have anything to do with work. Anthony is single, and Paul is drawn to him because Anthony needs Paul to help him. At first, Paul was pleased that Anthony asked him and enjoys Anthony's reliance and gratitude. Helping Anthony makes Paul feel good about him. Once Paul has worked on his codependency, he realized that Anthony's friendship isn't healthy. Paul has set boundaries telling Anthony that he is willing to help out at work, but he doesn't have time to help him after hours.

Fixing Problems

Look at your friends closely by writing in your journal. Are there any unresolved problems that you have been too afraid to talk about with them? Make a list for all your friends and process everyone. You have to decide if you can get rid of the problems you can't control you just don't want to deal with them. If problems are still there, try to approach them. If you learn to be more honest and forthright with your friends and they get offensive, you now to have information that could help you make better decisions about your friendship.

Before you start talking with your friends, you have to know what you want to achieve. What motivates you? If you are motivated to strengthen the friendship and resolve things by being honest, go ahead. If you feel brave enough to let them know they are being a jerk, just save your breath and let them go.

Look at Your New Friends

While you are changing, new people are going to come into your life. They will see you are compassionate, well-adjusted, and assertive; a person who is honest about how they feel and know their expectations and boundaries. This might not be what they are looking for. They may want to fulfill some codependency needs. They may want a friend who is codependent and will take care of them.

You now know enough about codependency to see red flags in relationships and friendships. Take care of any concerns you might have immediately. Remember to put yourself and your needs first and you have the right to stop any friendship that doesn't feel healthy at any time. If a new friend begins to cancel all the get-togethers you have planned at the start of the friendship, this might show that they aren't really interested in you at all. If your new friends begin to ask you for favors, this might show they are extremely needy. If new friends begin to talk about themselves nonstop, this isn't good either. If a new friend is offended easily, gossips about other friends get moody, misunderstands you all the time, these are all big red flags.

There is an old saying that goes something like: "Partners come and go but friends are forever."

Yes, friends are important for our emotional well-being, and some friendships do last a lifetime. Just make sure you pick your friends wisely.

Becoming Free from Codependency

Every person you meet in your lifetime and all the situations you face will give you an opportunity to fine-tune your freedom from being codependent. How can this change happen and what can you do to help it? Each year research finds something new about human behavior. Psychiatrists used to think that personality disorders can't be changed. Now, they believe just the opposite. The things that people believe can influence their behavior. At first, it was thought to be a brain thing. This it turned into an environmental/brain thing. Now, because of the advances in neurotechnology, research is newly excited about the brain. Many think neuropsychology will constantly evolve.

These changes that you have been trying to reach are very possible for you to achieve. Your goal is to develop and nourish your identity. Yes, you have an identity. Everybody does. You are only trying to remold your identity. Codependency traits are constant. You might be more or less codependent. You may show one or 50 codependency traits.

You have been given new insights, awareness, and tools that can help you fix your self-esteem, increase your sense of self, and be more confident. You will consistently be working on transforming by watching your behaviors, feelings, and thoughts. You make any adjustment you need to as you go along. You need to be present in your relationships and love. You have to value yourself. You have to find your voice. You have to learn to love yourself with all your flaws. You just might find that you have all sorts of power to expand your happiness.

Chapter 11 : Changing A Codependent Relationship

If you or a loved one is involved in a codependent relationship, the mental (and potentially physical) ramifications of staying in that unhealthy pattern of behavior are far too great to continue going on that way. You run the risk of developing mental and physical exhaustion, and the effects can be both short-term and long-term. Moreover, you may become neglectful in other important areas of your life, such as friendships, family, work, or health. In order to achieve a healthy relationship and an overall sense of wellness, you must be willing to adapt and foster your relationship so that it can move away from a place of codependency.

The detrimental impacts of codependency can become deep-rooted issues in a person's relationship, but that doesn't always mean that splitting up or ridding that person from your life is the only solution. Yes, sometimes the best answer is getting out of the relationship, especially if there is physical harm that's been done. But if both parties are able to recognize the fact that there is an issue present, and the relationship hasn't reached the point of physical abuse or intentional emotional abuse, then there's a chance that conditions can be improved.

Thus, without any conscious knowledge of it, a person can be carrying around behaviors that will lead to codependency. These behaviors and psychological issues may be difficult to bring to the surface, but there are means of reversing destructive actions and patterns.

For one thing, if you or your loved one is suffering from codependency, you've already made a move in the right direction. Education is the most useful tool that you can use in combatting codependency, and by reading this book, you're arming yourself with the power to improve a relationship.

Next, you must make a very difficult decision and determine whether or not you *can* stay in the codependent relationship, or whether you want to in the first place. Oftentimes, people are afraid to leave codependent relationships, either because they're afraid of the loneliness that will come afterwards, or they're scared that their partner won't be able to live without them, or both. Nonetheless, these are not worthwhile reasons to stay in a relationship. This is the most crucial aspect you must realize when it comes to overcoming codependency: you are not responsible for another's happiness. That being said, you *can* control your own happiness. If, after doing some soul searching, you come to the conclusion that you truly want to end the relationship (or if you've known it all along but have been afraid to truly acknowledge it), then it's time to move on.

Again, terminating the relationship does *not* have to be the answer. Oftentimes, a relationship becomes codependent overtime, possibly because both parties have fallen into a set of destructive behaviors. It is reversible, though, and codependency can be conquered with some hard work and dedication. If both parties choose to stay in the relationship and are willing to fix it, then it's likely that you'll both be able to make a full recovery from codependency. Keep in mind, though, that while you can control your own behavior and how much effort you'll put in to overcoming codependency, you cannot control your partner's level of commitment. Realize up front that it will be his or her duty to take responsibility as well.

If you want to improve your relationship, discuss the option of therapy with your partner. Couples' therapy can be extremely beneficial for overcoming codependency; likewise, individual therapy may also help codependents to recognize their destructive behavior patterns and provide techniques for banishing them. In individual or couples' therapy, parties may be led to examine some of the family dynamics that they were exposed to growing up. While it may be difficult to work through some latent emotions, bringing deep-rooted issues to the service will make way for reconstructing positive behaviors. This may also help both parties in the relationship learn to express a full, healthy range of emotions once again.

If your relationship has reached a level of codependency due to addiction, then treatment should become a priority. How you go about initiating treatment is up to you - sometimes, family members choose to stage an intervention. There's no easy, foolproof way to initiate this kind of conversation with an addict. Most likely, the addict already knows that he or she has an issue; unfortunately, you may feel that the addiction has reached a point at which you can no longer continue on in the relationship if the addict chooses not to seek help. Your relationship has reached a state of codependency, and without change, you won't be able to return to a healthy state.

If you or your loved one wants to overcome codependency, consider seeking other additional resources. Mental health centers and libraries may offer programs or materials to the public.

Overcoming codependency within a relationship may require a great deal of strength, commitment, growth, and patience from a person. If you're trying to change your ways to overcome codependency, you'll have to commit fully to embracing your own emotional, physical, and mental needs or desires. You may have to learn how to say "no" and stand up for yourself, and quit relying on making others happy in order to find self-worth.

One way to stay in a relationship that has become codependent is by encouraging each party to take part in his or her own activities or hobbies. In order to move away from codependence, a person must be able to regain his or her own sense of independence. Freedom is necessary in a relationship; otherwise, if a person becomes suffocated by his or her partner, feelings of resentment can build up.

The goal in overcoming codependency in a relationship is to make small changes. There's no way that you and your partner will be able to change completely within one day; yet, change *is* necessary. To avoid becoming overwhelmed, start with small changes that you can implement and be persistent with every day.

You must be willing to consistently ask yourself if what you're doing is for you, or whether it's for your partner. If you're moving in the right direction, you'll most likely develop a firm resolve. Keep in mind that you can be both firm and loving - it's just a matter of implementing small changes to regain your own happiness and sense of self-worth.

Also, avoid the pitfall of resorting back to old behaviors, especially if your partner encourages you to "go back to the way you were." If your partner is on board with overcoming codependency, he or she will need to be supportive so that you both can make effective changes. With enough resolution, you can overcome codependency in your relationship.

Chapter 12 : Being Aware of Codependent Thoughts and Behaviors

The fact that you are still reading shows that you are a courageous person. You are ready to at least think about how codependence could be affecting your life. Take a moment to feel good about your bravery.

Now comes a hard part of the process of overcoming codependence: recognizing your codependent behaviors. To begin, start a journal where you can keep track of your thoughts and actions. Do not judge your reactions. Merely state what they are, close your journal and get back to living your life. Here are some things to watch for and write down.

• When your partner makes a mistake, what do you do about it?

• What do you think and do when your partner criticizes you?

• How do you feel when your partner disagrees with you?

• Do you ever spend money on or go out to buy things for your partner that you know he shouldn't have?

- Which of your thoughts and behaviors are aimed at controlling your partner's problems?

- What do you do to help your partner keep his job?

- What do you think about when your partner hurts you either emotionally or physically?

- What do you think and how do you feel when your partner blames you for something?

- How do you feel and what do you think about when your partner is upset or angry about something that happened to him away from home?

1) If there are children in your household, what do you think and do when your partner complains about their behavior?

- What do you do to keep the peace in your household?

- What do you think and do when someone makes a request of you and you are unsure about whether you can help them? Do you say yes even if you don't feel up to the task?

- What do you think and do when you don't live up to your own expectations?

These are only a few things you might notice as you go through the next week. Be honest as you write in your journal. It is for you and you only. Study yourself carefully.

Remind yourself that facing reality is hard, but that once you do it, you can move on to getting healthier and happier.

Where Are Your Personal Boundaries?

A major part of codependence is having weak or inappropriate personal boundaries. Get your journal and something to write with for the next exercise. Mark on your page the numbers 1 to 10. Now, read the following statements and rate them anywhere from 0 and 10. 0 means you do not agree at all, 5 means you neither agree nor disagree, and 10 means you completely agree. Here are the statements to rate.

• What is mine is mine and what is my partner's is my partner's.

• I am not responsible for my partner's behavior.

• I am a worthwhile person with or without my partner.

• I have my own purpose in life aside from caring for my partner.

• I care about my partner's feelings, but I do not take them on as my own.

• I allow others to have their own personal space. I don't move so close to people that they back away from me.

- I am content with myself and with life in general regardless of the opinions of others.

- I agree to help others who ask for help when I can, but I say no when I do not feel comfortable helping or when the request is beyond my abilities.

- It is more important to care for myself than to please other people.

- Other people, including my partner can have their own opinions without hurting my feelings. I don't feel the need to have other people tell me I am right.

Were you honest with yourself? If so, add up the numbers to rate your acceptance of personal boundaries. The lowest possible score, of course, is zero. The highest possible score is 100. Where does your number fall? The higher your number, the healthier your sense of appropriate personal boundaries is. If your number is lower, especially if it is below 50, you have problems separating your own identity from the identities of others. This is an indication that you can benefit from working to overcome codependent thoughts and behaviors.

How Do You Feel About You?

People who are codependent usually have very low self-esteem. Codependent people often feel inadequate in their own abilities. It is only by managing their partner's addictions that they can experience a sense of self-worth. If your partner was no longer a part of your life, who would you be, and what would you think of yourself? Here are a few questions to think about as you consider your independent sense of self-worth. Write your answers in your journal.

- Do you make decisions based on your own set of values?

- Do you need others to tell you that you are attractive?

- Are you capable of making your own dreams come true?

- Who decides whether you are a good or bad person?

- How can you tell if you are intelligent of not?

- Whose needs come first – your needs or the needs of those around you?

- How do you feel when you fall short of perfection?

- How do you react when someone compliments you?

- Do you like to keep your own company? Do you get uncomfortable when others approach you to socialize? Do you isolate yourself to keep from getting hurt?

- Can you put aside any guilty feelings that come up when your partner has problems due to his addictions?

- Do you like who you are?

If these questions are hard to answer or make you think about yourself in ways that you would rather not consider, you are not alone. People who struggle with codependency tend to feel threatened when they examine their thoughts and actions in a constructive way.

It is much easier for people who are codependent with a partner to blame themselves or others than to own their feelings, thoughts and behaviors, and let others own theirs. Loving yourself and putting your own feelings first can be a radical departure from the way you have been thinking of yourself and others. It is a hard process to go through, but it is the first step to breaking free of codependency.

Evaluate Your Evidence
After a week is up, find a quiet place to be alone and sit down with your journal. If your partner does not like to give you privacy in your home, stop by a park and sit on a bench. Read through your journal and think about whether or not your thoughts, feelings and actions during the week fit the profile of codependency.

Notice the times you put others (especially your partner) ahead of yourself. Look for ways you took responsibility for your partner's addiction issues.

Did you say anything positive about yourself?

Or did you criticize yourself for the decisions you made?

If you are not sure whether or not you are displaying signs of codependency, read through the book this book again until you get back to this section. Then, look over your journal and honestly assess your level of codependence. Once you see the pattern, it is time to learn about enabling and how you can avoid it.

Chapter 13 : Dealing with Your Partner's Addictions

The first step to your individual freedom is to stop behaving in codependent ways. Your partner likely has addictions that cause problems between you. And in a sense, you yourself have addictions that hinder the relationship as well as your personal growth. If you struggle with codependency issues, you may be addicted a feeling of control over your partner. You may be addicted to the approval of your partner and others.

Whatever your own problems are, set them aside for a moment. For right now, concentrate on stopping the codependent behaviors. This idea can make someone who is in a codependent relationship feel anxious and out of control. You do not have to base your actions on these feelings. You can push past them to do what is beneficial to you and the people around you.

What Is Enabling?

Enabling your partner's addictions and general bad behavior refers to anything you might to do make it easier for him to continue his addictive ways. Enabling can take many forms. It can mean helping your partner to do the behavior or it can mean saying or doing things that make him feel justified in doing the behavior.

Here are a few examples of enabling by helping with the behavior:
Your partner is feeling depressed. You know that he always feels better when he drinks (at least for a while). So even though you don't like him drinking, you go out and buy him a bottle of booze to lift his spirits. Or, you hand him the keys and tell him it's okay to go out to the bar, just this once. If he is a gambler, you go to the ATM and get him a few dollars to go to a casino. You tell him to enjoy himself today and worry about quitting tomorrow.

These are examples of helping your partner feel justified in continuing in his addictive behaviors:
You criticize him about minor things. You manipulate him or trick him into doing things your way (i.e. not doing the addictive behavior). You don't let him have a social life. You yell at him to clean up his act. You berate him for being irresponsible. You punish him for his mistakes as if he were a child. You react to him the same way when he abstains from his addictions as you do when he gives in to them.

You probably do not do all these behaviors. Each person has her own way of enabling the addict. Take a moment to think of things you do that might make it easier for him to keep up or justify his addiction.

Write these things down in your journal. As you go through the next week or so, pay attention to your reactions. If you catch yourself doing any of them, make a checkmark beside each one you do. When you get to the end of the week you can look back at your journal and see which enabling behaviors you need to work on the most.

How to Avoid Enabling Your Partner's Addictive Behaviors
If you are in a codependent relationship, chances are you are enabling your partner to continue his addictive behaviors. Most people who are codependent believe that they are helping their partner. However, more often, they make choices that encourage the partner to hold on to their addictions even more tightly.

First and foremost, you need to find a way to quit feeling responsible when your partner falls off the wagon. You need to start owning your own responsibilities in the relationship and let your partner have his. Here are some specific ways to give up the responsibility for your partner's addictive behaviors.

- Stop making excuses for your partner.

- Do not be the one to call your partner's employer if he decides not to go to work as a result of his addictions.

- Let your partner be the one to make apologies for his addictive behaviors.

- If you have the thought that your partner's addictive behavior is your fault, remind yourself that he is responsible for his own behavior.

- Do not buy or arrange to buy drugs, alcohol or any other item your partner uses to feed addictive behaviors.

- Do not pamper your partner if he is hung over or otherwise suffering from the results of his addictive behavior.

- Do not nag your partner to change. Criticizing his behavior can easily prompt your partner to rebel and increase his addictive behavior.

- Separate your own thoughts and feelings about the addiction from your partner's thoughts and feelings about it.

What You Can about Your Partner's Addictions?

The things you have done in the past to try to help your partner overcome his addictions are no longer available to you if you follow this advice. You may feel hopeless and that your partner cannot recover from his addictions without you. Yet there are some things you can do to help him without being codependent. Here are a few ideas to try.

- Use "I" messages to tell your partner how his addiction makes you feel. For example, rather than telling him he is a worthless drunk (or drug addict, etc.) tell him something like this: I feel insecure when you put your addictions in front of our family's needs.

- Help and congratulate your partner when he is making good choices about dealing with his addiction.

- Do a hobby or other activity that you enjoy when your partner is feeling sorry for himself over the results of his addiction.

- Practice active listening when your partner honestly confronts his problems. This means paying attention to what he says and asking him questions if you don't understand something.

- Say no when he asks you to do something to help him continue in his addictions.

Even if you behave appropriately and avoid enabling your partner's addictions, there is still a very big chance that he will not stop them. If you want to be free from codependency, you have to accept that you can't make him do something he doesn't want to do. It is a hard truth to understand. Yet once you come to terms with your powerlessness over his decisions, you can stop enabling him and break free from the burden of feeling responsible for his actions.

Chapter 14 : Why You Should Not Be Codependent

Why did I write this book? Why do I want you to learn to explore the beauty of interdependence and quit codependency? Codependency is a dangerous trait to possess. Life has evolved at a blinding stage and our society right now is on the fast pace. We get bombarded daily with opinions, requests, offers of friendship and disappointments that it becomes simply too dangerous to tie your life inextricably with anybody else's own. What are the specific dangers that codependency may bring into your life;

- **Kills off self-esteem and confidence**

Allison Pescosolido writes, "Nothing erodes self-esteem quicker than an unhealthy relationship". When you hitch your happiness to a need to be needed, you soon begin to forget that you have self-worth. Codependency teaches you that your life isn't worth much beyond that of your partner. Codependents think only of their partners and new ways in which they may care for him. You lose your own sense of direction and your work may even begin to suffer. Worst of all, a lot of dependents take advantage of your urge and consistently berate and force you to do acts that further shatter what little self-confidence you possess. Codependents may even suffer constant sexual and physical abuse and yet, believe they simply can't exist outside the realm of their partner's need and affection. There is a voice at the back of their head telling them they are just an extension of their partners. They constantly need to seek approval and acknowledgement from their partners and derive lesser joy from their personal achievements.

- **Turns you antisocial**

The inherent need to seek approval and feel loved makes codependents decidedly antisocial. Codependency can easily turn you into a social recluse outside your partner's presence. Feeling insecure and decidedly unable to assess if their efforts are worth extra praise, codependents often turn to staying off social encounters. They miss engagements with other people, can be quite boring and unable to focus on conversations and generally exhibit a wide range of actions that suggests they would rather be left alone.

- **Relegates your own goals**

A codependent individual may be genuinely successful. He may break records, achievements and produce huge strides in the corporate and business world but deep down, codependency often leaves a yawning gap in their hearts. No matter the scale of your achievements, codependency teaches you to cherish the needs of your partners above every other goal. As such, you may find yourself unable to commit the same amount of resources and drive to attaining personal business. Codependents have been known to give up their work and life goals to focus on a partner with needs such as alcoholism. Codependency takes away your goals and makes your partner the sole center of your existence.

- **A helpless mindset**

Codependency makes you feel and act helpless. Codependent individuals become chained down by the weight of the expectations they have placed on their own heads. They develop a feeling of helplessness in the face of their relationship struggles. They hang on to their relationships because they can't seem to see any other option. They suffer neglect and abuse and still remain steadfast in their relationships because codependency tells them they have no option. An even worse aspect is that they see their partners as having no control over their actions. They treat their partners like children that have no control over what they do. They help them make excuses of not being in total control.

- **Can affect your health severely**

Codependency can be a health threat. Anxiety, depression and stress are three major psychological disorders currently on the rise worldwide, and depending on another individual to provide you joy and relief is a short path to overloading your circuit. By taking on too much worries and making themselves open to so many problems, codependents pile more stress onto themselves and this can easily escalate into depression and anxiety disorders. Insomnia is also never too far away from most codependents.

- **Leaves you firmly vulnerable to emotional injury**

Once you have taken control of your life and handed it over to somebody else's actions and inactions, you have set yourself up to be at his mercy. He/she can hurt you even unknowingly with the smallest of actions and you become extra sensitive to being hurt in any case. Opinions and criticism from any quarter also sting more. Your deprecated sense of self-worth and low esteem could also leave you in delicate quarters when it comes to emotions and feelings.

- **Makes you open to picking up bad habits and addictions**

Emotional injury and a loss of esteem aren't the only dangers that can arise from overdependence. A soft spot for a partner who has addiction problems could turn you into an enabler who helps him satisfy his addiction as a means of keeping him pleased. Even worse still, you could pick up the same bad habits in the hope of keeping him company. Addictions such as gambling, alcoholism and substance abuse can be easily picked up especially when your friend or partner already has a steady source. By becoming codependent on him, you could end up picking the same habits.

- **Refusing help from other people**

One of the primary demerits of codependency is the way it draws you back from seeking help yourself. Codependents are so enmeshed in a control complex that they totally adore being in control and would not admit to things being skewed with them too. They grow to be emotionally flat and cannot bring themselves to show any form of emotion. They learn to exist independently of any help from the people around them and lose the ability to ask for proper help.

- **A victim's mindset**

Codependents constantly feel cheated at all times. Their mind is a hodge-podge of conflicting emotions and they end up feeling underappreciated a lot of times. Codependency does not allow them pick faults with their partners and instead, they turn against the system. They help sympathize with their partners and teach them to look for conspiracy theories to absolve their partners of their misdeeds.

- **Stresses you out physically and mentally**

The human body has a threshold for the amount of problems and issues it can take at once. By adding more problems and issues outside of your own to your mind, you run the risk of maxing out your resilience and capability to withstand stress. Obviously, catering for a partner's needs will leave you with extra physical activity to carry out. Partners with problems such as chronic illness or alcoholism may need constant care that may task your physical capabilities beyond its limits. Of even more severe potentials is the risk of a mental overload. Piling up too many worries in your head can deal dangers to your psyche.

Chapter 15 : Conquering Codependency

Codependency may lead to different long-term problems such as depression, low self-esteem, health problems, career problems and relationship difficulties. Co-dependents often feel trapped, abused and they often feel that they are unable to trust anyone.

But there is hope. If you are a codependent, it is not too late. You can either end a codependent relationship or shape it to become healthier and more balanced. You can still reclaim your life and take control.

Here are the steps on how you could conquer and cure codependency:

- Acknowledge that there is a problem – Codependents are constantly in denial. They routinely deny that they have a problem. The first step in conquering codependency is to acknowledge it. You have to accept the fact that there is a problem. Be realistic. Realize that the relationships that you are in are not balanced. You have to recognize that the people you care about are taking advantage of you- your friends, family, spouse, kids, siblings or parents. Once you acknowledge and accept this, then you are on your way to recovery.

- Make a decision to do whatever it takes to conquer codependency – You have to make a tough decision to wage a war against codependency. After you have acknowledged that codependency is your problem, this is the time to decide to take steps that are necessary to end your codependency and make your life better. This is very difficult to do, but once you have made up your mind and you made the commitment to make positive changes in your life, there is no turning back. Everything will eventually become easier, lighter and you will be genuinely happy and feel more fulfilled.

- Get some help – It is necessary to talk to someone you trust about your codependency and the steps that you will take to end it. You can talk to an emotionally healthy family member or friend or you could see a mental health professional. You can also seek the help of spiritual leader that you respect and you can trust. The support of the people around you will push you into the direction of recovery.

- Focus on yourself – This is very important. If you want to conquer codependency, you have to focus on your own needs, wants and dreams. Take time to ask yourself – what do I really want? If you find yourself answering based on what your partner wants, ask yourself again and again until you get the real answer. If you are a codependent, you have spent so much time and effort focusing on other people's wants and needs that you have already forgotten your own desires and needs. Now is the time to be in touch with your own needs and your own desire. Do you want to go back to school or start your own business or maybe travel around the world? Acknowledge your needs, feelings, emotions and your dreams.

- Practice Self-Love – Self-love is not the same with narcissism. In fact, narcissistic people may appear confident on the outside, but deep inside, they despise themselves and feel inadequate. People who love themselves, on the other hand, accept themselves unconditionally. They do not take abuse and disrespect. They do not take advantage of other people and they do not allow others to take advantage of them. They are more direct in communicating their needs and their preference. While they clearly communicate their wants, desires, opinions and views, people who profoundly love themselves tend to respect other people's wants, needs and opinions. They do not judge others and they do not feel that they should change or fix other people. More importantly, people who constantly practice self-love have healthy boundaries. They do not allow people to meddle with their lives and they do not meddle with other people's lives. When you accept yourself completely, you do not have the urge or need to be accepted by others. Here's how you can practice self-love:

Say positive affirmations every morning – Positive affirmations can do wonders in your life. It can fill your life with love and happiness. You can find several affirmations online or you could make your own affirmations.

Take time to meditate – Meditation shuts off negative energy and allows you to focus on the positive.

Enjoy life – If you are a codependent, you have spent so much time taking care of other people that you have already forgotten to take care of yourself. Enroll in a yoga class, dance class or travel. Go to the beach often, if that's what makes you happy. Take time to hang out with your old friends and take time to go to dinner parties.

Learn something new – Expand your skills and make yourself better. You can learn a new language or learn how to play guitar, crochet or you can go to pottery class. You can also visit the local museums and libraries. Go back to business school if that's what you want or get a master's degree. Follow the desires of your heart.

Live in gratitude – To be happy, you have to appreciate whatever it is that you have. Take time to appreciate and be grateful for your job, family and life in general. Savor that plate of baked macaroni. Stop and appreciate the view. Be grateful and you will no longer feel the need to manipulate or to let others take advantage of you just to be happy.

Always do the things and actions that honor you and respect you – Do not ever allow abusers and toxic people in your life. Do not engage with people who bring you down. Do not participate in activities that are harmful to you.

Believe in your self-worth – Understand that your worth is not dependent on someone's approval. You have to know and understand that you are worthy of love and respect. Once you realize your own self-worth, you will be surprised with how your life will change in a positive way.

Let go of the need to change and fix other people – To conquer codependency, you have to let go of your need to control other people's lives. You must let go of your need or desire to change other people. This is one of the powerful ways to heal and cure codependency. Allow people to be themselves and resist any urge to try to change them and make them better. This means that you have to stop the care taking, rescuing, controlling, apologizing and pretending. You have to also avoid making rules for other people.

Create and define your personal boundaries- This is ultimately necessary if you want to conquer and cure your codependency. Personal boundaries are basically decisions that you make about the behaviors that you will and won't tolerate.

If you have weak boundaries, you will tolerate just about anything. You allow people to hurt you and disrespect you.

You also inappropriately assume responsibility for other people's mistakes, problems and experiences. If you have strong boundaries, you know where your responsibility ends and where others responsibilities begin. You draw a line between your concerns and the concerns of others. You stand up for yourself and you communicate your displeasure when someone is being hurtful or disrespectful to you.

Remember that setting boundaries is not enough. You have to enforce them. You have to communicate your feelings openly and honestly and call out people who violate them. Here are some easy steps on how you could create boundaries:

Decide what you will and will not tolerate. Take time to reflect and determine what behaviors are tolerable and what behaviors are absolutely unacceptable. Prepare a list of acceptable and unacceptable behaviors.

Watch and determine certain violations of your boundaries. Other people may not be aware that they are crossing your boundaries so it is important to communicate with others what your boundaries are. For instance, you do not want to take work related telephone calls during your day off. You must clearly communicate with your coworkers that you would appreciate it if they will not contact you on weekends about work-related matters.

Enforce your personal boundaries by calling out people who violate these boundaries. Respectfully but clearly communicate that you will not tolerate these kinds of behavior. Directly express your displeasure and then present a possible solution or alternative.

Be true to yourself – Most co-dependents have completely forgotten about their needs and desires. You have to maintain your personal integrity and be completely honest about who you are, what your dreams are, and how you feel. To heal a relationship, you have to be completely honest and become more genuine. You also have to stop caring about what other people think of you. You just have to live in the moment. Realize that it is okay not to be perfect.

Leave when you have to – Finally, when you think that you cannot change the course and the nature of your codependent relationship, it is time to leave and end the relationship. If you decide to end it, you have to end it in a healthy way. Experts say that a codependent relationship automatically ends whenever you stop responding to your partner in a codependent way. The relationship automatically ends when you set healthy boundaries and enforce it. Remember to avoid drama. Ending a codependent relationship should not be emotionally charged. Just stay calm and just communicate that if your partner could not respect your boundaries, wants and needs, then it is best to end the relationship.

Once you follow these steps, you will be surprised with the positive changes in your life. You will be happier. Your career will thrive. Your relationships will be healthier and you will be able to get rid of the diseases associated with codependency like depression, anxiety, and emotional pain. You will be able to travel more; eat in restaurants that you really like and pick out the clothes that you prefer. You will feel empowered and confident. In no time, your confidence will reach its all-time high and you can now put your painful, codependent past behind you.

Chapter 16 : Moving on With Your Life

When you come out of a codependent relationship, often your confidence can be at an all-time low, and you may find that you have lost a lot of yourself that was previously tied up in your relationship identity. Now is the time to re-discover who you are as an individual and firm up your needs and desires. You need to be gentle with yourself and start rebuilding your confidence.

Codependents are so caught up in what it means to be a couple, only focusing on the identity of their relationship and not on their own individual identities, that once you leave a codependent relationship, you may struggle at first to find your feet in this strange new world as a singleton. This is a common side effect of a codependent relationship. Be kind to yourself as you discover your new identity as an individual and not as part of a couple. Take time to discover your own wants and needs based upon your own personal feelings.

It is understandable that some people find it hard to establish their own desires, but I have included below some strategies designed to help you move forward and rebuild your self-confidence, allowing you to make choices and decision based on what you want. Building your self-confidence and self-esteem begins with learning to love yourself and wholeheartedly accepting yourself for all that you are.

Rebuilding your self-confidence

Stay away from negativity and negative people.

Negative people can have an adverse effect on your self-esteem and self-confidence. You want to stay away from people that bring you down and constantly challenge your actions. In a healthy friendship two people pull each other up when they feel the other is not doing something right, but negative people often challenge others for entirely different reasons. Try and limit your contact with these kinds of people.

Develop a positive attitude

You are starting a new stage of your life so try and develop a new positive attitude. Often, we listen to that negative voice in our own heads. When you hear yourself saying something negative or derogatory, try to turn it around and come back with something positive. Likewise, when you put off doing something new or that will take you outside of your comfort zone, try and approach the situation without prejudice and pre-emptive assumptions, instead flip it on its head and approach new situations with an open mind.

Accept failure

We all fail at some point in our lives. Instead of seeing failure as bad thing, try to reframe it in a positive way. Failure is not bad, and it only defines you if you let it. Pick yourself up and continue. Accept that there are just some things in life that are out of our control, take what you can from the experience and learn from it. The faster you accept failure, the easier you will find it to move on to better things.

Accept compliments

Most people are genuinely nice. If someone offers you a compliment, try and resist the urge to disagree with them, instead teach yourself to simply say thank you. People do not go out of their way to be demeaning, remember that they wanted you to feel good about yourself.

Compliment yourself

Give yourself a compliment every day. Try and find something you did well, or something complimentary about the way you look, for example 'That jacket looks very flattering on me', or 'I worked really hard on that project yesterday'. Learning to love yourself is essential to your overall well-being. Take responsibility for your feelings and acknowledge you are only responsible for your own feelings.

Coming out of a codependent relationship can be a steep learning curve. Understanding that you are only responsible for your own emotions and not the emotions of other people is a hard concept to understand. But you need to learn how to take care of you and let others determine what is right for them. You are not responsible for everything that happens in the world, nor anyone else's reaction to it. Just remember that you are too busy taking care of your own emotional health to interfere in anyone else's.

Don't compare yourself to others

As Teddy Roosevelt once said 'comparison is the thief of joy'. You are unique. There is only one of you in the whole world, so why compare your unique individuality to others? Stop concentrating on other people and start concentrating on being the best version of yourself that you can be. Comparing yourself to others takes the focus away from the most important person, which is you. Stop wasting your time measuring yourself by other people's standards and start making your own way in the world.

Let go of the past

Everything we go through in life, every situation we encounter makes us who we are today. Instead of shutting the past away in a box at the back of your head, let yourself feel the emotions connected with the past. Feel them - don't suppress these emotions, and then let them go. You are not who you were yesterday and you won't be the same person tomorrow. Understand that you will tie yourself to negative experiences from the past by not dealing with these emotions. It is ok to cry or feel angry about past experiences. Stop playing the victim. Make the decision to let past hurts go. Accept responsibility for you part in the situation and stop blaming others. Journal if you think it will help. Keep the focus on the present.

Practice good self-care

This is the ultimate way to express self-love. Make sure you are getting everything you need; the right foods, enough sleep, some exercise, connecting with others and the world around you and engaging in activities that will expand your personal development.

Believe in yourself

Who will believe in you if you don't first believe in yourself? Trust that you can do anything you set your mind to. After all, you managed to disengage from a codependent relationship and put down the framework for rebuilding your life. Stop listening to negative people and try and remember past successes and achievements and recall them every time you hear that voice saying you can't do something. Turn the sentence around. Instead of saying I can't, try saying 'I am working on...' Self-doubt is a big destroyer of self-confidence and the more you give into it, the greedier it will become, until it drags you down and you stop believing in yourself at all.

Learning to love again

At some point in the future there will come a time where you feel ready to start again and open yourself up to the possibility of having another intimate relationship. However, if you found healing from a codependent relationship tough, the thought of entering into a new relationship can appear terrifying. Breaking away from codependency doesn't mean not getting into a relationship ever again or becoming a relationship phobic instead it means that you can take your time to find a relationship that is right for you.

Avoid jumping straight into another relationship. If you have just left a codependent relationship and dive straight into a new romance without first taking some time to heal and rebuild your emotional health from the ground up, you will find yourself sucked back into the compulsive-obsessive cycle of codependency.

When considering an entering into a new relationship, think objectively and neutrally about your fundamental reason to be with someone new. Do you feel the need to play rescuer? Are you struggling with your new identity or feel like you have no validation if you are not in a relationship? Are you simply in love with the idea of being in love? These can be big warning signs that you are not yet ready and need to do more work so that you don't slip back into old behaviors.

If you do find yourself in a new relationship for all the wrong reasons, you need to take a step back and perhaps re-read the chapters on ending and healing from a codependent relationship, and begin to take care of yourself before thinking about committing to another potentially damaging connection that could wreck all the good work that you have done.

However, if you feel that you have put enough distance between yourself and your past codependent behaviors, and you feel confident that you are ready to start again, here are some simple ideas for taking that first step into a healthy, mutually beneficial relationship.

Try and visualize yourself in a new relationship that meets all of your needs

What does it your new relationship look like and how do you maintain the feeling of a connected loving relationship without needing to take over responsibility for the other person or their actions? Partners in a healthy relationship do not need to spend all their time together, they are happy for the other to spend time independent of them. In a healthy relationship neither partner is responsible for the emotional well-being of the other and this can be achieved without being cold or disconnected. You can have a bond with another person without the need to take on their needs as a duty that you must perform. Your obligation is first and foremost to your own emotional, physical and mental well-being.

Don't let fear of ending up in another codependent relationship put you off

You have new tools to recognize the warning signs of a codependent relationship, you can establish why you want to start again with someone new. Companionship? Mutual interests? These are great reasons for being in a relationship. Trust that you have not only managed to free yourself from codependency, but you have the toolkit to help you avoid being dragged back into that damaging cycle once again.

Define boundaries from the start

This time, you know what a healthy relationship should look like. This should help you set new positive relationship standards. Keep reinforcing to yourself that you won't associate with anyone who treats you badly or relies excessively on you for his or her needs. Remember why the previous relationship ended and identify early signs that predict a similar pattern.

Be open to new people

Learn to identify positive and nurturing relationships from negative and destructive ones. Spend time with balanced people who accept you unconditionally for who you are, not what they want you to be. Let down your guard and stay open to new people but stay away from people who display highly obsessive-compulsive traits or addiction dominated behavioral patterns.

Understand that you deserve the very best relationship

Believe that you deserve to be in harmonious, loving, healthy, nurturing and balanced relationship before you can be a part of one. Part of loving yourself is keeping away from potentially damaging situations and people. Believe that you deserve the very best relationship; one that meets your emotional needs, but doesn't drag you down. A healthy relationship is one where both partners get what they need but not at the emotional or physical cost to the other.

If you put these strategies in place, gradually, you'll find yourself coming out of the painful codependency cycle, and living a more rewarding, fulfilling and emotionally healthy life.

Chapter 17 : Common Misconceptions About Co-Dependency

As co-dependency lacks a concrete definition and is yet not recognized as a disease by the American Medical Association (AMA), there are many misconceptions about it. It is important to understand what co-dependency is not. Any definition of co-dependency may include people with one or more than one mental disorder. These disorders can include bi polar disorders, schizophrenia, anxiety issues and depression. A diagnosis by a professional is required for their treatment. This book does not attempt to elucidate specific treatment for these disorders that should be a job for the professional counselor or psychiatrist. What this book tries is to help the readers develop an understanding of the issue so they can identify the symptoms of co-dependency in their lifestyle. Co-dependency does not mean kindness, interdependency or care giving of any manner. People often complain being labeled as co-dependent because they were looking for a sick person or an addict. Co-dependent behavior in an exclusive situation does not make a person co-dependent. The evaluation of the co-dependency entails a study of the larger pattern of individual behavior and not isolated events.

It is not caregiving

Many people enjoy nurturing, caring and looking after other people. Mothers are naturally programmed to look after and provide for their children, starting even before the child takes birth. Co-dependent caregiving is different from looking after someone and the distinction needs to be understood. In the case of co-dependency, there would be more taking than any actual giving happening. So, the disease should not be confused with the breast-feeding tendencies of the mother, which is not co-dependency. Caregiving comes from abundance that all mothers have but co-dependency is a result of depravity and insecurity. Let take an example to understand the difference better.

Jack and Jones are two individuals. They quit their jobs, having to take care of their ailing parent. While Jack enjoys his job, he realizes that he is the only relative who can look after his parents. He prioritizes spending time with his parents during their last days above his job and hence quits. In order to take out some personal time, Jack employs a domestic help to look after his parents and socializes in his free time. He also pursues his hobbies and interests in the time he can take off for himself. He exercises, socializes and also looks after his parents to make the best out of his time home. This attitude nurtures both Jack and his parents.

On the other hand, is Jones who feels compelled to quit his job in order to look after his ailing parents. He blames this on his siblings who he comes to resent over a period of time for not sharing his responsibilities. Soon Jones begins to see his responsibility towards his parents as a burden and feels responsible for their medical treatment. The parents encourage Jones to get some rest but he feels obliged and pressured to look after them. This kind of a relationship is co-dependency where both Jones and his parents suffer. Their natural growth is hampered and they become dependent on one another. While Jones is seeking social gratification out of the service he provides to his parents, his parents seek medical and emotional support from Jones in their dying moment, yet each one suffers.

Jones co-dependent caretaking of his dying parents is inappropriate responsibility. He feels guilt-ridden and resentful for his parents, yet he neglects his responsibility towards himself. The relationship has control written all over it. He does not take help and takes the matter of his parent's treatment in his own hands for want of absolute control while feeling burdened under the pressure of caregiving. Co-dependents give until it begins to hurt. Then all that remains is a dysfunctional relationship that hurts the individuals involved.

Jack does not neglect his needs while looking after his parents. As a result, he does not grow resentful and neither feels guilty. Jack is not suffering from co-dependency, unlike Jones.

Co-dependency is not being kind

It is human nature to help others and display behavior of empathy and kindness towards all fellow beings. The man is a social animal in that respect. However co-dependent kindness stems from a sense of low self-esteem and deep identity crisis. Most co-dependents do not have a choice and they can't say no! The essential difference between kindness and co-dependency is determining whether the actions stem from a place of self-esteem or from fear, guilt, and anxiety. We will look at the example of Bill in order to understand this. Bill lets his wife make all the decisions like picking out dinner venues and weekend cinema shows so that she remains happy in their relationship. He fears to lose her and his abandonment. This is a sort of bribery he undertakes in order to make his wife stay in the relationship, satisfied. He can't let her know who he really is, what he really likes and what he does not. Even though this may appear to be a kindness on behalf of Bill o let his wife take all such decisions, it is essentially Bill's insecurity which makes him act in such a way. He is constantly veiling his true identity from his wife while trying to please her every day. Bill must realize that in doing so he is not making his wife love him but instead she loves an image, a fake persona of Bill, which he is posting in front of her. In order for a relationship to not become co-dependent, it is vital that the individuals assert their individuality to the other. In doing so, one drops all masks and veils revealing the true self for the partner to welcome or embrace. If the partner rejects the true self, it is better than dragging along a lie.

Co-dependency is not inter-dependency

Most relationships fall in between the spectrum of inter-dependency and co-dependency. Here we would take a look at the two extremes in order to understand the nature of a relationship.

CO-DEPENDENCY

It could be hard identifying co-dependent couple because they often appear to be intellectual, physically, socially and financially independent. In reality, they are two emotionally dependent and insecure adults. Often these relationships are marked by a power struggle or a power imbalance. There is no equality, closeness and faith. One person could anticipate the other's need and feel anxious, guilty or burdened about it. Such partners often directly or indirectly try to control the other in order to satisfy their ideas, needs, and demands. Such people feel experience lesser freedom in their relationships and end up fearing both intimacies as well as desertion. Such is the insecure nature of a co-dependent relationship

INTER-DEPENDENCY

In such relationships, attachment develops at an early stage between the partners. It is natural for people involved in a romantic or any other serious relationship to be worried about their partners. They express concern and miss the other. However, inter-dependent couples structure their lives around that of their partners instead of encroaching in their lives. They enjoy helping each other out and are confident of the other being there for them in their time of need. They are not insecure about the other's presence and often do not see their partners as others but just a reflection of their selves. Their habits and interests may differ and they give each other the space to pursue these different interests and inclinations. Their lives are inter-dependent. Such couples do not fear intimacy and neither fear abandonment. They are respectful and supportive of each other. They remain committed to the relationship.

Chapter 18 : More Tips and Advice for Overcoming Codependency

As you do these small things more and more, they will eventually grow into habits and once they are habits, they can help construct your emotional foundations. You do not need to do every single one of these things. In fact, some of them may not even work very well for you. These tips are more intended as suggestions and guidance. Let them inspire you to develop your own positive habits.

- Keep a journal: writing a journal is an excellent way to make the whole process of self-reflection a lot easier. You can use it as a reference and memory aid. And reading what you wrote a few days after the fact will help you to better reflect on what happened and how you actually felt in that moment. This will prevent you from minimizing pain you have felt in the past and from over dramatizing smaller events. So, as you write, remember to write down both what happened and what you feel. Getting in this habit will also help you to get better at identifying your feelings (something that many codependent personalities struggle with).

- Do something creative: creative activities can be immensely therapeutic and relaxing. It can also help give your subconscious emotions a means of expression. When you don't know how to say what you are feeling in words (or aren't even sure yourself what you are feeling), doing something creative can help you process those emotions in alternate ways. Plus, you will end up with something cool in the end. So, whether it's arts, crafts, or some sort of DIY project, take the time every week to do something creative. Who knows? You may discover some hidden talents in yourself. At the very least, you will discover some hidden emotions.

- Make to Do Lists: this might seem like it is coming out of left field but To Do lists can help more than you think. Each morning (or each evening before you go to bed), make a To Do list for the day. Include big important tasks as well as the little things. As you complete each task throughout the day, mark it off your list. This is a positive habit that will help you better realize just how much you really do get done in a day. It is a wonderful feeling to sit down after a long day and look at a long list full of completed tasks.

- Whether it is expressing a thought, saying no, finding a new hobby, or working on any of the other steps. Starting the day with the clear intention of how you plan to work on your recovery will not only help keep you on track but also help you notice the progress you are making. Think about it, after one week of doing this, you will have accomplished 7 goals that are helping your recovery. Add those 7 goals together and you are that much closer to recovery.

- Notice something beautiful: take the time every single day to stop and notice something beautiful or pleasant. It could be the sunset, a cute dog, a particularly artistic piece of graffiti, or even just an extra well-made sandwich eaten for lunch. Just remember to stop and take a moment to acknowledge how wonderful it is and let yourself just enjoy it without any outside pressure from anyone else. This is your own small moment of enjoyment and peacefulness that you can have all on your own without anybody else.

- Acknowledge an accomplishment: every single night, as you are going to sleep, think of at least one thing you accomplished that day. It could simply be accomplishing the small recovery goal you had set or it could be marking off everything on your To Do list. No matter how big or small, every accomplishment count. As you are going to sleep, you can use that time to appreciate what you have accomplished. If you can think of more than one thing, go for it. But always come up with at least one accomplishment from your day.

- Keep a dream journal: each morning, as soon as you wake up, write down everything you can remember from your dreams. This can be fun and enlightening. A dream journal will help you get more in touch with your subconscious and all those unexpressed emotions you are struggling with.

Plus, it can be an interesting way to pass the time to read through all the dreams you have been having the past few nights. As you reread them, look for any common symbols or themes. Alternatively, you can compare your dream journal with your regular day to day journal to see what in your life might be influencing your dreams. If you don't feel like an expert dream interpreter, you can take your dream journal (and your regular daily journal while you are at it) to your therapist to get his or her thoughts and opinions.

- Start up a savings for something you want: even if you do not have very much money to put away, this can be a very good exercise. Working toward a tangible long-term goal like a vacation or a new dress can help you build emotional strength and endurance. So even if you are just putting leftover change from the day into a jar, start saving money. And start saving it for a specific goal.

Even if you do not feel comfortable telling anyone what exactly you are saving for, you can still build up a savings and know for yourself what your goal is. Let it be a somewhat long-term goal, though such as a dream vacation or even just a fairly expensive piece of jewelry or another item that you want. Part of building up emotional strength is learning to appreciate delayed gratification and long-term rewards. Saving up for things you want to get in the future can help you develop that skill.

With these steps and tips in mind, you are ready to begin your own journey to self-recovery. This is one of the most courageous and inspirational decisions you could have made so congratulate yourself for coming this far and for deciding that it is time to change. This will keep you motivated and strong as you work through the process.

Conclusion

I have worked with individuals who experience the ill effects of codependency for certain years and it never neglects to stun me how satisfied these individuals are the point at which they think outside the box and venture past it.

Try not to empower individuals who don't attempt to improve their lives. Try not to put yourself down for not being who they need you to be. Be glad for what your identity is. That is the most important blessing you can ever give anybody on the planet.

There is much bliss to be had after codependence. On the off chance that you truly need to get past it, this book holds every one of the pieces of information. You should simply make the strides that are sketched out in the book and you will slowly discover your way back to wellbeing again and back to a solid perspective where you value yourself and set limits that help other people to regard you. This book was composed with a great deal of feeling since this is a passionate dependent upon me and to the people, I have needed to manage throughout the years who experienced the impacts of codependency. When you figure out how to proceed onward and to set down what are adequate limits, you help everybody – including that individual who may have started to underestimate you.

NARCISSISTIC ABUSE

Recover from Emotional Abuse, Mental Manipulation, and Toxic Relationships — a Guide to Surviving Psychological Abuse and Codependent Relationships

Introduction

If you have survived a relationship with a Narcissist, you should be proud of yourself! If you; however, live with a Narcissist or work with one, you'll find this book useful. Even if you don't know anyone with this disorder or you just have doubts that someone around you might have Narcissistic traits, you will be able to find answers through these chapters.

Narcissism can be defined as an obsessive concern with oneself. However, the important thing is to distinguish Narcissistic Personality Disorder from the Narcissism label that we give to individuals in our society. Some people don't really know the difference between the two, so this book is made not only for those who have suffered directly from Narcissistic abuse but also for the ones that might identify themselves as Narcissists.

Through the chapters of this book, you will encounter many definitions and classifications of Narcissistic Personality Disorder (NPD). Also, you will see what kind of influence Narcissists can have on your environment. Comparing examples from psychology studies, literature, mythology, medicine, and personal experiences through books and testimonies, this book represents your personal treasury on how to recognize, understand, and deal with the Narcissist.

Here you will find how other people dealt with their Narcissistic partners, or parents, or coworkers. You will find tips and pointers on how to protect yourself from Narcissistic influence.

Even if you have NPD yourself, this is a book for you! It offers an explanation on the causes of the disorder; it also helps you understand why your definition of emotional connection and concept of relationship is different and how can you be better.

Narcissistic Personality Disorder is associated with characteristics that undermine interpersonal functioning, but here you can see why it is like that and that it isn't entirely the fault of the person diagnosed with NPD. If you have heard that Narcissists lack empathy, that is true, but their lack of empathy isn't a product of ill will. Usually, this lack of empathy derives from some deeper and older problems.

But do keep in mind that anybody can be a victim of Narcissistic abuse. The aim here isn't to justify but to help both sides to understand each other so they can improve their quality of life.

This book tends to show the victim of emotional abuse some of the most important things on the path of recovery and to remind them that they are not alone.

After reading this book, you will hopefully be able to distinguish how and why people with Narcissistic Personality Disorder tend to use other people and why you have to be careful when dealing with them. You will be able to protect yourself from them and hopefully objectively understand why things happen.

In the end, we hope that if you ever realize that you are a victim of any kind of abuse, this book can be but a small reminder that there is hope as long as we can have the courage to seek it

Chapter 1 : What is Narcissistic Abuse?

These days, narcissistic personality disorder seems to be a relevant topic of discussion in almost every walk of life. Narcissism impacts family and friendship dynamics; it shows up frequently in our love lives; it permeates most all academic and professional fields, as well as all forms of social and entertainment media; and it certainly rears its ugly head in the realm of politics and government. Even so, the way most of us understand the disorder is a bit short-sighted, like mistaking an exaggerated caricature for the real thing. We recognize traits like vanity, self-absorption, and lack of consideration for others, and can easily condemn them, pity them, perhaps even laugh them off--but without scratching the surface and taking a deeper look at the root motivations of a narcissist, we may fail to realize the true dangers of narcissistic abuse, or to identify the abusive behaviors as such.

Defining Narcissism

Narcissism is a trait that exists upon a spectrum. All of us have it, to a greater or lesser degree, and the amount of narcissistic attitude that we display can fluctuate throughout our lives, as a reflection of age, emotional maturity, circumstance and mental health factors, such as grief or trauma exposure. There is a difference between a truly disordered individual and someone who is simply suffering from a temporarily over-inflated ego.

Below is a list of the nine-character traits that are typically used to evaluate an individual's likelihood of possessing pathological levels of narcissistic inclination. This isn't a foolproof test by any means, and shouldn't be used to draw conclusions about other people, or about yourself. A true diagnosis of NPD can only be made by a mental health professional who has had a significant amount of time to interact with the individual in question. Still, if you know a person who fits most of these descriptors, it's a good idea to stay vigilant while in their company, and perhaps to do some reflection on the impact this relationship has had on your life. To guard yourself against narcissistic abuse throughout your life, you must learn to recognize these traits as potential threats, not inherently evil characteristics. There are certainly some people with extreme narcissistic attitudes who truly pose no danger to anyone around them, but it is ultimately up to you to determine where you will draw the line and what types of treatment you will tolerate from the potential narcissists in your life.

- Grandiosity - A narcissist has an overinflated, unrealistic sense of self-importance. They may expect to be recognized as a brilliant expert in a particular field without commensurate education or experience; alternatively, they may expect to be seen as the most attractive or sexually desirable person in a group, despite a failure to attend to their own hygiene, eat well, exercise, or dress sharply. Some narcissists will proclaim these sentiments boldly and unapologetically, using superlatives to describe themselves; for example: "I think I'm the best person to host Thanksgiving this year--no one is better at cooking or organizing parties than I am, and my home is definitely the largest, most comfortable venue for it."

- Obsessed with power and success - Narcissists often harbor over-the-top fantasies of acquiring status markers or positions that might grant them unlimited power. This might translate into an obsession with acquiring and hoarding financial wealth or a fixation on achieving unrealistic beauty standards; it might

287

look like an unquenchable thirst for degrees, awards, and accolades, or a desire for international fame. It's important to note that for a narcissist, these needs are never satisfied, and the things they desire are generally unattainable; they are working towards a god-like degree of power, which no human can ever grasp, even if they become the richest person on the planet or win the highest political office in the land.

- Arrogant attitudes - Some narcissists are smart enough to know when to turn this off--they can catch more flies with honey, after all, and will not want to offend powerful or elite people around them. But generally, narcissists look down on other people and aren't shy about making this known if the circumstances allow it. For example, a narcissist running for local political office may do their best to appear humble in the public eye, yet act haughty and condescending towards the wait-staff in the restaurants where they dine, or with the domestic workers in their own home--perhaps they'll even patronize and insult their spouse, parents, and children. The narcissist is able to improve their own self-image by belittling, dismissing, and dehumanizing others.

- Feels special and unique - Narcissists often harbor the extremely unrealistic notion that they are somehow different from most everyone else on the planet, cut from a cloth of superior quality, and misunderstood by humanity in general. It's important to note that most people toy with this idea from time to time, with a healthy degree of narcissism that allows them to have faith in their own abilities, to overcome hardships, and to combat existential anxieties. The difference is that people with healthy degrees of narcissistic inclination are most often relieved to find people who actually do understand them, and are happy to find commonalities with others, enjoying the feeling of belonging to a group of equals who share mutual respect and appreciate differences. By contrast, the narcissist takes pride in being unique and is never happy to be one among the crowd. They often believe that they should only associate with other similarly elite people, but even within that group, they will see themselves as extraordinary and distinguished by comparison, whether or not others recognize them as such.

- Constantly envious, but feels enviable - Everyone experiences bouts of envy now and then, but narcissists feel envy as a constant since there is no realm in which they don't wish to be considered the best, or the winner. For example, a narcissist who is in a seemingly happy, successful relationship with a trophy spouse might still feel envious of a friend in a new relationship, even if the friend's new lover is a less suitable mate for the narcissist than their own partner. Narcissists also tend to project feelings of envy onto other people, in order to explain their lack of love or admiration for the narcissist (which confounds the narcissist, of course). For example: "Don't hate me because I'm beautiful," or "He won't tell me why he's upset with me--I'm sure he's just jealous of my success."

- Entitled - The narcissist feels that they are deserving of special treatment and that others ought to be aware of this fact. If they don't offer the best accommodations, they'll either demand them or confidently help themselves to whatever they feel is owed to them. This can be done through mundane behaviors: cutting in lines, interrupting other people's conversations, or ignoring commonly accepted social norms, such as tipping for good customer service. It may also show up in more extreme displays of entitlement, such as demanding to be seated in a crowded restaurant without a reservation (at the expense of those who did call ahead to reserve a table), expecting to be the center of attention at someone else's wedding or birthday party, or taking shortcuts to success while others have to put in hard work and time to achieve the same goals. Narcissists often act as though the rules that apply to others shouldn't apply to them. They also expect total, unquestioning compliance from others, and are hurt and angry when this expectation isn't met, or whenever their entitlement is challenged. For example, think of a wealthy person pulled over for driving while intoxicated, expecting to be let off the hook by the police officer, who ought to immediately recognize them as too important to suffer the same punishment as any other reckless driver. When the police officer fails to do so and prepares to place them under arrest, the narcissist might fly into a rage, saying: "You don't want to do this--you're making a big mistake here! Don't you know who I am?"

- Needs excessive attention and admiration - Everyone needs validation and praise once in a while, but narcissists need far more than is reasonable. They will demand attention and commendations, even when they haven't been earned, or when these demands inconvenience other people. Again, think of the wedding guest who insists on being the center of attention, even if they aren't a part of the wedding party--perhaps a guest who wears a white dress to upstage a bride, or makes a scene, or starts a loud fight during the event. These are the actions of a person who needs attention so badly that they don't care who else is impacted; they may not realize that their hunger for personal significance can only be satisfied at the expense of the two people getting married, but if they do, this knowledge doesn't trouble them. Narcissists will want constant attention, whether it is positive or negative, but they'll also have an endless thirst for superlative praise. Hearing "nice work!" every once in a while, won't cut it; they need to hear that they are the best, the most beautiful, the most powerful, the most successful, and they need to hear these praises over and over again--the bucket is never full. If others fail to offer these compliments, many narcissists aren't above praising themselves publicly, just to be sure the message is heard. For example: "Look at me! Don't I just look like a million bucks in this outfit?" or "Check out my new Italian leather briefcase! I bought it as a gift for myself when I beat out ten other chumps for a promotion, figured I deserve a reward; and now that I'm at the top of my field, I need to look the part, right?"

- Lacking emotional empathy - This is one of the traits that truly sets a pathological narcissist apart from those who simply dabble in narcissistic behaviors from time to time when their egos need a little boost. Narcissists aren't incapable of understanding or recognizing other people's emotions, but they do have a tendency to detach from them or ignore them when other people's feeling become inconvenient or get in the way of their pursuit of personal goals. For example, a narcissist might recognize that a close friend is distraught over a recent divorce, and even try to offer some emotional support or condolences--but then fail to understand or accept the fact that this emotional stress prevents their friend from wanting to come out and celebrate the narcissist's birthday, or help the narcissist to pack for a move. This lack of empathy may also lead them to misread social cues and fail to recognize when they are crossing other people's boundaries. It also allows them to cause discomfort, pain, or suffering in others and remain unbothered by feelings of guilt or shame. Their lack of empathy doesn't only show up during periods of emotional turmoil, though. In everyday life, narcissists tend to dominate conversations and fail to recognize when their endless monologues are exhausting the people around them. If they do allow others to speak, they may ask a lot of invasive or overly personal questions, or show a callous indifference to the nuance of other people's identities--for example, laughing at an impoverished person's story about financial hardship and stress, and asking why they don't just take an impromptu tropical vacation, quit complaining, and try positive thinking.

- Interpersonally manipulative and exploitative - Since narcissists lack empathy, it is fairly easy for them to lie, cheat, and take advantage of other people in order to pursue their personal goals without feeling remorse or shame for the damage these behaviors cause. Having some cognitive empathy, but very little emotional empathy, they are able to predict the emotional reactions of others, but remain detached from them, allowing them to use deception, blackmail, or bait-and-switch tactics to control people. Narcissists are likely to maintain relationships for purely strategic reasons, such as professional connections or access to a friend's financial resources, and can unceremoniously cut ties after they're done using the connection or when the potential for future exploitation is withdrawn.

Again, it's important to understand that this list is a general set of guidelines for evaluation and that there is plenty of room for misdiagnosis if it's applied incorrectly. A person with narcissistic personality disorder won't just have exhibited these qualities once or twice--these characteristics would describe their overall outlook on life and motivate the majority of their observable behaviors. Don't beat yourself up if you read this list and recognize some of these traits in yourself. It's perfectly natural to feel envious of others on occasion, to crave attention and admiration, sometimes, or to desire success and strive to achieve ambitious goals. The key difference for a person who suffers from pathological narcissism is that these traits define their personality, and the need for superiority is compulsive; their self-centered attitudes overshadow their ability to be rational or self-aware and can show up in wildly inappropriate circumstances. For example, you may have exhibited some of the behaviors listed above while on vacation and drinking more than usual, but you'd feel compelled to apologize later on if any of your behaviors hurt your loved ones, and set aside the entitled attitude when you return to work on Monday morning. By contrast, a narcissist would be unlikely to apologize for missteps in any kind of sincere or meaningful way, and would continue to behave as though they're on vacation after returning to the office.

Abuse as A Byproduct

Since narcissists are so self-involved, it's entirely possible for them to justify abusive behaviors by claiming they were all unintentional. How could they be purposefully hurting other people if they never think about anyone but themselves? Some malignant narcissists may indeed have sadistic inclinations that allow them to enjoy causing pain in others, but meanwhile, many narcissists are truly unaware of the fact that their abusive behavior is a choice; instead, they see these behaviors as reflexes, or actions that anyone in their position would naturally take. The impact of the abuse is far less important, in their view, than whatever justification or catalyst they use to explain their motives.

This is part of the danger of narcissistic abuse. Narcissists are experts at rationalizing their own actions, no matter how horrible they are; in order to excuse their habits of disregarding other people's needs, exploiting others for personal gain, and skirting consequences, they must believe wholeheartedly in one a priori assumption: that they are superior, and everyone else is virtually worthless. If you, as a victim, spend enough time communicating with someone who is thoroughly convinced of your worthlessness, their attitude will eventually start to warp your own sense of self-worth, especially if they trap you in abusive cycling of idealization and devaluation. This is emotional abuse. Narcissists don't need to be physically violent to damage their victims; instead of fists, the weapons they use are mind-games, pathological lies, slights, insults, and intimidation tactics to establish control and superiority, draining the victim's energy, destroying the victim's faith in their own sanity, and constantly diminishing the victim's capacity for self-love.

NPD is sometimes called the "second-hand smoke" of personality disorders; unlike other cluster B disorder types, narcissism has an almost contagious element. While those who spend time with a narcissist may not be so seriously impacted as to be diagnosed with the disorder themselves, many victims of narcissistic abuse and members of narcissistic regimes will mimic and adopt the behavior patterns of the narcissists in their lives; this may be done subconsciously, or it may be done decisively as a means of self-defense. Either way, the disorder has an insidious way of seeping into the lives of everyone it touches, often working its way deeply into the minds of victims before they are even aware that any form of abuse has taken place.

If you share a relationship with someone who has a narcissistic personality disorder, abusive behavior is almost guaranteed; however, abusive dynamics can also persist without the presence of the disorder in any of the involved parties. A victim of narcissistic abuse can easily pass on the behaviors of narcissistic abuse to other people, without truly harboring the internal mental markers of the disorder; likewise, a person suffering from grief or trauma may unknowingly inflict abuse upon those around them, despite being deeply empathetic and considerate under normal emotional circumstances. Strangely, some people may exhibit the behaviors of narcissistic abuse with only one or two people in their lives, or only under a few sets of very specific circumstances, while being otherwise rational, humble, and compassionate.

The purpose of this book is to help you recognize and stop the cycle of abuse, rather than to diminish the abuser, who, in some cases, may truly be innocent of any malicious intent. Many abusers may have suffered under even more extreme forms of narcissistic abuse in childhood than that which they pass on, so it isn't always productive to classify them as evil or nefarious; still, it's important to recognize that it isn't your personal responsibility to be an emotional punching bag for someone who has suffered at someone else's hand. Within this dynamic, it doesn't matter who wins or loses, who accepts fault or points the finger of blame; instead, we must realize that in the continuation of a toxic relationship cycle, nobody wins, and neither party can grow or change without first breaking their unhealthy relationship patterns.

Chapter 2 : Reality of The Narcissist

In order to understand people who are suffering from Narcissism, it is important that we know what kind of person we're exactly talking about. Narcissism is a mental disorder. The person who has this disorder displays a lack of empathy for others and if you offend them, they won't react in a nice way. Narcissists are always looking to get you to pay attention to them and they think that they are the most important person out there. The thing is, the Narcissist can't comprehend the issue of hurting your feelings. They don't have an empathy switch and some of them don't even understand if they're hurting someone. People with this disorder can cause various problems in every aspect of life. Whether it is at work, school, family, or relationships, Narcissists believe that their needs are above all others. And if they don't receive the attention and admiration that they think they deserve; things could get ugly.

The thing is, everybody is a little bit Narcissistic and it is our self-care trigger. But if you are extremely preoccupied with yourself, it will make you cut off others and you will care only about your own satisfaction.

Sometimes it is hard to differentiate between a person who is self-absorbed and a person with Narcissistic Disorder. There are many guides and lists on how to recognize a Narcissist. Some people, whether they are professional psychologists or just people who have had experience with a Narcissist have written a lot about the different characteristics used to determine Narcissism. All of them agree on a few main ways for recognition: The Narcissist is going to be someone who is the center of the universe and he (or she) is going to be totally absorbed in it. If you are dealing with an extreme Narcissist, that person will see you as a thing to be used, not a human being that needs love and care. Keep in mind, that this kind of behavior mostly isn't the product of the ill intentions; it is just that to a Narcissist, the only important thing is their needs and meeting them.

So, if Narcissists feel that you can give them the attention that they want, you will find yourself charmed until they get their objective. Since they don't understand the concept of traditional human relationships, once they get what they want, they'll stop being considerate. The most common cause of this disorder is childhood trauma or some other big and consistent event in their lives. Even though they are usually socially skilled, they have issues with attachment. You can find them in different environments and they can be quite adaptable in order to achieve their goals. Narcissists can change their identity depending on the situation. They can be nice and get along with others. Sometimes they can scare and intimidate, or they can even act like they really care about other people's well-being. They can be comedians, party bringers; they can look friendly and approachable. But in reality, they are not. If you start asking them personal questions, they'll find some way to avoid them. They will cut you off if you try to get close. They are not the kind of people who will talk much about their personal lives and if you insist, they'll just exclude you.

Narcissists are more interested in controlling people, even though they can convince them that they care and they act friendly. Their issue isn't a lack of social skills; it is a lack of empathy. Some of them just want to be in control or to reach success, while others like to be admired. However, if you don't react according to their desires or if they don't find you useful, they'll just walk away. There are many reasons why dealing with Narcissism is hard. Especially when you realize that you're just a means to an end.

For a Narcissist, taking advantage of others is not a desire, but a need. And they don't care how others will react. Since they think that they are important, more important than others, they think that others envy them and it turns out they are envious of others in the process. Narcissists often behave arrogantly and they'll look down on you. If you spend time paying attention to their behavior, you will realize that this type of personality has a really different image of confidence and that extreme self-adoration can leave other people affected on multiple levels.

When Narcissus Isn't A Myth but A Child?

There is a big chance that when you were in school you've heard about the Myth of Narcissus. As the name suggests, this disorder was named after that myth. The poet Ovid was the one who wrote the Roman version of the myth. In order to reference the disorder, we call Narcissism we'll review Ovid's telling:

Narcissus was a son of a river god and a nymph called Liriope. His mother Liriope wanted to know what kind of future awaits her son and went to see a prophet. She was told that Narcissus would live a long life if he fails to recognize himself. Narcissus grew up and became beautiful and loved. Still, he thought that there was nobody to whom he would return the affection. He was so gorgeous that even the nymph Echo fell in love with him. Echo was cursed and she couldn't speak. She could only repeat the sounds and words of others. She tried to reach out to Narcissus as she followed him through the woods, but she could just repeat his words. When the nymph appeared and tried to hold on to Narcissus, she was rejected. The gods were furious at Narcissus and they condemned him to be denied by anyone he loved. One day, while he was hunting, Narcissus bent down to drink water from the woods. He fell in love with his own reflection in the water. He was so amazed by this person that he saw. He tried to grab the reflection, but he failed. Narcissus stayed in the water for days. He wasn't sleeping, he wasn't eating. He was so obsessed with the person that he saw that he started to talk to the reflection and promised that he'll never leave. As Narcissus was saying his farewell to the reflection, Echo appeared and repeated his words. He died, and as the nymph mourned him, a flower appeared in his dying place.

There are many psychological studies that use this myth as a reference and its elements have many symbolic meanings. More than the other myth, the story of Narcissus was used by the scholars of human behavior. For them, this myth represents dualities, such as illusion and reality, passion and coldness, wanting love but rejecting love, subject of desire and an object of desire, etc. Narcissus represents self-knowledge as death and shows the role of empathy. It also symbolizes twisted self-love and perils of physical beauty. Narcissus has become the synonym of the concept of destructive self-love. According to some researchers, the relationship between Narcissus and Echo was a premise for the Narcissistic family model. In this story, both of the characters have excluded the ability to see, hear, or react to the needs of another. So, as some studies suggest, Narcissus represents the parent system getting its own needs met. This can happen for various reasons: alcoholism, drugs, stress on the job, mental illness, etc. On the other hand, Echo represents the child. This child will do anything to gain the attention and approval of his parents and in the end, it becomes their reflection. Unlike children living in healthy families, children who have parents with a Narcissistic Disorder have to meet the expectations of their parents. These parents believe that their children are responsible to fulfill what they want, not the other way around. Since they are role models for a child, they have a major influence on how the child will grow to view it. Having a role model is the way in which a child learns what is acceptable and unacceptable in their behavior.

In comparison, children who come from Narcissistic families become reactive and reflective grownups. The consequence of those kids learning early that they need to meet parental needs is that they usually never develop trust in their own feelings. Their feelings become a source of discomfort because they can't get any validation for them. Looking up to your parents and mirroring some of their attributes is normal to some extent. However, in the Narcissistic family, this mirror reflects that the child isn't able to meet its parent's needs and often provokes the feeling of failure.

Children who are raised in Narcissistic families usually have issues with intimate relationships. They don't develop trust when they are young so in adulthood, they have problems forming relationships. Have you ever heard of Maslow's hierarchy of needs? It is a psychological system developed by Maslow, one of the greatest psychologists. His hierarchy describes that the need for psychological and physical safety is an essential part of the development of trust. For a child raised in a Narcissistic family, this safety often means unlearning trust, rather than never learning to trust.

There are certain behaviors, like embarrassing the child and getting drunk, that will produce a crisis for the child. This kind of situation produces dysfunctions for the child, especially when you are raised with this event happening on a daily basis.

Let's see a concrete example. Here is the story of Mary, a girl who was raised in a Narcissistic family. Mary remembers her mom. But when we asked her to describe her relationship with her mother, she said: "my mom was just... there." As Mary explained, her mother was doing the usual house stuff but that she felt like she could never get close to her. Mary then said that it felt like her mother was there and cared for her, but not really. The reaction of Mary's mother on some big life events for her made Mary realize that her parent was doing "parent things" from the "parent book". Mary realized that her mother looked like she cared but she didn't really care. Mary's story isn't one of dramatic abuses, rather it is an example of an emotionally unavailable parent. As Mary was growing up it was clearer to her that her mother didn't pay attention to her and that she can't meet her emotional needs.

Still, there are many cases that illustrate abusive families. There are a large number of examples of overtly Narcissistic families that are dealing with alcohol and drug abuse, and even incest and other assertive behaviors.

Chapter 3 : Symptoms and Patterns of Narcissistic Abuse

What we haven't talked about is either the symptoms of narcissistic personality disorder in a general manner nor the ways that these can manifest into abuse.

Note that all abuse is negative and even if your abuse doesn't fit these criteria, there's still a good chance that you're being abused if you even have to read this book and ask the question.

The first thing that we need to talk about before diving any deeper into this chapter is that this is not an easy topic to discuss with yourself. You have to prepare yourself mentally in order to realistically address these problems and these symptoms. Realizing you've been the victim of abuse is extremely difficult and stressful, and it can be difficult to internalize. Your knee-jerk reaction may be to simply tell yourself that none of these things are so bad, but you can't do that - if you do, then you're just doing what the abusive partner wants you to do and allowing the cycle of abuse to continue.

Instead, what you need to do is mentally prepare yourself for the distance required to assert the situation in an honest way. This is easier said than done, by far. It's not easy to summon up the mental distance required to allow yourself to look at the person in an objective light rather than just in terms of what you want them to be and in terms of how you automatically internalize trauma.

Now, onto the actual symptoms of narcissistic personality disorder. There are nine key symptoms of narcissistic personality disorder. We're going to look at all of these as well as how they might manifest in terms of narcissistic abuse. Afterward, we're going to look at the general ways that narcissistic personality disorder can also have abusive tendencies unrelated to the symptoms.

The first major symptom is when a person experiences excessive grandiosity. What happens, in this case, is that the person has a massively inflated view of themselves and their proclivity to do this or that. They may experience excessive grandeur in the way that they see themselves and expect other people to treat them as though they're superior. This can come back to being an abusive component in the relationship because of the fact that it's very easy for their personality to tend towards expecting you to treat them preferentially to every other person in life, as well as validating their ideas that they're superior to everybody else.

The second major symptom is that the person is fixated on fantasies of power, intelligence, being extremely attractive, and so forth. This one is a bit trickier to understand in terms of abuse, but it becomes a bit easier to digest when you prelude this with the understanding that neglect in and of itself is a form of abuse. The person may be so caught up in their own desires and pursuits that they may fail to properly give you the attention that you're wanting or needing. In essence, they may be so busy attending to whatever their fantasies are that you become merely a thoroughfare to the fantasy or worse, an accessory to it. This is a form of emotional abuse because it causes you to feel immensely devalued in terms of not just the relationship but in general. A relationship thrives when both people feel like they are being pushed forward and loved by the other person.

The third major symptom is that the person has a general perception of being excessively unique or superior to others, as well as being connected with people who are seen as very high-status. This is often used as a means of projection and can be used in your relationship as a tool of abuse because of the fact that it may be used as a means to make you feel like you're less than they deserve. While this doesn't come out as outright abuse, generally, it still can functionally be abuse.

The fourth major symptom is the person in question needing the constant validation or love of others. They may go out of their way to demand attention from you and may get mad if you serve as anything but a pedestal and a yes-man for them. This is insanely unhealthy if not outright abusive because it leads to the person being codependent on your validation, and the cycle will only become worse and worse if you feed into their incessant demands for validation. This is not a good deal and you need to break the cycle if you can do so in a way that will result in your safety.

The fifth major symptom is that the person has felt as though they're especially deserving of either special treatment or of others being directly obedient to them. This may manifest in terms of abuse as the narcissist demanding that you treat them as though they're above everybody else in your life, essentially causing the eventual closing of contact with other people. This is far from preferable because it works reflexively with abuse. The more of your attention they demand, the more that you drive other people away and this leads to you having less and less of a support network, which ultimately makes it much harder for you to leave whenever it would be healthy for you to leave. Also, if you aren't obedient to everything the narcissistic person wants, they may decide to punish you in one way or another, which could turn even physical or be much more subtle in the form of mental cutdowns and psychological abuse.

The sixth major symptom is that they'll have no problem exploiting people or doing whatever it takes for them to get what they want. This can come up as abuse in multiple channels. On one hand, your regular validation of them and their narcissistic thought patterns may be construed as something they want, and they'll have no problem manipulating and gaslighting you so that you remain in their life. Gaslighting, for the record, is a common practice among manipulative people where the person will make you feel as though you misremember certain events or basically rewrite history in order to make you feel bad about yourself. On the other hand, they may end up manipulating you in order to have you help them with their exploitative goals.

The seventh major symptom is that the person will either not want to or will be unable to empathize with the feelings of people in general, but also especially you. This can be one of the biggest sources of tension and one of the biggest mental justifiers behind their abuse. They may, for example, regularly do things which hurt you for their own personal benefit without stopping to think about how you might feel about it.

The eighth major symptom is that they will be intensely jealous of other people, and also assume that everybody else is just as jealous of them. Because of their obsession with being the absolute best, they will often want anything that somebody else has. This can manifest as an abuse in a relationship pretty horribly because they not only are generally jealous but are also in need of your validation, which means that if they sense that you even mildly are attracted to somebody else or at risk of leaving that they'll double down on their abusive tactics so that you stay with them.

The ninth major symptom is general pomposity and being arrogant in a general sense. This usually doesn't manifest directly as abuse, but when it does, it's normally in the form of them minimizing the things that you like and telling you that you're wrong for being the way that you are. There's a difference between debate and argument and general abusive behavior.

Firstly, you need to know that there are three general realms of abuse: emotional abuse, verbal abuse, and physical abuse.

Narcissists will generally opt for the first two until they're backed into a corner. This is because they are a much more subtle form of abuse than the first two and cause more long-term damage and neediness on the end of the other person than simple physical intimidation does. While a victim of physical abuse may fear for their lives, a victim of emotional abuse and verbal abuse will begin to feel like they're absolutely worthless and aren't deserving of anything better. That's not to divide the three; they almost always occur in tandem. It is verbal and emotional abuse specifically which cause people to stay in relationships.

Emotional abuse in the realm of narcissistic personality disorder will normally manifest as either intense neglect or intense neediness, as well as a general disregard for your feelings. Tensions will constantly be high when you're with the person in question and you'll feel as though you're walking on eggshells not to say the wrong thing after a while. This normally doesn't happen at first, but as the person shows more and more of their narcissistic side and devalues your interests and feelings more and more, you're going to feel as though you aren't cared about.

Emotional abuse will often come up, too, as gaslighting and various forms of psychological isolation. Their jealousy and desire to be the best will often result in them being mean to you or cutting you down so that you can't be attracted to anybody else or you feel as though you can't leave them. If you fail to validate their narcissistic fantasies, they will get mad.

The scariest part of narcissistic abuse is in how the person reacts when you don't fulfill their fantasies. As I said before, narcissistic personality disorder is often comorbid with other personality disorders. It's also often comorbid with things like substance abuse disorder (addiction), major depression, bipolar depression, and anxiety disorders. Because of this, reactions can be particularly scary. They may present as irrationally angry, irritable, depressed, or any other number of undesirable emotions, especially in the face of having their narcissistic persona challenged. This can present a big hurdle for somebody who is on the receiving end of an emotionally abusive relationship.

One form of emotional abuse is manipulation. For example, if you try to leave them, they may threaten you with suicide, even in a subtle way. This is to make you feel like you can't go anywhere and that you have to stay with them. After a traumatic or abusive experience, they'll try to rationalize things by making them your fault.

That's another pillar of narcissism that frequently comes up in abusive situations: the displacement of blame. If nothing can ever be their fault and something always has a way of coming around and being your fault instead, then there are questions to be asked about the validity of the arguments that they're having. Chances are good that they actually are just having their narcissistic side come out and are unable to rationalize that they could be wrong regarding something, or else a gigantic hole would be placed in their perfect image of themselves.

Verbal abuse ultimately comes down to whatever things that they say which directly serve to cut you down or make you feel small. In the context of narcissism, this may be subtle; for example, they may just constantly talk about their own successes and what they've done in order to make you feel small in comparison. While this is normal to an extent— though not to the extent of the narcissist—if they do it intentionally in order to make you feel bad, it is most definitely abuse.

Physical abuse is any use of physical intimidation in order to make you do whatever it is they want you to do, or to just intimidate you into staying with them. It also is using physical punishment in the context of a relationship to make the victim subservient or obedient. Physical abuse is in all cases abuse. It's never okay to lay hands on somebody in a non-consensual manner.

Narcissistic people thrive ultimately off of people that they can manipulate and have their way with. They look for anything that they can perceive as a sign of weakness in a given person and then they start to run with it in order to make them a permanent fixture in their sphere and continue to manipulate them. The best offense to anything is a good defense. Fortunately, most narcissists won't be physically abusive, but the mental and emotional side of abuse are incredibly real. Narcissists will be oblivious to your emotions, will have irrational reactions to criticism, and will be in general very tense and hard to get along with.

Do note that a narcissist doesn't necessarily have to have all nine symptoms to qualify as a narcissist. Any of these symptoms are maladaptive if they're practiced in a negative and maladaptive manner. Just because somebody doesn't meet the formal criteria for a diagnosis of narcissistic personality disorder doesn't mean that they aren't abusive. Use your best judgment in determining your path forward.

Chapter 4 : How Narcissists Work

Narcissists project a strong, over-confident, and selfish image that can easily get out of hand. This is malignant narcissism, the sort that leads to misery when the narcissist cannot get their way, or when challenged in a way the forces them to look at their own weaknesses. To prevent that, the malignant narcissist will go to great lengths and sometimes do some outrageous things.

They'll come off as know-it-alls who are above the rules. They'll project an image of great superiority and imply that everyone else is somehow beneath them. They win favor very easily at first, then that wears off once their lack of empathy is seen. That's what this chapter is about, some of the more common things you can expect from a malignant narcissist.

Nature or Nurture

During infancy, we have a totally devoted caregiver who treats us as the center of the world, making us feel as though we are all-powerful and can do anything we like. Under normal circumstances, as we mature, we begin to understand that we are separate from our caregiver, losing these notions and establishing trust as we learn that our caregivers are different people, establishing boundaries and eventually experiencing push-back to our demands and actions. By this process, we establish a healthy ego and begin to take steps toward realistic and mutually rewarding adult relationships.

Narcissists don't experience this maturation. This is usually when the caregiver cannot cope with the responsibility of completely caring for another person. They don't develop trust in their caregivers and never manage to learn that they are not all-powerful and that they cannot control others. Instead, they tend to remain stuck in their infantile belief that they are the center of everything and will manipulate the people around them to remain at the center.

Manipulation

When dealing with a narcissist, you have to expect at least some level of manipulation. They are attention addicts who are intent on protecting their vulnerable inner self, which translates into pushing or cajoling the people around them to pay the narcissist the attention they crave, to live up to their vision, and most of all, to refrain from doing anything that might force them to admit that their vainglorious image of themselves is wrong.

It really doesn't matter to them if the people they manipulate suffer from it. Their attitude is simply that you can't make an omelet without breaking some eggs. If the person they are manipulating pushes back, stands up to the manipulation, and makes the narcissist face their own ugly behavior, the reaction is usually violent, not necessarily physically, but intense and often vicious. They may slander the person, blame them for the narcissist's own actions, or demean them, whatever it takes to cow them into silence.

The manipulation tactics used by the narcissist are many and varied. Some can be quite pleasant, others are subtle, the rest awful. They may be used alone or in combination and will be changed as needed for the narcissist to achieve their goals. We've divided these techniques into three categories based on how the subject is made to feel: The Good, the Bad, and the Ugly.

The (not so) Good

- *Love-bombing Their Partner.* The victim has never felt so loved in their life. The narcissist will do this to hook their victim and reel them in quickly. The narcissist doesn't want to give them a chance to reflect, to look closely at what is happening, or to ask a lot of questions.
- *Idealizing Their Partner.* They build up a fantasy ideal of their victim and treat them as if they actually live up to that fantasy. Like love bombing,

this can be quite pleasant for the victim until the narcissist turns on them, which will happen once the reality of a relationship sets in and they begin to see things about their partner that they want to change or eliminate.

- *Subtle Flattery.* Like idealization, this early-stage tactic opens the door to other things by making the partner feel good about themselves and about the narcissist, good enough for them to allow the narcissist greater access into their life.

- Mirroring Their Partner. The interest and attention usually die away once the narcissist attains the love of their love object, but in the beginning, they are avid in studying their partner's tastes, values, and beliefs in order to mirror those traits back at them with the goal of making them think they found their perfect match.

The Bad

- *The Victim Play.* The narcissist deliberately plays the victim to arouse the sympathy of the person being manipulated, often throwing the pity party of the century in order to get them to do something.

- *The Obligation Game.* The Narcissist's penchant for tit-for-tat and their ability to play upon our sense of fairness comes to the fore as they do something nice in order to obligate someone to do something for them, sometimes against the self-interest of the other person.

- *Making Excuses.* Slightly different from the narcissist's victim play, here they are trying to excuse or justify their behavior by deflecting the blame and arousing the pity of the abused party. "If I had only received the money, I'm due," or "If you had just kept your promise not to...," the excuses always leave the narcissist as the victim.

- *Lowered Expectations.* In any relationship, the last thing a narcissist wants is expectations from their partner. By lowering those expectations, a gradual process of diminishing returns in which the partner gets used to receiving less and less from the narcissist, they end up expecting little or nothing at all while the narcissist continues to extract what they want from the relationship.

- *Playing on Hope.* By itself, lowering expectations is a sure-fire way to kill a relationship with anyone. Eventually, they realize there is no point to it and move on. Since the narcissist is drawing a kind of sustenance from their partner, that is really the last thing they want. So, like any good parasite, they have to balance feeding off their host without killing them. To do this, the narcissist will occasionally turn on the charm and be everything their partner wants to erode their defenses and give them something to hang onto when the narcissist's normal behavior reemerges.

- *The Silent Treatment.* The narcissist doesn't always get their way. Their partner may do or say something that dings their defenses. They may even have simply refused a demand. The reaction is rage. Sometimes, that comes out verbally or physically, and sometimes, it's expressed when the narcissist stops interacting with their partner. This is a kind of bullying behavior that is meant to sow the seeds of doubt and uncertainty in the mind of the partner. The idea is to keep them guessing and anxious about what will come next.

- Word Games. The narcissist plays with their partner's sense of reality. On the extreme end of the spectrum, this takes the form of gaslighting, which we will deal with below. On the more benign end, they use words to confuse, belittle and degrade their victim, often claiming that they are "joking" or that they "misspoke."

The Ugly

- *Devaluation.* The narcissist's word games can be used to undermine their partner's self-esteem. They do this by purposefully saying, or not saying, and doing, or not doing, things that make the victim feel worthless. Nothing could be taken as a joke or as a mistake, this behavior is overt and personal, from pointedly ignoring some accomplishment to questioning their taste in clothes to comparing them unfavorably to others. In addition to making the narcissist feel better about themselves, the point is to force their partner to feel as if they don't deserve better treatment.

- *Deny Everything and Demand Proof.* When the victim confronts the narcissist about their behavior, the usual response is denial and demands for proof, which will then be twisted to either excuse the behavior or turn the blame for everything back onto the victim (see Gaslight is More than Just a Movie below).

- *The Triangulation Game.* Here, the narcissist introduces other people into the relationship specifically to upset the victim and arouse their jealousy in a bid to assert control. This could be someone that the narcissist uses as an example to belittle their partner, or someone who supports or even helps the narcissist (see Beware the Flying Monkey below).

- *Creating Guilt.* Like the stereotypical Jewish mother, the narcissist will weaponize guilt. The idea is to deflect blame for their behavior and break down resistance by making the partner feel as though the problems between themselves and the narcissist is their fault, which makes them vulnerable and more willing to agree to the narcissist's unreasonable demands.

- *Bullying.* Sometimes, in the face of blowback or defiance, or if their precious defenses have been breached, the narcissist will become aggressive, intimidating, perhaps even violent. This is done as much to punish their partner as to leave them anxious and fearful in order to get them to do what the narcissist wants them to do.

- *Slander.* Along with the bullying, under certain circumstances, the narcissist will also begin a smear campaign against their partner. By reaching out to others, usually close friends and family, they hope to convince these people that something is wrong with their partner and that any problems are their fault.

- *Systematic Targeting.* This is a rather general tactic that goes along with bullying, word games and other forms of attack. The narcissist systematically seeks out and then specifically target the victim's real or perceived flaws and insecurities. This is done to undermine their self-esteem and keep them off balance and unable to respond.

- *Pure Deceit.* While normal people tend to tell the truth most of the time, narcissists have no problem lying when it suits them. They will lie by making something up, by leaving out important details, or by being vague about what they are asserting. Now, while it is likely that the narcissist actually believes the lies, they also do it to get an advantage over their partner or the people they are otherwise involved with, to protect themselves, or to cover something up.

- *Projecting Negativity.* This is another deflection tactic. When the narcissist does this, they are pushing any negative thoughts, emotions they might have, or anything negative that they might have done or are doing onto their partner. This goes hand-in-glove with Creating Guilt.

- *Shifting Standards.* A gaslighting tactic (see below), this is another way for the narcissist to maintain control over the victim. By "moving the goalposts" in this way, the narcissist seeks to confuse and humiliate their victim, often to the point of inducing depression, apathy, and other psychological problems in the victim.

- Harsh Judgement. When listening to the narcissist's stories about other people, including their past relationships, their partner heard a lot of harsh judgment against those people. At the time, they were likely moved to pity by the tale, unaware that this facet of the narcissist's personality would one day be aimed at them. This is one of the more common ways the narcissist makes the victim feel inadequate because it fits in with their sense of superiority. They constantly complain about what they think is wrong with the victim, implying that they are sub-par and that they could be better if they only tried.

These are among the more common tactics that narcissists use to get under the skin of their victim, but two more deserve a little more explanation: Gaslighting and the Flying Monkey.

Gaslight Is More Than Just a Movie

In 1944, Ingrid Bergman starred in the movie adaptation of the play, Gaslight. She played a woman whose husband was trying to convince her that she is insane by manipulating things in the house and denying that anything has changed when she asks. The name Gaslight comes from the way he would slowly dim the gas lights in the house while insisting to her that nothing had changed.

Since then, it has come to mean manipulating a person's perception of reality, making them second-guess their choices and even their sanity, all to increase their dependence on their abuser, who is really seeking full control of their victim. Abusive narcissists who gaslight their victims use a variety of techniques, but the most common are:

- Information control to maintain the narrative that the narcissist wants to promote. This includes:
  o Withholding information
  o Trivializing information

- o Twisting information
- Undermining the Victim, which includes:
  - o Verbal abuse, which can be subtle or overt and often comes in the form of jokes and back-handed compliments
  - o Diminishing the victim's self-esteem
  - o Impairing the victim's physicality and mental processes
  - o *Impeding and distorting any attention the victim might get from others*

Some of the things you are likely to hear if your narcissist is trying to gaslight you are:

- *You're just insecure/jealous.* When you hear that, they're telling you that the issue is not their behavior, not their flirtations, affairs, sexting, or other infidelities, it is your faulty interpretation of their behavior, so get it together and stop bothering them about it.
- *You're too sensitive/overreacting.* The rough translation here is "I really don't care. I did it, I'll do it again, and if you complain, I'll make you pay." Doing this will make the narcissist's partner doubt the severity of their abuse, undermining

their perception of what's been happening to them.

- *You're nuts/insane/delusional.* This is the dark side of "playing doctor." Here, your narcissist is saying that your perception of what they've done to you is not only wrong, it's delusional, no doubt from some deep, underlying mental illness you've been hiding all this time, and I will tell you exactly what that is. By convincing you that you are delusional, they can continue to avoid any responsibility for their own actions.

- *You can't take a joke.* Your narcissist is telling you that calling you something horrible and demeaning is really no different from harmless teasing and that you lack the wit or even the intelligence to understand that. Again, this undermines your perception of what is really going on in your relationship.

- You're harboring something that's in the past. The message here is that "you're nursing an old wound that is your own fault anyway and you need to get past it so I can move on to what I want to do next." By doing this, the narcissist trivializes the pain their partner suffered and tries to mask the truly cyclical nature of the abuse.

If you see any of the abuses cited above in your own relationships, either as the victim or the abuser, you will want to take a closer look at your situation and those involved and make some changes before it goes too far.

Beware the Flying Monkey

Just because someone's a narcissist, that doesn't mean they have to act alone. Called "Flying Monkeys" by Christine Hammond, MS, LMHC after the creatures dispatched by the Wicked Witch to go after Dorothy. Obeying without question, they do her bidding.

It works the same way with narcissists, and even more so with sociopaths and psychopaths. After all, by sending a loyal henchman out to take care of the dirty work, they can at least appear to have clean hands.

You've seen this in action, though you may not realize it. How many times have you seen some spokesman for a narcissistic entertainer, politician, or CEO coming forward to make their boss look good after some scandal? What was Michael Cohen when he was helping to cover up Donald Trump's affair with Stormy Daniels? These are all examples of flying monkeys.

The question is, given the often-public floggings they risk by carrying out their narcissist's orders or covering up their actions, why do they do it? Because there is a pay-off for both parties, at least for a while. According to Hammond, these flying monkeys often have their own psychological disorder, and that allows for each to feed on their relationship in some way. The list includes:

- *Narcissistic Personality Disorder.* As long as they can garner power, influence, money, prestige, or some other benefit, the partnership works. Once those benefits are lost, or a greater benefit is offered, the narcissistic flying monkey flies away and could even turn on their former idol. Cohen is a good example of this in that he turned on Trump when it benefitted him more to do so.

- *Generalized Anxiety Disorder.* In this case, the constant anxiety of the flying monkey is attracted to the arrogance of the narcissist, but it lasts only until the anxiety eases.

- *Co-dependents.* The co-dependent feeds on the narcissist's need to be served and adored. The narcissist feeds on the co-dependent's quest for purpose and satisfaction by way of taking care of others. Of course, once the co-dependent recovers and turns from their people-pleasing ways, the disappointed narcissist will leave.

- *Addicts.* Just like a drug pusher on the street can make their addicted clientele do anything for the next fix, if the narcissist is the one supporting the addiction, the addict will slavishly do or say whatever will keep them on good terms with their supplier. This relationship ends one of two ways: The addict gets clean and no longer needs what the narcissist provides, or the addiction worsens, and the narcissist cuts them off because they get too needy.

- *Dependent Personality Disorder.* The narcissist loves this one because the dependent makes them feel so superior because in addition to obedience, they either include the narcissist in every decision they make or leave the decision entirely up to the narcissist. These relationships rarely if ever end.

- Sociopaths. Here, the narcissist is useful to the Sociopath, who will use the outrageous behavior of the narcissist to veil their own nefarious deeds, orchestrating everything while allowing the narcissist to think they are the one running the show. These relationships tend to end when circumstances change, and it benefits the sociopath to get rid of the narcissist.

The Uses of Anger

Anger. It can manifest naturally when the narcissist is disappointed, much like the tantrum of a spoiled child; but it usually shows up when the victim claps back at them and either threatens to expose the frightened little child that lays at their core or worse, actually do expose it. It can also be used as a carefully orchestrated way to intimidate their victims into compliance.

When it comes to anger, there are two types of narcissists we need to consider. The Grandiose narcissist, with their inflated ego and sense of entitlement, and the Vulnerable narcissist, who is covering up their inadequacies.

You Can't Always Get What You Want (But You Get What You Need)

Under normal circumstances, when we are disappointed in something, we either tackle the problem (Problem-focused Coping) or we deal with our emotions (emotion-focused Coping). Either way, we cope with the disappointment, put into some perspective, and move on. That, however, is not necessarily how narcissists react.

It would be easy to say that the typical malignant narcissist's reaction is rage, especially at those they believe have managed to block their plans. It is an emotion-focused coping mechanism that might make the narcissist feel better for a while, but it doesn't solve anything, and it alienates the people who have to deal with the narcissist and may, actually, be able to help the situation. That said, it is a tad more complex than that. Studies have shown that grandiose narcissists and vulnerable narcissists deal with disappointment differently.

The grandiose variety, with their over-inflated egos and heightened self-esteem, cope with disappointment better, adapting to changing situations in ways that vulnerable narcissists, with so much of their energy going to covering up their own sense of inferiority and low self-esteem, simply cannot.

Chapter 5 : Understanding the Abuse Cycle

The next thing that we need to explore a bit is the narcissistic abuse cycle. This is a pretty straightforward thing to look at, but there are some complexities to understand as well. The execution can be a bit challenging along the way, and the victim is going to be the one who fairs the worse, mostly because they are going to be a bit blindsided by the cycle. Many times, the victim isn't even going to see that the cycle is happening to them at all. It is not that uncommon for the victim to get stuck in the cycle for years, and by the time they realize what is going on, they may feel like there is no way to get out.

Being able to first recognize, and then leave, the cycle can be hard for the victim. This is because they are stuck dealing with the emotions, the fantasy, the reality, and the logic of their situation. Emotions are going to hook them into the relationship to start with. The narcissist made sure that there was a lot of passion, intense feelings, and more towards them, and they are not likely to let this all go. However, as the victim starts to see that there are some slips from the narcissist, and these slips will happen at some point or another, the logical mind of the victim will start to take over some of the emotions.

This is a bad thing for the narcissist because it means that the victim is going to start thinking for themselves. They will want to be free of the cycle, and they will stop supplying the narcissist with the attention that they need. In many cases, when the logical side starts to take over, it is going to lead to the victim doubting the validity of their emotions and they will start to wonder if it is all a lie, or if the emotions are truthful.

The narcissist is not going to give up that easily though. They are going to make sure that the cycle goes on, and many victims, at least in the beginning, who hear that logical voice are going to turn it off in favor of their addition to the moments of praise and pleasure that they get during what is known as the love bombing phase with the narcissist.

Many times, the victim is going to know because of their logical mind that the narcissist is toxic and abusive. However, the emotions are going to come into play, thanks to the work of the narcissist, and the victim is going to start doubting reality. They will stay in the relationship, mainly because they are so willing to follow their heart, rather than seeing what the situation really is. if there are higher traits of co-dependency with the victim, the option of leaving is going to seem super painful, so the victim will stay.

Outline of the abuse cycle

Now that we have talked a bit about the victim and how they get stuck in the cycle of abuse, it is time to go into some more details about what this cycle is. There are going to be five phases that are present in the abuse cycle. These are all connected together, and they need to be present in order for the victim to be caught with the abuser for longer than they should. The parts that come with the abuse cycle will include:

1. **Idealization**
2. **Devaluation**
3. **Discarding**
4. **Destroying**
5. **Hoovering**

These five steps are all going to be a part of the narcissistic cycle of abuse. They are going to be present in all cycles, and the victim is just going to go back and forth, in a circle, between them. If you are the victim, then you need to pay some attention to these cycles so that you can start to see them as they happen. This is going to support you in having a better understanding of the abuser, and can make it so that you actually see what they are doing. When you know more about the cycle and how it works, it is much easier to find the power that you need to end the cycle of abuse and actually get up and leave that relationship.

Idealize

The first part of the abuse cycle is going to be idealize. This is going to make it so that the narcissist will appear better than who they really are. When we enter this stage, the narcissist is going to do a process that is known as love bombing. This means that they are going to try and create an ideal relationship for the victim. They do this by showing tons of affection, love, and interest. This is going to lead the victim to feel a deep sense of trust to the narcissist, and can make the victim feel like they and the narcissist are connecting on a deeper level.

The victim is going to feel like they are in love here. They are going to try and share many things with the narcissist, letting go of their deepest secrets, fears, and hopes. The narcissist may appear to be sharing information as well, but it is rarely genuine and often it isn't even the truth.

The narcissist is going to string their victim along for some time, making up a relationship that is almost too good to be true. They want the victim to feel comfortable with them, and they will take the time needed to do this. The connections and even the ecstasy that is shared between the two of you is amazing. The victim is going to feel like they have met the one, someone they are able to connect with on a deeper level, with plenty of physical chemistry in the mix.

The main point of doing this for a narcissist is to get you comfortable with them so you are connected, and to collect as much data as possible. During this phase, the narcissist is going to hold onto all the things that the victim shares with them, and will use it later when they get to the devaluation period. They want to make sure that you have some time to create an environment that is secure, so that you feel like you have everything that you need and want. But once the victim is hooked, they know that it is time to move on to the next step. The victim is now ready to do anything that they can to protect that relationship, and this is means that they can move on and get more of what they want.

Devalue

Once the narcissist is sure that the victim is hooked and invested in the relationship, it is time for the narcissist to move to the devaluation phase. This is when they are going to take some time to chip away at the perceptions of the victim, making even the strengths of the victim look like flaws. This is going to be a slow process going from idealization to devaluation. The narcissist knows that if they make the switch too much, they are going to end up scaring

340

you off. There are going to be small little changes, ones that are almost impossible to see, so that the victim stays around.

The narcissist is going to start out with all pull and no push, reeling the victim in and ensuring that they are going to come back for more. Over time, this is going to start changing. There is first going to be ten percent, then twenty percent, and then thirty percent, and so on. The narcissist will increase based on the victim's tolerance for the abuse when it gets started. if someone comes in with low boundaries to start, then the narcissist is going to move through the process a bit faster. But they may move at a slower rate if they are dealing with someone who comes in with stronger boundaries.

However, the narcissist is going to win, and the victim will usually not recognize this until it is too late. The narcissist, over time, has conditions the victim by building up their tolerance to the abuse, and because it is so natural and gradual, it is going to happen without the victim noticing as much. If the narcissist decided to do it too fast and didn't take the right amount of time, then the victim would start to see the abuse and would run away. Even if the narcissist is impatient, they realize that losing the victim is bad for them, so they work slowly and strategically.

Once the narcissist has looked at the situation and realized that they have reached a push and pull ratio that they are happy with, they are in a state of control. The narcissist is going to feel like they have all the power in the relationship, which causes them to just get worse and worse. They are going to take full advantage of the fact that they seem to be in control over the relationship, and the process is going to become greater. Often the push to increase the ratio of their own power is going to be quicker during this part.

It is common for the narcissist, in this stage of the game, to start looking for some other victims that they would like to lure in. this way, once they are in the devaluation phase with their first victim, they are still able to get the right attention that they need. This ensures that the narcissist is going to get a lot of attention all the time, while the victim feels lost.

This phase of our abuse cycle is going to be painful when it comes to the victim. Often, they are going to be turned away from the things they used to enjoy. If the victim was sexy and confident before, they are going to start believing that they are vain and cocky. If the victim was once intelligent, they are going to think that they are a know it all. The narcissist is able to use this phase to gaslight their victims, which means that the victim is going to start believing a reality that is just not there.

There can be a bit of back and forth when it comes to this phase. The narcissist will have to determine whether the victim is in the hole for this one or not. If the victim is completely under the control of the narcissist, then the narcissist will keep in the devaluation state. But if not, then it is likely that they will go back and forth between the devaluation phase and the idealization phase to make sure that the victim stays put.

Discard

As the devaluation phase gets worse, the victim is likely to become desperate here. They want to make sure that they are able to get themselves back to the idealization phase where they felt really good. But during these attempts, the narcissist is often going to discard their victim. Because the victim is dealing with feeling insignificant and insecure, the narcissist knows that the victim is going to do anything to seek their approval. This is going to condition the victim to seek excessive admiration from the narcissist, which gives them more control.

It is common during this time for the narcissist to withdraw, telling their victim that everything they have done for them is a sign of failure, and they will blame the victim for not making them feel good. This causes the victim to blame themselves when things don't go right. As the victim still continues to try and seek validation in a desperate manner, the narcissist is going to use these attempts as they way that they seek their own praise, admiration, attention, and validation. Basically, while the victim is trying to get back on the good side of the narcissist, and they are trying to keep themselves happy as well, they are fueling the fire and are not really giving the narcissist a reason to be nice.

This kind of behavior is going to support the narcissist when it comes to scooping out all of the remaining qualities inside the victim that don't serve with the agenda of the narcissist. The narcissist knows that their victim is desperate for attention and affection, and that they will do anything to win it back. The narcissist also knows that there is a good chance that the victim has no idea how low their self-esteem and self-confidence have gotten at this point.

From the point of the victim, there is really nothing that they can do at this point in order to make the abuser happy. The abuser will keep setting their standards higher, making sure that these standards are slightly out of reach of the victim the whole time. As this blame shifting is going to continue, the victim is going to have a lot of confusion and desperation, which the narcissist will use to turn themselves into the victim.

At the same time, the narcissist is going to work in order to let other people into this dynamic. During any time apart, they are going to bond with other potential victims and start a new love bombing phase there. In the mind of the narcissist, they are creating a new backup plan in case their first victim doesn't come back. When the victim and the narcissist get back together, they will claim that second person is close to them, but it won't affect your relationship. This allows them to keep two people, at the same time, trapped in this cycle. The narcissist will have no problem switching back and forth between which one of you gets the pleasure of filling their needs.

There are some cases where the victim is going to decide to leave the narcissist first. Rather than waiting to end up in the discard phase, they will figure out what is going on and choose to leave. This happens when they start to struggle to find reasons to stay because the narcissist is so bad to them. If the victim threatens to leave and then doesn't, this is going to anchor in the narcissists attempts to devalue their victim.

But, if the victim does end up leaving, it won't be long before the narcissist starts the hoover phase. Through this phase, the narcissist is going to try to harass the victim until the victim starts to give the narcissist attention one more time. Then the idealization phase is going to start again so that the narcissist is able to hook the victim back into that cycle one more time. The more success we are able to find in the hoover phase, and the victim is hooked, then stronger this hook is going to grow and the harder it is for the victim to go through the discard phase when it does happen again.

Destroy

When we get to this phase, there is a strong possibility that the other relationships that the narcissist has been working on have now developed a bit more than before. The narcissist is going to have more than one source of narcissistic supply, and it is likely that they will become less dependent on that one victim.

During this phase, the narcissist is going to put more pressure on the victim to take all the blame. They are going to dig more into the devaluation process, using all of the vulnerability and weakness as a chance to drive the abuse down deep. They are going to switch back and forth between these two phases with the victim, which makes that victim feel like they are worthless and that they have nowhere to really go. The narcissist is going to make this worse because they are going to make the victim feel like they should leave because they are no longer welcome.

Here, the narcissist is going to be able to take all of the insecurities they have about the victim and use them. Everything that the victim shared during that idealization phase is going to come back. The narcissist has no problem using it to haunt the victim, to cause them pain, to cause them to doubt themselves, and to turn the strengths of the victim into flaws. If the narcissist, for example, knows that the victim is afraid of being seen as needy, they will use the desperate attempts that the victim is using to seek validation in order to amplify this insecurity and peg them as excessively needy. They are going to exploit all of the fears, insecurities, and the past to work against the victim

At this point, it is likely that the victim is going to believe them. The spirit is crushed and the hope is going to be destroyed. It is likely that the victim is going to see that the narcissist is their own cure, and that they need the narcissist in order to undo what they have done. Because of this reason, the victim will keep working on trying to please the narcissist, to get their acceptance, and to try and make it all better.

Many of the victims who are at this stage feel like they don't even have the strength to walk away, and it seems impossible to undo all of the pain and the hurt that is inside of them. The victim will seek out the narcissist as their remedy, even

347

though they may also withdraw a bit because they are scared of being hurt or of the narcissist lashing out at them again. This is a very uncomfortable phase where the victim needs to get the validation of the narcissist, but they may feel that it hurts too much to talk to them even.

During the destroy phase, the narcissist is going to take some time to try and make their victim seem unwanted and unworthy by everyone. They won't just use phrases that show their own displeasure in this person. Perhaps they will say something like "No wonder your mother doesn't like having you over anymore" or "This is why your friends don't hang out with you anymore." This makes it seem like the victim doesn't really have anywhere else to turn. Even though the narcissist is the reason that those people quit interacting with you, the narcissist is able to turn this around and make it seem like you are the one to blame.

Hoover

Once the narcissist is done with the destroy phase, and the victim is able to get away from the relationship for a bit, then the victim and the narcissist are likely to spend some of their time apart. For a bit, it may seem like the narcissist has stopped and you are abandoned for now. If you are coming out of this phase for the first time, know that this is not done. The narcissist may have some other victims that they are working with as well, these are the back up. It is likely that they are not done with the first victim.

The hoover phase is actually one where a lot of the trauma is going to happen, even though it is true that the rest of the cycle is going to be traumatic and exhausting as well. Here, the victim is not able to fight their addiction, or the need that they have for validation. Some may be able to escape the narcissist for a few weeks, and maybe even for a few months, but most are going to end up returning.

No matter how hard they try, it seems like they have a life that is empty when the narcissist is not around because they are no longer being used and abused in the manner that they were conditioned to do. The narcissist is good at their job, and they were able to condition the victim into needing to be in that abusive situation, which works well for the narcissist. The victim, after some time apart, is going to miss that relationship, even though it was bad for the, and they will go back to it.

Soon, the victim, wishing for the relationship to go back to the way that it was, is going to start idealizing the relationship in their own mind. They really miss that person, the narcissist, so they are going to learn how to ignore all of the bad and the negative experiences, and will just focus on the positive ones. They are going to romanticize that idealization phase, while hiding the rest. After enough time has passed, the narcissist knows that the victim is going to be able to downplay the abuse in their own heads. And this is the perfect time for the narcissist to come back.

While the narcissist waits for this to occur, the victim is often going to find that it is a big challenge to get back into the normal world. Their independence is going to be challenging to get back, and since they are going to have a low amount of confidence, it is hard for them to get into a new relationship. The words of the narcissist are going to ring through their minds, reminding them to feel that they are not really worthy of any love or affection.

Chapter 6 : Narcissistic Abuse in the Family

A number of people fall victims to narcissism early in their lives. When we're children, we have almost no control over anything happening around us. Having a parent that suffers from NPD is simply a terrible hand to be dealt in life.

This does not mean everything is lost though. Healing is always possible and, more importantly, recognizing the signs of narcissism in either your parents or with other family members is an important first step to healing.

This chapter is going to help you spot the signs of narcissism in family members and also educate you on how you can make the situation better in order to end the abuse.

Signs

We usually associate narcissism with romantic relationships, so it can be difficult to think of this from a parent and child context. However, this does occur more often than you might think. With a parent-child relationship, the parent is not always conscious of their narcissism and simply views their approach as the normal one. Indeed, the parent might have grown up with it and are simply following what they know.

Narcissistic parents usually marginalize the achievements of their offspring and are engaged in some sort of competition with them. A lot of people who suffered such abuse detail that the parent always seems to want to prove that they're better than their child in some form or fashion. Another form of parental narcissism is trying to live vicariously through the child and pushing unrealistic expectations on them.

While every parent sets up expectations of success for their children, a narcissistic parent's dreams and wishes for their child are set with the aim of validating the parent's own identity. The child, as an individual, doesn't get much of a say in what they want to do. Undermining the child's individuality is a key sign of abuse as the parent tries to dress the child as an extension of themselves or of their projections.

Nitpicking and constantly criticizing the child is another sign of parental narcissism. In this case, the strategy is to marginalize the child since the parent might be threatened by the child's potential or abilities. Such abilities might be a direct threat to their parental authority so criticism and making blanket statements implying that the child will never be good enough are the methods by which the narcissist will try to regain the upper hand in the relationship. The other side of this coin is to try to set unrealistic goals and then criticize the child when he doesn't meet those wild expectations.

This leads to a streak of perfectionism in the child which will cause him to sabotage himself in the long run. This is a more covert tactic that is used since openly criticizing the child might provoke rebellion but cloaking the undermining of the child with a veneer of improvement leads to the child believing that their parent has their best interests at heart.

Picking on the slightest excuse for grandiosity is another classic narcissistic move. In the context of a parent and child relationship, an example of this is when the parent chooses any achievement their child garners and uses this as proof that "we," or the parent and their child, are better than "them," or everyone else. This brings the child into the narcissistic envelope and severely damages their ability to form normal relationships.

Using their child to show off and validate their own image as superior parents is another narcissistic move. In this case, the narcissist hides their true motive by presenting themselves as a proud parent but is actually using their child to assert their superiority over others. The child, in this case, is expected to adhere to a perfect image and any deviation from this leads to criticism or hostility.

A narcissist never does any favors for free. Everything has to be paid for in a sense. This is no different when it comes to their children. Expecting a lifelong debt to be repaid in return for raising a child is something a narcissistic parent will expect as par for the course. Reminding the child constantly about how ungrateful they are or how much they've done for them is a classic tactic.

Using unrealistic expectations, the parent will also guilt trip or shame the child into believing they aren't good enough. Statements labeling the child a shame to the family or blaming the child for their own unhappiness occur quite frequently in narcissistic parent and child relationships.

Given the importance the child plays as one of the revolving cast members of the parent's life, spousal jealousy is common with a narcissistic parent. Any romantic relationship their offspring engages in is viewed as a direct threat to the parent's stature and a guilt trip or emotional drama of some sort always follows. Such tantrums may be thrown even in the case of a career change or when the child has to move far away from the parent.

As the parents get older, the relationship becomes codependent, and the narcissist will shame their offspring every step of the way whether they are still taking care of that child or not. This is because they recognize that as they get older, their ability to control their child diminishes and thus, the degree of negativity goes up a notch to exert greater influence over the child.

Generally speaking, any behavior that displays unrealistic expectations and completely disregards or undermines the child's right to exist as an individual is a clear sign of a narcissistic parent.

We can't choose our family. Given the fact that we spend our formative years with them, it can be extremely hard to recover and move on with our lives. While cutting off poisonous non-familial relationships is simple, this is not the case with family. It is about as difficult as cutting away a portion of yourself from your existence. However, it needs to be done in order for you to move forward.

The following tips will help you through this difficult task.

- *Expect some type of stalking: The narcissist will never simply let you leave. You are, after all, their primary source of oxygen, and they need you to survive. Expect your wishes to be left alone to be ignored and for them to constantly guilt trip you. If this doesn't work, they will spread all sorts of lies about you and slander you.*

- *Remain strong: In the face of all this, a lot of people cave in and initiate a little contact and tell themselves that they won't take it further than that. Before they know it, they're right back where they started. Use emotion to fuel your desire to improve your life and resist the urge to fall prey to their tricks.*

- *Find support: It is crucial that you find some form of support or else you will make your task doubly harder. Regardless of whether it's a support group of like-minded people or friends or a spouse, find somebody you can rely on to stay strong and inspire you to do better.*

- *Be selfish: Remember the golden rule: Never harm yourself. Put your wellbeing first and foremost and don't be apologetic about doing so.*

You might also be hit with visits from other people close to your family in an effort to try to triangulate you. These third persons will not know the entire situation and will view the whole thing as if you're the one who's being unfair or unreasonable.

The best thing to do here is to remember that these people themselves are being triangulated and to not give in. Don't waste your breath arguing or even engaging. Remember that emotion is what feeds the narcissist, be it positive or negative. You venting your frustrations at them doesn't hurt them back, it only emboldens them. Therefore, the best way to deal with them is to be indifferent. Simply showing that you cannot be provoked will take the wind out of their sails, and you'll have some modicum of peace in your life.

Aside from family, another place we're really vulnerable is at the workplace. Whether it be a colleague or a boss, our professional reputation often hangs in the balance in such situations so it's important to take a look at workplace narcissism next.

Chapter 7 : Narcissistic Abuse in the Workplace

Workplace bullying by narcissists is distressingly common if you happen to have worked at any large multinational corporation. The problem with workplace bullying is that it isn't as easy to simply pull the plug. A lot of people need their jobs for financial purposes, and finding another one at the drop of a hat is not practical.

This is especially the case when the economy goes south. In such situations, narcissists will often feel emboldened, and you will be forced into a tight corner. In this chapter, I'm going to discuss the sources of bullying in the workplace along with what you can plausibly do to handle this.

Dealing with Abuse

Some companies' HR departments are equipped to handle workplace bullying incidents, but more often than not narcissism in the workplace is covert and passive-aggressive and cannot always be openly pegged as bullying. Given the nature in which the abuse is carried out, often the victims themselves question whether it is appropriate to report such behavior, especially if the victims happen to be male.

The initial interactions follow the same pattern of narcissistic abuse where the victim is reeled in using the love bomb. While there are no flowers or gifts being presented here, the narcissist will do their best to endear themselves to the victim by getting them to divulge all kinds of information about themselves.

More often than not, it is the best and most efficient employees who are targeted, so if you happen to be highly qualified for the job then you will need to be on your toes. Once the narcissist has gained enough information about their victim and is close enough to them, the rumors will begin, and you will find yourself being undermined by them.

Initially, this might happen in a meeting where the abuser takes credit for your work or subtly undermines you in front of your bosses. In such cases, when you do stand up to them, you will find rumors circulating about you and people talking about you behind your back.

This is doubly challenging if your abuser happens to be your boss. While a boss will be threatened by your competence, the higher authority they have will reassure them a bit about the security of their position, so you might not find the same level of rumors being circulated. After all, not many people become close to or socialize with the boss outside of work.

A key sign to look for is the classical narcissistic tendency of loving you one second and hating you the next. If you disappoint them in some way, expect the floodgates to open and for the criticism to be exceptionally personal. Self-centeredness is another giveaway. If every conversation finds its way back to how amazing they are or how much better than you they happen to be, then you're definitely dealing with a potential abuser.

A lot of companies require evaluation forms, and some even have forms where feedback needs to be provided about your boss. This is a great moment for you to spot the narcissist. They will simply be unable to take any sort of criticism and will be extremely upset about it. When it comes to co-workers, look for signs of someone who absolutely wants to be in charge and accepts nothing less.

Such people may or may not be qualified but the qualification part is secondary. What matters the most is the fact that they get to lord over everyone else. Unfortunately, modern workplaces reward this sort of behavior since it is viewed as a form of ambition and positive energy that must be harnessed for the company's benefit. All it does is make everyone's life a living hell, unfortunately.

An important point to note is that not all narcissists will be bullies. A lot of covert narcissists will be content with simply undermining their co-workers and moving forward at all costs. In most workplaces these days, name calling of any sort is grounds for being fired immediately so any sort of verbal harassment like this is unlikely to be practiced by a skilled narcissist.

Often, such people will be in positions they are sorely unqualified for and will cause the inevitable mess. A lack of contrition or any sort of action where they accept responsibility is a flashing sign that the person is a narcissist.

Dealing with Workplace Narcissism

The easiest way to deal with a workplace narcissist is to avoid them as much as you can. This is not always possible, especially if the person involved happens to be your boss. Dealing with such a situation is extremely tricky, and unless it is a job that you cannot dream of leaving, then finding something else as soon as possible is the best way forward. Ultimately, you will not have the same energy levels as the narcissist does, and you will be the only one exhausted after all the maneuvering.

When dealing with a narcissist in the workplace, you may receive advice from well-meaning friends about not letting yourself be spoken to that way and so on, but this will only make things worse. Instead, try to divert the narcissist's attention back to the task at hand as much as possible. This is especially for those moments when their criticism starts getting personal. You will achieve nothing by screaming back or demanding they apologize. So, don't expect it.

Instead, get them to focus on the task at hand and avoid them as much as you can. In the case of coworkers, record each and every piece of work you do and every action you take along with all of the ideas you suggest. This will help you ground yourself when you confront the coworker and tell them to stop piggybacking off of your ideas. If you don't do this, they might cause you to get confused and make you question your own thoughts.

If your coworker is the problem, then approach your bosses with your ideas first, instead of sharing it with the coworker ahead of time. Be brief or even misdirect any questions your coworker asks you about any ideas. Don't ever give the impression that you're ready to slug it out with them, though. Remember, any emotion is fuel for them. Your best form of defense is to engage as little as possible and to be as indifferent as you can when you do.

Given the narcissists' ability to manipulate and to cloak their power hunger as ambition, your bosses will, depressingly, often fall for it and promote them. If you notice such promotions happening constantly, then you have to resign yourself to the fact that you will not receive a fair shake at your current workplace. In such situations, it's best to line up something else as soon as you can.

Of course, in many instances, it is your boss who is a narcissist. If some work-related task fails due to your boss's incompetence, then directly criticizing them will achieve nothing. If anything, it will put you in their crosshairs, and you'll find your life becoming more and more miserable. When proposing new ideas, present them in such a way so as to not insinuate that their idea was poor and didn't work.

It is even better to cast doubt over your own idea and then leave it up to them to make a decision as if you're asking for their advice. This will increase your chances of being viewed favorably as well as getting things done.

Ultimately, all of this tap dancing around is ridiculous and you owe it to yourself to find a better place to work. Remember that being kind to yourself involves placing yourself in the most conducive environment for your abilities to shine through, and a workplace which is littered with insecure little bullies is not one of those places.

Given the preponderance of workplace narcissism, be wary when you're new to the job and don't readily divulge details about yourself to coworkers or bosses. You might be viewed as a bit aloof at the start, but in the long run, assuming the workplace is right for you, you'll be more than able to make amends.

While family abuse and workplace abuse are sticky situations, there are none stickier than finding yourself in a romantic relationship that has turned abusive. Given the huge amounts of emotion we invest in our relationships, these are the toughest to extricate ourselves from.

Chapter 8 : Narcissistic Abuse in a Couple Relationship

Throughout this book, we've been looking at how narcissists abuse those they're in a relationship with. Narcissistic abuse within romantic relationships is given a lot of attention since this is where the majority of people tend to experience it. Given the deep emotional investment people make into relationships, it is understandable that this sort of abuse tends to leave the deepest cuts.

In this chapter, I'm going to give you things to look out for not just in your partner but in yourself as well. A lot of the time, we are far too caught up in ourselves and cannot separate ourselves from the situation objectively. Thus, the best thing to do is to monitor ourselves for subtle signs of manipulation and our reactions to it.

Patterns

All narcissists follow a pattern. It begins with love bombing and then deteriorates to neglect and manipulation. If you're lucky enough, you will be able to spot the signs of love bombing and exit the relationship quickly. The best way of dealing with narcissists is to simply get out of the way and disengage completely. Even a little emotional investment will be seized upon and used against you.

If your abuser happens to remove their mask as the relationship progresses, then this is a tough situation to extricate yourself from. By this point, you're fully invested emotionally, and it will be painful to cut the cord.

Romantic narcissistic relationships tend to be about punishment and minor rewards. The narcissist will find ways to punish their partner if they don't get what they want or even without any reason. Techniques such as withholding affection or "losing" or "breaking" something that belongs to their partner are ways in which they seek to exert control.

All of this is just a precursor to gaslighting, wherein they will turn their victim's accusations against them and get their victims to question their reality. Sometimes, the bid to control is overt, and the narcissist will make threats against their partner. Mind you, these threats don't need to be delivered via gritted teeth. It can be a friendly reminder that they'll reveal something embarrassing to a group that will undermine their victim, for example.

Overt threats might be something like threatening to seize their partner's possessions or anything else that the couple might share, such as their home or custody of their children. Another tactic that is used is to violate their partner's privacy by checking their communications and messages.

This is usually a diversionary tactic and is done after their victim accuses them of being unfaithful or questioning their whereabouts. This way, the narcissist deflects the accusations and turns around and accuses their victim of the very same thing, which is, in other words, projecting their own faults back onto their victims.

Victims of narcissists in relationships are also isolated and cut off from their usual support network of friends and family. This can be gradual, so it is very difficult to spot over time since the victim simply gets used to it or buys the narcissist's story that it is the support network that is at fault and is threatening their relationship.

Narcissists will engage in love bombing after a series of fights and will follow up these arguments with excessive displays of affection. Things like buying gifts, unexpected surprises, and the like will be showered on the victim. All of this will seem a bit out of place, but a lot of victims will refuse to accept these signals as being signs of manipulation because of the fact that they've already invested so much time into the relationship.

By carrying out such actions, the narcissist is simply reeling their victim back in, and once the victim displays affection, the narcissist simply goes cold. and it's back to the same old routine with the victim left scratching his head and wondering what he did wrong. Other common narcissistic tactics are to divert attention and to keep changing statements in order to avoid responsibility.

The narcissist will do almost anything to avoid taking responsibility and will seek to misdirect the victim at all times. So, an accusation of being unfaithful will be met with an argument that the house is dirty, for example. This might sound nonsensical but in a deeply emotional argument, the implication that the victim is the one at fault will not be missed.

Once the victim loses all her energy and cannot fight back anymore, the narcissist assumes full control, and this is marked by the narcissist controlling their shared resources. At this point the victim is fully isolated and almost ceases to exist as an individual, having been fully absorbed into the narcissist's feeding group.

Examine Yourself

Emotion has a way of scrambling our brains, however. The best way to safeguard yourself is to monitor yourself for any signs of abuse. This way, your focus remains inward and you won't have your judgment clouded by the other person's impressions.

The first sign of abuse is usually when you repeatedly find yourself defending your abuser to your friends or family. Mind you, I'm not talking about defending minor transgressions like forgetting to buy the milk; I'm talking about repeated concerns that your support network brings up.

A lot of victims will defend their abusers to extreme levels since they'll interpret this as a personal attack on them and their choices. This is exactly what the narcissist wants since it serves to alienate other people from their victim's life. So, if you find yourself in this position, remember that there's a good chance you're missing something or ignoring it.

Another explicit sign of abuse is if you're no longer invested in your own goals and dreams and instead associate them with sadness or regret. This is a classic sign of abuse since it means the narcissist has successfully turned you against yourself and has assimilated you into their emotional feeder network, or network of people who give the narcissist the validation they want.

If you constantly blame yourself or suffer from anxiety or depression, look for signs of abuse in your relationship. The narcissist's aim is to constantly undermine you and erode your self-confidence. If you've begun to notice this sort of behavior within yourself, it might be a sign of abuse. Another subtle sign is if you notice your partner behaving differently around a group of people than with you.

A lot of victims will blame themselves for having offended the narcissist, and this only fuels the anxiety cycle, followed by draining arguments, followed by a love bomb. And then it's back to the same place of blaming yourself.

The best way to deal with all of this is to first ask yourself whether your partner is doing this intentionally or unintentionally. A lot of narcissists simply aren't aware of their behavior, and in some cases, counseling will help. If they do truly want the relationship to work, even a narcissist will seek to implement change and will genuinely be sorry for what they're doing. This scenario is, of course, an exception.

A huge clue is to notice how they both react and make you feel when you accuse them of something. If you end up feeling terrible and think it's all your fault or if they deflect and misdirect, the odds are pretty good that they're a narcissist. Try pointing this out as calmly as you can.

If there is no motivation within them to change, you have to cut the cord. This will be very painful, but remind yourself of the first rule, always: Never cause self-harm. You will be accused by the narcissist of being selfish, and if you have kids, this will be doubly painful as the narcissist will do everything in their power to use them against you.

Do not make the mistake of doing something for your children's sake. If you choose to stay on, all they're learning is the wrong way to deal with narcissism, and you're only setting them up to be either narcissists or victims themselves. So be selfish and practice self-compassion.

Chapter 9 : How to Handle a Narcissistic Partner

Once you have been able to learn that you are in a relationship with a narcissistic partner and that they are going to be very manipulative and controlling the whole time, you may be wondering how you are supposed to handle this kind of partner. The narcissist is going to handle the world differently than anyone else. And it is likely that they have spent a good deal of time trying to control you, rather than letting you be an individual and have your own life even while in the relationship.

Handling a narcissistic partner is going to be difficult to deal with. The narcissistic wants to be the one in control, the one who is admired, and the one who gets all of the attention and love. And they don't want to give any of it up to the other person in the relationship at all. As the target in this kind of relationship, you have to be willing and able to stand up strong the whole time, and really not give in to the narcissist, in order to get ahead and maintain your own autonomy along the way. Some of the things that you can do to help handle a narcissistic partner include:

Seek Some Help

One of the first things that you should consider doing when it comes to dealing with a narcissistic partner (once you find that you have one of these partners) is to seek some professional help. Most of us are not used to dealing with a narcissist in our lives, and it is likely that there is a lot of emotion and more when you learn this is the reality of your relationship now. It is important to seek some help during this time so that you can really get the help and the answers that you need to navigate this relationship.

A professional is able to help you recognize some of the signs of narcissism in your relationship, will give you some tips and skills to use to fight against the narcissist and regain the control that you want in the relationship, and can even help you if you decide it is time to leave that relationship and start over fresh without the narcissist.

This can be seen as a time of fighting against the narcissist. And as you start to visit with this new support person, the narcissist and some of their actions are going to become more apparent over time. The narcissist may not even like that you are seeking help in the first place, and there could be some issues there. having a professional therapist will be able to step in and help you to maintain your own identity and your own control in the relationship, even when the narcissist is fighting against it and trying to regain the control that they want over you.

Set Your Boundaries and Stick with Them

After you have had some time to seek help for dealing with a narcissistic partner, it is time to consider what boundaries you would like to choose, and then work on putting them up right away. Up until this point, the narcissist has had a lot of free range to do what they want with you. They have been able to cross boundaries that others would not, they have been able to say and do whatever they want, and respecting your privacy, and personal space was something that never crossed your mind.

Doing this has put you in a position that is not comfortable and can make maintaining the relationship hard. And putting up these boundaries are going to make a big difference in how much control you are able to have during that relationship. You have to decide what kind of boundaries that you are comfortable with, and which ones you want to set. And once you decide this, put them into place, and then stick to your guns and don't give up on them at all.

Now, remember that you are going to get some resistance when you work with a narcissist. The narcissist has had some free reign up to this point, and they are not going to be happy when they find out they have lost the control and they are not allowed to do whatever they want. They are going to fight this a lot, and things can get ugly. You have to hold your ground and keep these boundaries in place if you wish to be in that relationship any longer, or the boundaries, even with the slightest bend from you, will be pushed down by the narcissist trying to get what they want.

Don't Think They Are Going to Change

The narcissist is not going to change. Now read that again. There are a lot of targets who get into this kind of relationship, assuming that they can be the one who will change the other person, the one who will make a difference and finally get the narcissist to open up and be a better person. They may realize that there is something wrong with the narcissist right now, but with a little bit of love and encouragement, things will get better.

It is never a good idea to get into the business of changing other people. This isn't going to happen in most cases, and will just make you feel tired and miserable in the process. Plus, often the work that you put into changing someone is just going to cause you more heartache and pain in the process while helping the narcissist to get more of the admiration, love, and attention that they are looking for.

Realizing right here and now that, no matter how much love and attention and work you put into the narcissist, they are not going to change, is going to be one of the best things that you can do for your health. You can then set up those boundaries and decide whether you want to maintain that relationship or not. But just by seeing that the narcissist is going to maintain their current way of life, that they don't see anything wrong with their words, actions, and choices, and that they aren't going to change no matter how hard you work can be freeing on its own.

Understand That They Don't Understand Your Emotions

One thing that you have to remember when you are working with a narcissist is that they are not really going to understand the emotions that you have. You can spend all day, talking until you are blue in the face, about how hurt you were and how they should change. And the narcissist may agree with you and "promise" that they will change, but this is never going to happen. All that will happen is that you will get hurt, and the narcissist is going to continue on with the path that they have done so far.

This is a big mistake that a lot of people will make with the narcissist. They assume that if they just sit down and explain what is going on with the narcissist and that they explain how they were hurt and why it hurt you, then the narcissist will understand, feel bad, and will give up on their ways and be better. Then these same people are heartbroken when they are working with the narcissist again, and things have not improved and have not gotten better.

The thing is, the narcissist doesn't have empathy, and they don't really understand how they are harming you. What is even worse is that most of them don't care that they are causing you this harm in the first place. As long as the narcissist is able to get what they want out of you, they are going to continue to do it. They aren't really capable of understanding your own feelings, and they just expect you to view the world the same way that they do. Explaining your feelings and so on will just waste time because it won't change a single thing.

Rather than doing this, you should focus on yourself and what you are going to do with this situation. Realize that the narcissist is not going to change on their own, and your hurt feelings will not get them to make these changes either. If this is too hard to deal with, and you can't understand why they won't do this, then this is a good sign to get out of the relationship before things get even worse.

Determine If You Can Stay in the Relationship or Not

At this point, it is time to determine if this is a relationship that you want to keep up with or not. There are a lot of people who worry about leaving a relationship with a narcissist. They think that this is the only relationship they can gain some value from, and they assume that if they don't stay with this person, they will never be able to get anyone else to love them and want to be with them again. This is a sure sign that you are with a narcissist because they have changed the way that you think, and have found a way to keep you right under their control in the process.

If you have read through this guidebook, and you have determined that you are with a narcissist, it is time to determine whether you think you can set up your boundaries and stick with them, or if it is time to leave the relationship and work on improving yourself. You have to stick to your guns in either place, though. The narcissist is not going to be happy with the change, and they are going to try and push back against you.

For example, if you decide to stay and put up some boundaries that you expect the narcissist to follow, they aren't going to like that they can't just walk all over you any longer. This makes them mad because it takes away some of the control that they had, and it gives that control back to you. They will try to push against thee boundaries, to see how strong they are. If the boundaries are not strong, then they will keep on going with their current habits and behaviors. But if you do put up the boundaries and stick with them, then there is going to be guilt-tripping, shame, blame, yelling, fights, and more to try and get you to put those boundaries down.

This can be hard to stay. The narcissist is not going to change, mostly because they don't see that there is anything wrong with the behavior that they are using. And when you put up those walls and set those boundaries, you have to get ready for the narcissist to get mad and resort to any tactic they can in order to get what they want. This can be a challenge to stick with, and if the narcissist thinks that they are losing the control, then it is likely that they are going to take any measure to get it back, and this can include physical abuse, even if it wasn't present in the past.

This is why a lot of people choose to leave. Maybe they aren't strong enough to maintain the boundaries that they need to set, or they tried to do the boundaries, and things with the narcissist got too hard to handle. When this happens, they choose to leave the relationship, hoping to get a break and some relief from the narcissist.

379

This is a good road to take because it allows you to focus on your own health and mental wellbeing. But the narcissist is not going to let you go without a big fight in the process. And this can be hard. The narcissist will promise to get better to change and to do things your way. This is just going to be done to win you back; they have no want actually to change and they definitely won't, even if you get back together with them.

You have to stand strong and find a good support group here. This will ensure that you are able to avoid the narcissist and that you can build up the life that you want, even if the narcissist is bothering you. Eventually, the narcissist is going to learn that you have no real want to be back with them, and you will stop fulfilling your purpose. This can take some time, but once it happens, they will eventually let go because they will divert their time and attention to someone else who can meet their needs. This will be hard, and you always have to be wary against them, but if you stand strong, you can regain your freedom and your life from them once again.

Handling a narcissist is not going to be easy. Staying in the relationship often means that you are putting your own choices and your own freedom, and a life without manipulation, on hold for some time. This is why so many people choose to just leave the relationship, instead of fighting for something that can be managed, but is often a challenge for the rest of their lives, and often won't improve.

Chapter 10 : The Stages of Recovery with Narcissistic Abuse

Now that we have talked about a few of the topics that you need to know when it comes to narcissistic abuse, it is time to take a look at some of the steps that you can take in order to recover from this issue. Narcissistic abuse is going to take over a lot of the different aspects of your life. There is someone who comes into your life and sweeps you off your feet, but then, before you know it, they have trampled on you and started to take away your self-worth and your self-esteem.

Once you start to realize that there is something that is going on with the relationship, and you know that it is time to get out of there and move on, there is going to be a stage where you are working to recover from the abuse that you feel. The first thing to realize here is that you actually went through abuse. Even if it doesn't feel that way, and even if there are no scars from the encounter, you did go through abuse.

When it comes to the stages of recovery from narcissistic abuse, there are going to be three stages that you need to pay attention to. These are going to be the victim, the survivor, and the victim. Let's take a look at each one so you can learn which one you are in, and what you can do to get yourself through all of this abuse.

The first stage: being the victim

As a victim, there are going to be a lot of different emotions and feelings that you are going to go through at this time. You may feel like you are being betrayed by the one you loved so deeply. You may feel like your family and friends are victimizing you. It is also possible that the victim during this stage is going to feel some rage, feelings of rejection, uncertainty, denial, hurt, and humiliation depending on the tactics that the narcissist decides to use against them.

There are going to be a lot of blame that is placed on you doing this time. It is true that the narcissist is there, pulling the strings and making sure that they are the ones in control. But when you are hurt, or when something goes wrong in the relationship, they are never going to be willing to take the blame for that situation. This causes the blame to be switched over to you, and this can be hard on the victim.

Because of this, the victim is going to spend a lot of time accusing themselves for all of the bad things they think are happening in the relationship. they are going to be angry at themselves because of all the lost time and love that they were able to give the narcissist, even though they now know the truth. They are going to have some panic psychologically and financially. And if there were children in the relationship, there may be some worry about the way that the plan of action is going to affect them. Even though the future is going to change for the better, the victim is going to feel scared about what the future holds. There is going to be an intense fear by them that they are never going to find another partner to be with and they will be all alone forever, and they worry that even their friends and family will leave them behind.

These are normal feelings to have as you start to recover from the abuse. The narcissist spent a lot of time and trouble trying to implant these ideas in your head, because they would often be enough to keep you from leaving and to get you to stay. Learning how to own those fears, and making a good plan of action will make a big difference in how well you are able to move on and get through the other stages.

Now that we know some of the fears that the victim may be going through during this first phase, it is time to know some of the ways that you are able to overcome these issues. If you are able to overcome some of the accusations and some of the fears that you are dealing with, you will find that it is much easier for you to go through with your decision, and not look back at the narcissist and that relationship at all. Some of the steps that you can do to overcome your fears if you are a victim of a narcissistic relationship includes:

1. Learn more about narcissistic abuse and some of the signs that are going to show up with it.

2. Dwell more into the details of what happened. You can check out some of the behavioral patterns. You may find that there are some new things that you are able to figure out about your partner and the relationship that you were not ready for, which means that you need to be prepared to get a shock.

3. Accept the reality and understand that you are not alone.

4. Take the time to question yourself. What made you be the victim that the narcissist picked out of all the others? Study a bit more about the narcissist and how they pick their victims, and then figure out if you can pinpoint what happened. This can show you exactly how the whole thing started, and gives you some insight into how to change for later.

5. If you have some questions about the relationship, then it is important to make sure that you are able to get all of then answered, either

by the narcissist, by a therapist, or by someone else.

6. Work on the steps and the plan that you are going to take in order to get out of that abusive relationship, and to make sure that you don't get drawn back in.

This stage is going to last until you are actually able to get out of that relationship. Just because you know you are with a narcissist, and you are aware of some of the signs and symptoms that you need to watch out for, doesn't mean that you are actually going to be strong enough, or ready, to get out of that relationship. Once you do finally get yourself out of it and moving on with your life, you will be able to move to the next stage.

The second stage: the survivor

Now that you have a better understanding of how you became a victim, it is time to learn how to survive all of this. First, we need to take some time to look at how you are feeling right now. This is going to ensure that you are going to really understand what is going on in your life. For example, are you dealing with any trust issues? Do you have some events from your past that are bringing out your anger or your fear? Do you know the proper way to give yourself love and to take care of yourself? Have you actually taken some time in your life to meet new people?

Dealing with abuse means that you need to be able to handle a lot of different things at the same time. You need to worry about how your mental capabilities are, how your physical body is, and even how you are emotionally. The narcissist wanted to make sure that they could get ahold of you, and keep you around. This means that they were more than happy to push you through anything that it took to help keep you there.

This means that when you are trying to get away from the narcissist, it is important to realize that there is going to be some mental aspect of the whole situation that you are going to need to deal with. And if you are not prepared for this mental aspect, you are going to run into some troubles. There are a few things that you can consider when it comes to looking into how prepared you are mentally for the issues you are dealing with. For example, are you working on some self-soothing approaches? Do you notice that you are self-aware and confident or are you dealing with feelings of depression? Are you noticing that there is a lot of hyperactivity going on and you have a constant worry about meeting with another narcissist?

This is all hard for the victim to work on, and this is why many decide to find a therapist to work with, someone who is going to help them get through the whole situation. There are a few things that you as the victim need to learn to overcome in order to get through some of the stress that comes with abuse. And these include:

1. Seek out a therapist. You want to make sure you are working with someone who is able to help out with post-traumatic stress disorder.

2. Work hard so that you are able to let go of some of the things that the narcissist did to you, and get back your older self.

3. Try not to keep yourself isolated at this time. This is going to make you feel worse, and can make it easier for the narcissist to get back in your life. Try to get back together and reconnect with your family and friends.

4. Go out and enjoy life.

5. Continue to learn more about emotional abuse and about narcissism, this will make it easier for you to understand what went on in that relationship.

6. Understand that you are vulnerable. Feel the gratitude and experience happiness. Try to live in the moment.

7. It is sometimes hard to forget and forgive the situation that you went through. But holding onto all of this is just going to make you feel miserable. It isn't doing anything to the narcissist. If you find this difficult to do, divert your attention over to something that you love to do.

The third stage: The Surthriver

When you reach this third stage, you need to go through and figure out what has happened in the past, and what steps still need to occur in order to help you get through the experience. For example, do you feel like there are a lot of negative emotions that come up on a regular basis? Are you really angry and resentful about yourself, and about the one who made you feel this way? Do you feel that you should be embarrassed because of the fact that you were a victim of the abuser and are you ashamed that the narcissist was able to abuse you? And even if you have left the relationship and are still struggling to go back to work and rebuild the life that you need?

It is likely that during this time, you have left the narcissist and you are trying to regain some of your own life back so that you can feel happy, and not be under the control of the narcissist all of the time. this is a lofty goal to work with, but it is one that is going to be really hard to work on. The narcissist spent a lot of time trying to make sure that their victim will not run off. And it is likely that you will spend several years or more with the narcissist.

Because of all the abuse, and how long the victim stays in the relationship, it is no wonder that they are going to feel like it is hard to go back to the way that things once were. And this can make it hard on them to stay as a survivor and actually see the results that they are looking for.

The first question to ask here is do you feel like you have not become the person you had wanted to be? Some things to look at when trying to figure out this question will include:

1. Do you feel that you are never going to be able to forgive your abuser, no matter how much time has passed? Or, do you feel like you really have no want or need to forgive that abuser?

2. Do you feel that when you are around others, they are always judging you because you are not able to move on in the way they expect, and you are not working on creating your own brand-new life after the narcissist has left?

3. Do you yearn to really be free, and to be able to stoop and enjoy a lot of the things that you once enjoyed in the past?

4. Do you want to have the ability and the drive to pursue some passionate dreams again?

Once you have been able to answer all of these questions, it is time to go through and figure out how you are able to overcome this issue. It is not going to be easy, and it is going to take some time. And there may be situations where you will think you are better, and then something pulls you back down. But with the right perseverance and hard work, you will start to see some results.

Chapter 11 : Break the Addiction to abuse

The most important thing to realize now is that it was not LOVE; it was ADDICTION. This addiction is like a drug; so, when you decide to leave the abuser, you will go through a withdrawal like you are going cold turkey from an addiction. It can go on for days and months so you better get a good hold of that. At first, it feels miserable. You know that this person is not good for your health, your sanity, your work performance, your peace of mind, your social life and your appearance but you still feel like you can't help from controlling yourself to not respond to their contact.

Addiction is always about the feeling one get from the substance and it's the feeling that give you distraction to things that you don't want to pay attention in your life. This is what you really need to work on. You have to get really clear and honest with yourself. You have to honest about things like 'What are you getting from such abusive relationship?', or 'what are the feeling you are avoiding by staying?' Avoidance is the trademark of anxiety disorders. Anxiety is always the sign of present or past abuse. So, if you are dealing with anxiety and are not in the present abusive relationship, then you need to go back and look on the past trauma that you haven't deal with it yet. Always remember, an advice for your life, if you want to get out of pain, you have to go through it. You just can't ignore or avoid or run from it because this will further lead to more pain. Just face it, feel it and let it go in its own. Avoidance leads to anxiety.

Trauma only survives in the darkness and with what it is hidden and that is what exactly you need to find and conquer it. Maybe this person will show up again in your life and they will do something through which they convince you that they have changed (which they have not) or you convince yourself that they have (please don't do this, BIG MISTAKE!). You accept them and you will find yourself right back where you were maybe next day, next week (sometimes next hour). This contact with abusive person will inevitably lead to harm you. You will set yourself for another dramatic brain mishap so that's why it is important to break the contact.

There are some steps that you could adopt when you are in the safe place so that you won't get sucked back in.

1. GET LUCID Get out of the fog. Don't trick with yourself. Realize any communication with them could prove very harmful. Accept this. Realize it's all the game. If out of 10 characteristics of narcissist or any other abusive people your

393

abusive partner does not match to 2-3, don't trick yourself into thinking that they are not toxic. High chances are you are still not able to decipher their manipulative behavior completely. Realize it's a game. This is the game that you learn to play. They hate it completely. One of the most important things to accept that they will never agree to the fact that any game is being played, so it's up to you to stop playing. This means that you don't try to bring up past stuffs because you will always be told that you are sensitive, overthinking or need help and they are right. You don't try to acknowledge them (forget the responsibility that they should take) their words and actions because a/c to them, they haven't done anything.

Most of them cannot perceive what they are doing to you (and will not). They might appear to acknowledge (very complainingly) that they may have said or done something wrong but they will never change or stop doing that until and unless they seek some serious s

Therapy which is a very far distance thing for them to do (because you know, there's nothing wrong in them. It's EVERYONE around them.

You will end up paying the price for your attempts to bring the relationship into a right place. They cannot acknowledge the fact that they are driven by a compulsion to make others feel bad about themselves. In their unconscious mind, they are dirty, flawed, vicious, evil and horrible. They are filled with jealousy and envy and if you try to make them acknowledge this, you will bring out a monster from them.... with you being a victim, they fully intend to eat.

2. NO CONTACT Get away. Get far away. Do not disclose your new location, your address to them or flying monkeys. Delete and block them from every social networking them.

If you absolutely cannot cut off contact with this person, like they are co-worker or co-parent to your child, then you need to set clear and strong boundaries. Keep contact to bare minimum. Only necessary contact. When you are having contact with this person, gray rock it out. It means be boring or uninteresting. This really turns off abuser. Maintain strong and clear-cut boundaries or you will end up being hurt and manipulated again. Chances are you will learn this lesson at least one-time hard way in order to get feed in your head.

No contact is your power. This is the one thing that they absolutely cannot control, only if you don't go for the bait.

3. DETOX. Get rid of everything that they have ever given to you (Please). Get rid of all the photos, saved texts, clothes anything that reminds you of them. (Do not invite them to take their stuffs back, because even if once they make you taste the drug of addiction, you will be pulled right back in).

4. Learn something new. Pick up something that you have never tried it before. Reconnect with yourself. Embrace yourself, your support system, and your life. Spend time with yourself alone. Get to know yourself. Discover what your passions are, what you live for, what are your life purposes. Dream about where you want to be (that's why you got out of such abusive relationship – to fulfill your dreams). Discover your mission. Get back to basics. Meditate. Exercise. Take yourself walk to the museum or book store (if you are a book lover, WOW!) or café. Hydrate your body with enough clean water. Fill your mind with peaceful things. Write yourself motivating letters. Get adequate amount of sleep. Spend your time and energy with loving friends who uplift you, who you admire, who inspire you. Learn from others and feel motivated. Get out and meet new people. Lie down to the ground and look at the sky.

5. Travel. Travel if you have time. Travel alone. Travelling really soothes you. You go and take your own decisions and do not get influenced by others. It really shapes you out of your reality. You start seeing life from a new different perspective. Forget luxury and live with the place. You will observe there's so much more to life than all of this.

Chapter 12 : Redefining Yourself after Abuse

After you have been in an abusive relationship, you probably have lost touch with yourself. For someone outsider, it's like finally freedom to abusive person and abuse but for survivor, the real journey is now beginning – the journey to within. Narcissist destroys one's core values and soul and survivors often look for closure that they can never get. There's no closure with the abuser (please accept this). You will go looking for exposure with them and you will find either pulled yourself back in, or rather more teared apart (they probably discard you). Closure is a joke. The only apology you need is the one you owe to yourself for staying long. The only person you now need to meet is yourself. "Don't keep dancing with the devil & wonder why you are still in hell."

The journey to within, let's be honest, is tougher and painful in some ways than the abuse itself. You will find that when some wounds are healing, some new wounds actually get emerge. So, defining yourself again could prove frustrating and tedious. It requires one to incorporate all the awful things happened to them into who they are, without letting all that define them. It requires completing building self-concept that requires analysis of victimization without allowing yourself to become a victim. It requires courage and faith to let go of one concept of yourself and build a new one.

This wasn't love and you are sure of that now. But it could be heartbreak for you. Loss of innocence. Loneliness that you may be facing. But the best thing you could do now is don't let all of that defines you. It was really undeserved of you but hey, do you know who are successful people? they are those who don't let themselves defined by what happens to them, instead what they choose to become out of what happens to them. So, it's really in your hand. Decide that you are not going to stay where you are. It's the first step to go where you want to go.

Learn to live with yourself. That's the first thing you need to do. Spend some healthy time with yourself. Maybe you could take yourself out for a walk or go out watch a movie. If you have constantly this desperate obsession to be around people, this is the best time to work on this. When you were in an abusive relationship, somehow your identity has been slowly eroded and that's why it is crucial to spend some time alone.

REALITY CHECK. If you want to know what you have become or how you were acting during relationship time, ask your close friends and family members. They will surely tell you that you were not the same person, or you are behaving differently. It's maybe because of depression, or exhaustion, or maybe you have developed some health issues, or due to anxiety. Maybe you are constantly obsessing about this person and your true friends and family is going to notice that and hopefully call you on that.

Spend some time alone and also with loving, understanding people, so that the next time when someone going to point that you are overreacting or being oversensitive, you could see the mask fall off.

Also, people will tell you to "get over it" when they find you constantly whining about the relationship or abusive person, it might piss you (or feel exhausted and sad) that people aren't able to understand you or see the behavior of toxic person. Remember one cannot comprehend easily what it feels like to be abused until and unless they go through it. Don't take their words to your mind and heart. They are simply not able to get you. Now, what you can do in such situation is that spend time with people who are really encouraging and support you. When you go through the self-healing, your relationship dynamics with others are surely going to change. It might shock them for a while because now you are not going around and absorbing anything and everything. Now you are redefining yourself after abuse. You are going to be selective and set boundaries. You are going to become a different person. It's like an act of phoenix who is going to rise from her own ashes. This recovery will make you self-empowered. It is going to bring you to yourself. You will start making own decisions, forming and sharing your own opinions, allowing others to hold their own troubles and worries instead of taking it for them. You will become confident, secure and humble.

So, you have to give room to yourself to evolve. Nothing is wrong if people are sad, angry, confused or offended by your new ways.

Eventually the dust will settle and light will adjust. And so, do us.

Boundaries need to be formed.

Allow this to happen to you.

Chapter 13 : Mistakes to Avoid on The Road to Recovery

It is not an easy thing to end a relationship with someone who was a part of your life. However, it is about the things you do after ending the relationship, which determines whether you can recover and move on with your life or stay obsessed with the emotional predator and the sad situation. You get to decide whether you want to move ahead or not. You have the control here to free yourself from the burdens of your past. If you want to regain control of your life and want to move ahead, then there are certain mistakes you must avoid on your road to recovery. Before you learn about the mistakes you must avoid, there are certain things about narcissistic recovery you must keep in mind to move ahead in life.

Please ensure that you don't overwhelm yourself by reading a lot about narcissism and narcissistic recovery. All the information you need is given within the book. Instead of overwhelming yourself with an excess of information, it is a good idea to focus on the points shared in this book. Please don't ever agree to "staying friends" with the narcissist.

If you are an empath, then you might find it a little tricky to sever all ties with the narcissist. However, take a moment and rationally think about it. How can you ever stay friends with someone who subjected you to narcissistic abuse? Do you think your friends would ever treat you the way the narcissist did? Would you want someone you love and care for to be with a narcissist like you were? If you answer these questions honestly, then you will be able to clearly see that staying friends with the narcissist does you no good whatsoever. In fact, staying in touch with the narcissist will only harm your recovery.

If you have any ideas or are thinking about ways in which you can keep a narcissist in your life, then you need to reconsider it all. You must not allow someone else to ruin your chances of recovery. Severing all ties with the narcissist and putting some physical distance between yourself and the narcissist is a wonderful idea. Your intentions, regardless of how pure they are, will only give narcissist the idea that the manipulation can go on, and you have no objections. Please don't believe that you will be fully healed the moment you end the relationship with the narcissist. You will need time and will need to make a conscious effort to heal yourself from the trauma you suffered. Now, that we have cleared all this up, it is time to look at some common mistakes you need to avoid at all costs.

The first mistake a lot of people make while recovering from narcissistic abuse is their inability to come to terms with the manipulation they were subjected to. Victims of narcissistic abuse at times struggle to accept the fact that the narcissist in their life is not only dangerous to their mental wellbeing but is a threat to their emotional and physical wellbeing as well.

On the surface of it, no one is fond of the highs, lows, or the uncertainties of life with a narcissist. However, there comes a time in the life of victims of narcissistic abuse were living with the narcissist becomes a habit to them. They start thinking that the life they are living with a narcissist is how things are supposed to be, how they must be, and how they will stay the same. Think of it as an addiction. Your mind will come up with different versions of events and all sorts of reasons as to why you cannot leave the narcissist. You must understand that your reactions need to be based on reality and not your perception of reality. You must stick to the facts, notice all the red flags, and not let anything melt your resolve of breaking all ties with the narcissist.

If you view a situation as being tragic, then you will respond accordingly. If you think of yourself as a victim of circumstances, then that is precisely where you will get stuck. If you think of your life as a journey and yourself as a student, then you can view all this as a learning experience. The way you think influences all the choices you make and the way you respond to situations. The moment you feel like you must go out of your way to prove your worthiness to your partner, it is a red flag you cannot afford to ignore. If your partner loves you unconditionally, as they are supposed to, then they know your worth, and you don't have to prove anything. If you ever catch yourself wondering about whether you made the right choice by ending the relationship, think about all the misery and suffering the narcissist subjected you to.

While recovering, people tend to have unrealistic expectations about the time it will take before they can start feeling better. Ending a relationship with a narcissist is quite different from ending a relationship with anyone else in your life. Please don't make the mistake of setting any unrealistic goals or expectations about the speed of the recovery. Who wouldn't want a magic pill that can put an end to all their misery and suffering? Who wouldn't want to wake up in the morning and feel like their usual selves again? Everyone would love this, but alas there is no such thing as a miracle cure. The process of recovering from narcissistic abuse will take time and effort. Don't lull yourself into thinking that it will be quick and simple. It will take time and effort, but you will feel infinitely better when you recover. If you set any unrealistic expectations for yourself, you are merely setting yourself up for failure.

As much as one would wish for a fairy godmother to fix their situation, recovering from narcissistic abuse is a gradual process. As with any transformation, the process of healing yourself is a journey of gradual success, which will take time. The recovery time tends to vary from one person to another. Instant recovery is seldom possible. The reality is that when you end a toxic relationship, you not only have to work on healing all the damage the toxicity caused, but you also need to face all the issues which led to that problem. The process of recovery will take time. It is the amalgamation of several small and practical steps you need to take each day. It is about motivating yourself to move forward instead of getting stuck up in your past. Please be kind and patient with yourself.

Victims of narcissistic abuse tend to avoid the hard work of having to move on with their life because they feel like it will make them lose their identity. They feel like they will lose themselves when they end the toxic relationship. For a lot of victims, the process of having to move on causes an identity crisis because the toxic relationship was all they knew about, and it was their life. Regardless of how miserable they were, it was their way of life, and everything they knew would change the minute they decide to move on. The truth is recovery isn't possible unless you want it to happen. A lot of people stay the way they are because of all the sympathy and pity, which comes their way from their loved ones. This tends to make the victims feel like they matter and are worthy of love. So, in their bid to hold onto that feeling, they tend to stay put in toxic relationships. This kind of thinking seldom does any good, and it will effectively put an end to any recovery you make.

You must answer this question- "Am I ready to allow myself to heal?" Are you ready to take all the steps to heal yourself and move on? Are you willing to make the necessary changes and put in the effort required to free yourself from the clutches of the narcissist? Don't fear to hit rock bottom. Once you hit rock bottom, the only way is up! Once you acknowledge the damage you have suffered, only then will you be able to start recovering from it.

You must understand that you have the right to live your life on your terms. In fact, you deserve to live a happy life. You have the right to move away from anything or anyone who harms you in any manner. You deserve to be happy. You deserve to live a life that's free from all forms of abuse. You deserve a chance to grow. You deserve a chance to love and be loved.

Conclusion

Congratulations!! You have made it to the end of Narcissistic Abuse! Hopefully, the information you found within these pages has helped to open your eyes to the insidiousness of narcissistic abuse and all of the harm that it can inflict on those who suffer from it. If you are a victim, you may now be able to see the signs of abuse within yourself. If you are not a victim, perhaps you have realized that someone you know is. No matter what, you will be prepared to identify victims in the future, so you know that you can treat them with the compassion and kindness they will need to escape their own abusers.

Throughout this book, you were provided with a wide range of information. You learned some key parts of narcissistic personality disorder, as well as how to identify a narcissist in your midst. You learned how the narcissist abuses those around him, hoping to keep them within his grasp and under his spell at all times for his own selfish uses. You learned about how he sees people around him as little more than tools meant to be abused and discarded when they are no longer useful. Your eyes were opened to the possibility of physical abuse within a narcissistic relationship, as well as several of the different ways the narcissist's abuse can hurt another person.

Along with learning to spot the abuse, you were taught how to handle the abuse. You were given several skills to handle abuse at the moment as well as how to make yourself less desirable as an abuse victim to avoid the abuse altogether. There were several tools here for you, ranging from cutting off the narcissist to managing your expectations when an interaction is required for some reason.

You were also guided through how to recover from narcissistic abuse. You were taught about the stages of recovery, acknowledgment, determination, compassion, and modeling for others. You were given tips on how to heal from narcissistic abuse, ranging from self-care to finding support groups and practicing mindfulness. Lastly, you were taught how to move on from the narcissist and get on with your life.

All of the content in this book is intended to help you on your journey to healing. As you wrap up this book, do not forget to acknowledge your own worth. No matter how much the narcissist may tell you otherwise, you are worthy of love. You are worthy of happiness. You are worthy of respect. No matter how hard the narcissist tries to convince you otherwise, know that things can and will get better. You can see a world in which you are happy again. You can escape the narcissist's grasp and free yourself. It will take patience and perseverance, but you can free yourself from the narcissist's grasp if you are ready to take the leap. If you are ready, hold on to this book and everything you have learned within the pages, and jump into the unknown. It may be scary, but there is a whole world waiting for you once you escape from the narcissist's grasp. Good luck on your journey!

ANXIETY IN RELATIONSHIP

Learn to Cultivate Empathy and Security in Relationships. How to Cure and Manage Anxious Attachment and those Behaviors that Trigger Jealousy, Anxiety, and Fear of Abandonment

Introduction

Are you hopelessly in love? Has the person you've been crushing on for so long finally realized you two would make a great couple? If so, then congratulations! Being in a relationship is one of the most amazing experiences a person can go through. But it all had a beginning, didn't it? You saw how he showed some amazing qualities, how well he treated you and how respectful he was with your friends. You realized the feeling you had was more than mere infatuation; you daydreamed for quite a while about him and you being together; and when the moment for you to tell him how you feel finally came, you felt as if your heart was about to come out of your chest.

Isn't it great to remember all you went through just to have them in your arms? And yet, you might still feel like your partner is not as committed to the relationship as you are. "How's that even possible?" you ask yourself. "I do a million things for him and I would do a million more, but I'm afraid one day he will turn around and leave me." While it is normal to feel attached to your significant other, you understand that this type of attachment is going to an extreme. After all, your partner has told you time and again that you don't have anything to worry about and that he would also do a million things for you.

Do the reassurances of your partner seem to fall on deaf ears? Do you feel it's difficult, if not impossible, to trust in your partner? Do you feel you always have to be constantly checking for reasons to doubt what your partner does for you? Don't despair! You are not alone! You can successfully overcome these difficulties that make being in a relationship seem more like a prison than the union of two great, trusting friends.

In this book, you'll learn to identify behaviors that trigger anxious concern in you, you will also be able to learn how to manage jealousy and the fear of abandonment that embitters of many couple. You'll see that it is possible to connect with your partner and that, with a lot of effort, come to the realization that he loves as much as he says he does, if not more.

Chapter 1: Self-Esteem and Insecurity

Are you an insecure person? Are you shy? Do you fear the thought of being in front of people or speaking to someone special for fear of being rejected? The reality is that we all have felt this way many times during our lives. Fear of rejection and social anxiety is much more normal than we think. You can see it at school when peers don't want to come in front of the class to give a presentation. You can see it during the teenage years when your friends struggle to ask someone for a date, even asking the teacher seems like they want to avoid at all costs. But why? Where does insecurity come from?

There are many reasons why a person is insecure. The environment where he was raised plays an important part. Perhaps this person was born in a family where social skills were never emphasized. Parents tend to a lot of emphasis on academic achievement, which is not bad, but sometimes, they make the mistake to put more emphasis on academic skills than social skills. The kid grows up believing that all he needs to do is study or comply with the house's rules to be completely happy. This idea is only further emphasized when the kid is rewarded with presents that only fuel his desire to be in a bubble. After all, why would he have to go out if he has everything he needs to be entertained while at the same time being supervised by his parents?

Overprotection seems to go hand in hand with what has been described. Again, it's not bad at all to protect the people you love, but can a person realistically shield someone from all harm? The outcome is going to be the same in any case. What do you think will happen when the kid finally grows up and has to face the world? Do you think he will be prepared to tackle life's problems? Or do you think he will shudder at the first problem? Do you think he will continue trying after failing? Don't you think it's more reasonable to believe that he has gotten used to his parents' help so much that he might crave for someone's help? It will be so easy for him to be attached to someone who helps him navigate life. Wasn't that the way his family raised him? He was always being watched and his goal was always to make someone else happy so it's only natural for him to find a significant other who makes him feel like "home" again.

Another reason for insecurity is the fact that people are taught by society that it's wrong for them to speak out because no one will care what they say or because of fear of being criticized or even harmed. They grow up in an environment of fear and isolation, which is the perfect breeding ground for anxiety. Ongoing ridicule is also a factor. Teased due to their physical or cultural differences, these people grow up with the idea that they are somehow inferior and nothing they say can be really taken seriously.

In the context of a relationship, people can become insecure if they have recently faced rejection or even unfaithfulness. They convince themselves they don't have any value in other's eyes, an idea that's very damaging to one's self-esteem. They ask themselves how this could ever have happened to them when everything seemed to be right. But here there's another underlying issue: perfectionism. Perfectionist people want their friendships, academic goals, relationships, to live up to their own unreasonable standards. They think that by doing so they will achieve a greater goal and be happier, but in reality, they are setting themselves up for failure and heartbreak.

When expectations aren't realized in a relationship, one can suffer tremendously. "I thought we were perfect, why is this happening to me?" is one phrase that has been voiced by people with high and unrealistic expectations. Thinking that love and companionship will solve all their problems is a beautiful idea, but it's an unrealistic one. These people will end up disappointed and might easily give up when the relationship goes encounters difficult problems. Not being able to find the relationship they have always dreamt of makes them wonder if they can ever be loved, and so the insecurity of finding someone they can share life's moments takes hold of them.

Self-Esteem

Insecurity and low self-esteem are related. When a person doesn't think their feelings don't matter to anyone, that person is undermining his own self-esteem. He views himself as someone with no worth or value. This distorted view of himself can push him further into desperation and anxiety. It is common knowledge that a person with low self-esteem doesn't feel encouraged enough to try new things, to get out of his comfort zone and to be dependent on others.

Being dependent on others because you place no value on yourself is a risky scenario. You're giving up your own life to someone totally different, your life becomes "his property" and so you end up feeling used. On the other hand, you might feel constantly jealous because you think other people are better, more interesting, and more important than you.

The key to understanding insecurity is to accept it. It's helpful to remember that we all have faced rejection, ridicule, fear, and doubts. We are humans and so we have felt insecure in one way or another. The key to overcoming insecurity is knowing that it can be overcome, is knowing that what other people might insultingly say about you does not define you as a person, is knowing that even harsh criticism doesn't mean you're a failure or have no worth. The truth is that insecurity can be overwhelming sometimes, but if you're willing to fight it, you will end up feeling you have accomplished one of life's greatest challenges: knowing who you are and how much you're worth.

How Insecurity Undermines a Relationship

A relationship is the union of two people who willingly accept each other's fails and learn how to put up with one another's differences. To some, this definition of a relationship might sound too cheesy, but there's much that can be found in this saying.

Accepting each other's fails to mean you understand the other person is as imperfect as you are and so he's bound to make many mistakes. There might be times when his words might hurt you and you might rightfully feel indignant or angry. But what about accepting your own failures? Is it easy for you to be modest and admit to your own mistakes?

Differences in upbringing might also show that both you and your partner have different communication styles: he might be someone who prefers discussing an argument after the water had calmed down, while you may be someone who wants to address any issue that seems to threaten the relationship. Therefore, finding a balance is key when dealing with problems in a relationship, whether they can be considered "minor" problems or "serious" ones.

Insecurity lends itself to the doubts and uncertainties you see in the relationship. He is not in the mood for talking much lately? "Must be something I did" is what you wonder. But what if he has told you already that it's because he feels very stressed out and he needs some time for himself to feel recharged. Will you happily admit that he also needs time to relax or will you continue guessing why he doesn't feel like talking to you?

Do you like double guessing your partner's intentions, no matter how good they seem to be? Do you think he's always trying to hide something from his life? Do you think he doesn't trust you anymore? It's easy to let yourself be consumed in these ideas, after all, there are many things that you just don't know about his day, you don't know what he's thinking. But what all of these questions only do is foster more insecurity in you. If you let yourself fall in the trap that the answers to these questions are worth scrutiny on your part, then you will be undermining one of the bases of any healthy relationship: trust.

If you've only dealt with the type of person that's always open to you and tells you everything, how will you be able to deal with a partner that's not secretive, but prefers to keep some things to himself?

Some measure of privacy and respect will always be appreciated in all relationships. Your partner will be grateful for showing respect and you'll be able to see that you also need some time for yourself to grow and develop as a person. Relationships other than the couple also need to be maintained to have a healthy environment where both know they are respected and interested in one another.

In the worst-case scenario, a relationship can even be destroyed if one makes a pest of himself by always checking the other's relationships and by thinking that there cannot be any uncertainties in their relationship. It's all too common to see how a relationship is brought to an end just because someone doesn't trust his partner and doesn't respect his right to make his own choices.

You don't need to become the one who will destroy the relationship. Avoiding that is possible if you learn how to manage the behaviors that lead to more insecurity and jealousy.

Chapter 2: Attachment and Emotion Management. Three Steps to Follow to Be Less Jealous and More Open to Listening

One manifestation of insecurity is being overly attached. There's nothing wrong with wanting to spend some time with our partner; actually, feeling connected to someone and demonstrating it is vital if you want to have a healthy and loving relationship. This becomes a problem when it's taken to an extreme. Being overly attached poses a danger to your relationship and you need to learn how to manage this.

If you remember what was discussed in the preceding chapter, you'll recall that a person who's always being told what to do with the sole purpose of making the other happy has relinquished his own free will. His decisions and opinions are not taken into account because he has learned to leave it all to others to decide what's good for him. That person has become a puppet and has put his life in other's hands. He's as vulnerable as the other person wants him to be and his self-worth is almost non-existent.

Even though this is usually an extreme case, this scenario repeats itself countless times. A relationship doesn't have to be like a prison, where one person feels he cannot move a single finger without consulting with the other whether it's right or not. Yes, there are certain circumstances where mutual agreement will definitely be necessary, but not all decisions in life require to be examined with an overly-judgmental eye.

You're in no better position if you feel you're the one commanding. In a relationship, both will suffer. The one commanding and examining every movement is just showing how insecure he or she feels. The truth of the matter is that the relationship is not healthy. Just as an unreasonable boss is never satisfied with the explanations of his employee, the one demanding constant explanation from his partner will never be quiet, rather, he'll be finding excuses not to believe any explanation.

A mother might think that she's shielding his son by maintaining him in a "bubble" where he is safe from threats, temptations, and danger. But the son will have to grow and mature. He will have to understand that life is also enjoyable outside the "bubble" where he was raised. By being overly attached to your partner, you might think you're protecting him from temptation or danger to your relationship, but you're just stifling his enjoyment of life. You're just making him wonder what it feels like being outside of your relationship. In other words, by being overly attached, you're giving him more reasons to end the relationship.

A prisoner might reassure himself by thinking about the day when his release will come. Don't let your relationship be like a prison where your partner finds reassurance only when he thinks about the day when he leaves the relationship.

You Don't Possess Your Partner

By being overly attached many people come to think that they are in possession of their partner. No human can be fully possessed by others. This goes against our own desire to be and live free. A relationship is not the union of master and slave. Do you really see your partner as someone who has to render an account to you? Do you feel like it's nothing less than a crime and an insult when he makes a decision without consulting you? Why do you feel you have control over your partner?

If you think your partner has voluntarily come under your control by accepting being in a relationship, you have fooled yourself. Being in a relationship doesn't mean your partner has come to you to surrender all his rights and goals, it means he has come to you because he wants to share them with you. He has grown up to be a person who wants to share life moments with you, not for you take them out of his hand, but to understand that he sees you as someone very special in his life.

The other way around is also true. You're being possessed by your partner if you're so attached to him that you want to follow everywhere, he goes and supports every decision he does just because you feel you have to be with him. Doing that might make you feel you're in a position of control; after all, you know exactly what he's doing, who he's been with and where. But in reality, you're surrendering your own freedom, you have left your decisions aside to follow your partner's. You've become possessed by your partner when all you wanted to do was to be sure he's been doing right.

Emotional management

Feel like emotions can sometimes be overwhelming? Emotions are proof that we feel and are able to enjoy basic human experiences. When someone falls in love, he embarks on a roller coaster of emotions that might make him feel exhausted. Being in a relationship is not the end of that roller coaster. Although it provides a measure of security, you both still need to keep working if you want to make a success of this relationship.

Happiness and joy are normal feelings that follow after beginning a new relationship. But if you're an insecure person, these emotions soon turn into anger, frustration, or jealousy; but how? An insecure person will never be satisfied with her partner reassurances whenever he makes a mistake or apologizes. Also, she might find it difficult to believe her partner.

Three Steps to Be Less Jealous and More Open to Listening

1. Realize your worth and avoid comparisons: You may not be perfect. You may not have the perfect body. But surely there's a lot your good at. Realize that you have a lot of value in the eyes of those closest to you. You have qualities that make you special to your partner and those qualities set you apart as someone different, interesting, and attractive to your loved ones. With that being said, don't compare yourself to others! Do you feel that the fact that someone looks better than you or has better clothes than you make them a more important or better person than you? Outward appearances tend to matter little when choosing a life-long partner. Realize how much you're worth and continue working on your good qualities.

2. Try to get more involved with people: Spending time with people will yield great benefits for you and your relationship. Having an interest in others rather than yourself all the time will help you have more meaning connections and will boost your self-esteem. The more you get to know people, the clearer you'll see that we all have the same problems and the less you'll worry about your own insecurity. Do good things for others!

3. React to criticism in a proper way: Since we are all bound to make mistakes, it's only natural to expect that sooner or later we will receive criticism. What matters here, though, is how you react to that criticism. Sure, there's criticism that's designed to just put you down. You can turn away and ignore it if you certainly realize that it is totally unfair, untrue, or diminishing. On the other hand, if the criticism is well deserved, strive to listen to it and improve. An occasional mistake doesn't make you a failure as a person.

Striving to be a better person is not an easy task, but you can learn how to manage your emotions when you're confronted with criticism. Socializing will be a great tool in understanding how others see you, but remember that, the closer we get, the easier it will be for you to see where your friends fall short, and they will see that about you too. Your good qualities already endear you to many people, especially to your partner! So, don't be afraid of showing them to the world!

Chapter 3: Improving Empathy and Communication in a Relationship

You may have heard of the value empathy has in some relationships. Do you know what empathy is? Several dictionaries define it as "being able to experience the feeling of others." It comes in handy in every relationship we form with anyone. After all, don't you feel happy when your best friend finally receives the promotion she's been waiting for so long? How do you feel when others congratulate you on your success? If you've ever tried to put yourself in other's shoes to try to understand what they're going through and how you'd be able to help, then you've been training your empathy. Empathy is what makes us feel pity when we see people suffer and rejoice when others dear to us are rewarded. In contrast, a person who only cares about himself and what he can get out of other people without thinking about the consequences of his actions and how these can affect others can hardly be called empathetic.

Therefore, it shouldn't come as a surprise to some that empathy is also very important in a relationship. Yes, it is true that the needs of man might be different from those of a woman. And it is also true that we cannot read minds so as to know what exactly is needed to say or do in certain circumstances. But basic emotions and hardships are so common in all of us that, even though we may never have been through them, we can easily understand them and provide the comfort and words of encouragement the other person needs. You may know how hard it is for anyone to lose a loved one in death. You may know how stressing a 10-hour job can be. You realize how difficult it is for someone to move out of the city or even the country. And you may know how heartbreaking it is to be rejected.

Everyone who has experienced these situations knows very well how desperately they needed the reassurance or comfort of a good friend. And what if the friend wasn't able to utter the right words at that moment? Just being there, just presence can be enough to show that you really care. "If you need to talk to someone, just call me." Showing your availability even after the first days is of great help and is to be commended.

"But, what does empathy have to do with a relationship?" You may ask yourself. Well, an empathetic person knows that her partner might feel stressed out after a long day. She may try to understand how difficult it can be for him to put up with a demanding boss, horrible colleagues and long hours stuck in traffic. And all of that could even be worse if he's working on something, he considers boring or monotonous. What could an empathetic girlfriend do? Will she batter him with constant questions about his day? Will she start asking about everything he did? Will she start complaining that he is lazy for being on the couch after coming home? She can be more understanding, can't she? How would you act? Empathy can help us answer that question. Empathy prompts us to ask: "How would I like to be treated if I were him?" Will you come up with an easy answer?

Every day we're encountered with situations that can put to the test our resolve to be empathetic. Since a relationship is one of the closest connections anyone can have, empathy needs to be displayed every day. Doing good things for your partner, having his needs in mind, will endear you to him and will surely have better results. To know his needs, consider what he considers important and think about them is showing how important the relationship is for you.

One way to understand his needs is getting to know him better. There's no knowledge of what a person is like if there's no communication. How could you improve communication between you and your partner? How can you get to know your partner?

Communication is Essential

There's no way to getting to know another person other than communicating with him, spending time with him and see how he interacts with others. In all of these instances, communication is key; but not just the superficial small talk, an occasional conversation that randomly occurs. Meaningful conversation is what needs to take place if you really want to see what the person is like.

Meaningful conversation is not accidental. Yes, there are times when small talk will turn into deep and interesting conversations, but having a goal in mind is necessary. What about a relationship? Since both of you may already know a bit about each other, is it still important to continue getting to know each other? Yes, indeed.

Communication shouldn't stop after getting into a relationship. Actually, after getting into a relationship, there's even more, to know about your partner than ever before. You start to see how his qualities shine but also how his flaws come to light on certain occasions. There will be times when you both will have to discuss some issues; some more important than others. Likewise, problems will arise, how can you handle all of these in a peaceful constructive manner?

433

Be Clear with Your Intentions

Some people have a harder time to catch what their partner is trying to say. Don't think your partner knows what you're already thinking what bothers you. Don't assume he knows what you need. Sometimes, you will have to spell it out. Assuming your partner knows everything about you and what you need is just another form of "mind-reading". Just say what you need.

Be Completely Engaged in the Conversation

Your partner is ready to have a conversation with you, are you? You may be doing another activity, but isn't your partner deserving of your full attention? And don't pretend you're listening. Rather, ask your partner to wait until you're fully available to have that conversation. When you're finally having that conversation, don't try to interrupt your partner. Resist the urge to interrupt or disagree with him. Wait until it's your time to speak. Asking questions will come very in handy. By asking question you are showing your partner that you care about him and that you're really interested in the outcome of the conversation. It will also help you clarify what your partner is talking about.

Try to Get the Message

When an active and meaningful conversation is taking place, more than just words are being expressed. Body language and tone of voice are factors to consider. Depending on the tone of voice, a message as innocent as "It's fine" may really mean "It's not fine." "You never call me" may really mean "I feel you're not interested in me." Try to get the message behind the words so that you can understand what the problem is all about.

Don't Give Up

Continue listening to your partner. Resist the urge to disagree. Be kind and use tact when it's your turn to speak. And don't give up easily.

A relationship is nourished when both parts are eager to discuss problems and disagreements in a respectful, kind, and attentive manner. The outcome of these conversations usually strengthens the relationship and also help them understand each other even more. It's also important to communicate your fears. You'll be surprised that one of the most common fears is the fear of abandonment. How can you deal with it and overcome it?

Chapter 4: Managing the Fear of Abandonment

Fear of abandonment may have many causes. Seeing how your parents split is one of them. You may know how hard it is for everyone involved. After years pass by, some kids grow up to think that they can never feel secure in a relationship because it will inevitably end with one partner leaving the other. On the other hand, there are some who try to manipulate their partner so that he can never leave the relationship.

Both courses of action stem from the same basic emotion: insecurity. An insecure person is sometimes afraid of uncertainty and what might happen is he lets his partner continue with his own separate life. Leaving with that constant fear is already very damaging to anyone's health. What can you do if you feel this fear is taking over you?

Don't Be Resentful

Pat experiences of parents splitting up or a former partner leaving may still be fresh in your mind. Truth is, this is very common and happens all around us all the time. Rather than being resentful and angry about those people you think "did you wrong", learn to forgive and let go of the anger. Just consider what might happen to you if you don't learn to let off those feelings. A person who's always angry will easily become a bitter individual. He will also become prone to anger and will not manage stressful or difficult situations with the needed clarity of mind. Rather, he will readily let his emotions cloud his judgment and get the best of him. Learn to forgive.

Associate with People You Love and Love You Back

Spending time with people you consider important in your life will give a great boost to your self-confidence. Friends and family members are the best examples of how you are able to be loved, respected, and considered important for who you are, despite your flaws and imperfections. The love and companionship they provide will also make it clear to you that the fear of abandonment is sometimes unfounded.

Beware of Easy Escapes

Self-destructive behavior might seem like an easy way to unwind yourself from all the anger you're still holding within you. Heavy drinking, getting into fights, isolating yourself and drug abuse is not the right to cope with your emotions. Do not be afraid of asking for help if you need it. Professional help is also to be considered if needed.

Learn to Trust Again

Don't think "all men are the same". Granted, you might have suffered a lot when your former partner left you, but that doesn't mean that everyone is just like him. Don't come to the conclusion that you can never be safe in a relationship. You might even have some male friends that are great examples of loyal behavior. Sure, learning to trust again is not going to be an easy task, but giving yourself the time needed to forgive and forget is a very good first step. And when you're ready to have a relationship again, rather than wondering whether one day he might leave you, concentrate on the present and think about the potential that your relationship has now and in the future. Concentrate on his good qualities and he has shown them time and again. That will endear you to him and convince you that there's no need to fear.

Talk to Your Partner About Your Insecurities

If you're in a relationship and still feel insecure, don't hesitate to communicate your fears and insecurities to your partner. In a kind and respectful manner, tell him what bothers you and what activities of him might make you feel you have for your insecurities. Don't conclude your partner will only be defending himself. He might try to reassure you that your fears are unfounded. Strive to listen to his reasoning and learn to trust in what he says. After all, he also trusts you.

Trusting is sometimes easier said than done. You might still feel like you cannot trust your partner, no matter how hard you try. One thing that will help you is understanding that in every relationship a measure of trust and loyalty is expected and required not only from your partner but also from you. Trusting means more than just letting your partner do whatever he wants with his life. It also means that you respect his decisions and support them wholeheartedly.

In the long run, the way he uses his spare time and the decisions he makes will enable you to see how he feels about the relationship and how committed he is to it. Only if you learn to trust in your partner will you experience how he chooses to be loyal, not because he is obliged to be loyal, but because he **wants** to be loyal. So, learn how to trust your partner again.

The fear of abandonment is a very common one. Never feel like you're the only one who feels afraid to see someone leaving. Letting go of hurtful past experiences, spending time with friends and family, learning to trust your partner and seeing how we willfully choose to remain with you will surely lift you up and help you cope with your fear of abandonment.

Chapter 5: The Influence of Social Media in a Relationship

Nowadays, people are more connected than ever before. We have the privilege to live in a time when information is at the palm of our hands and we don't need to wait a very long time to get it. Every day, we're bombarded with news about our community and the world around us. We get the good, the bad and the ugly. The internet has amazing places where you can find the answers to many questions and tips on how to make your life a bit simpler, but at the same time, it can trigger feelings that might otherwise never come out.

The issue with being connected is that we like it and yet it's difficult to manage. We enjoy feeling like we're connected with as many people as possible because that helps us keep in touch with the latest news: the birth of a new member of the family, the engagement of one of your friends and even getting promoted. But all of this information can also become very difficult to handle when it's just too much information coming all at once.

Social media has become ubiquitous. To some people, social media **is** the internet. That means that almost all, if not all, the interaction that they have on the internet is through social media. They get all the information they need from social media. The problem with social media is that, as it is unregulated, it is the perfect breeding ground for false or altered information. This "altered" information doesn't include political or economic news only; even people try to "alter" what they are in social media.

Not Everything That Shines Is Gold

There's nothing wrong with posting on social media things that you would want to celebrate anyway. You may feel like you're sharing with your loved ones and friends your joy for what it's happening to you. The problem appears when you see that almost everyone on social media is keen to post only the best moments of their life. By taking a look at some of your friends' posts, you might think that they don't have any problem at all. By browsing social media for a while, you might think that everyone is living their best life, having the time of their lives traveling around the world, going on a cruise, having amazing vacations. The picture of a happy family might make you think that they don't seem to have any problem and that their family life is perfect. Seeing wedding pictures might make you believe that the couple has been happy since the day they met.

In reality, as you already know, life is far from perfect. Many people post certain content to make their lives look as everything is perfect. They create a new persona, a fake identity. This is multiplied throughout all the internet and so at the end of the day, you get millions and millions of people presenting the best of what's going on in their lives, consciously leaving aside the sorrow and pain or even the boredom of everyday life. This might make you think that you also have to live up to a certain standard of excellence.

See that beautiful model on her most recent post? She seems to be always accompanied by a lot of friends and a handsome boyfriend. Do you feel you have to be that attractive to have the attention of your partner or friends? Does it make you feel like a loser if you're not living life to the full just like her? Look at the comments. She seems to get a lot of attention from everyone. Do you envy that attention? Do you want it?

Have you recently spotted a seemingly fabulous wedding on social media? You can see that they are really happy. Does that make you feel you also need to get married to be truly happy? Are you asking yourself when that's going to happen to you? Do you crave to find someone who is just as happy to be with you as the couple is to each other?

If you see many friends posting about how they are having the time of their lives with their partners, you might begin to feel lonely. Do the posts make you feel you are a failure because you're not in a relationship? If you're considering breaking up with someone, but everyone seems to be in a happy and committed relationship, will you feel you are not doing something right?

Living up to a Standard

Do you like posting pictures on social media? Then you are one of the millions around the world who do so every day. It's just natural to want to share the joys of life, and one of those is being in a relationship.

As time goes on, you might find yourself posting more and more about you and your partner. After all, isn't love to be celebrated? You may have posted about your anniversary or any other special date, possibly a trip that you both took together, a present that he gave to you, a gift you gave to him and so on.

Your friends might naturally feel delighted that you had found the love of your life; it seems so looking at the pictures. And they share in your joy by commenting on your posts, liking them, and even wishing you the best for your relationship. In other words, everyone on the internet that has access to your profile knows that you're in a relationship, that you're happy being in it and that you both are going strong.

Scenarios like this are repeated every day. People just seem to like advertising their relationships. Interesting enough, there's an overwhelming amount of posts about the joys of being in a relationship, but when looking for the breakup, the cheating or the problems, people seem to be mute.

Breaking up is just another part of life, why don't people also post it on social media? Yes, it is something personal and intimate, but it seems to people that you would announce everything about your relationship, isn't it normal then to also announce your breakup?

Truth is people are ashamed to announce they had split up. They had been posting for a very long time that they were very happy and everything seemed to go alright in the relationship. Judging by the post, they didn't seem to break up. They think that, since everyone on social media is having a perfect relationship, this shouldn't be happening to them, so they prefer to be silent on the matter.

What is worse, some people don't even want to break up with their partner just because she might feel she's letting friends and family down. They prefer to save face, to keep up appearances, rather than disappoint. Have you ever been in the same situation?

Thinking that everyone is happy just because they look happy on their pictures and posts is foolish. Social media only shows a picture of the moment. A picture that can easily be manipulated or changed to make it look like everything's going fine. They don't show the many challenges that all relationships must go through. They are not the exact representation of what might be going on in the relationship. They can never show the disagreements, the hard feelings, and the sadness that each and every couple has to endure.

Don't be fooled by the idea that if you're not in a relationship, you're a failure. Don't fall into the trap of social media that makes you think that everyone around you is perfectly happy. And don't think you're disappointing anyone, not even yourself if you decide to break up with someone. There's much more to life than what you see on social media. Do not try to live to the standard of perfection that is only unrealistic but also very unhealthy.

My Boyfriend Likes Using Social Media

As noted earlier, social media enables millions of people to be connected and to share any type of content and information. Your partner may be just another person who enjoys spending time on social media. Have you been worrying lately about his use of social media? Are you left wondering what he does or who he's talking to? Do you want to know who's trying to reach your partner?

If you're both on a couch watching TV but your partner is laughing at his phone, it's only normal to wonder what he's laughing at. Curiosity pushes you to ask but you are left with more doubts if he only gives you a vague answer. But you don't really need to be mad at him. Don't think he's being unfaithful or that some colleague of his is trying to get closer to him. Even though social media makes it easier to communicate, there's a great chance your partner is just using it as a distraction rather than a tool to get out of the relationship.

You don't really need to be worried if you see something that first seems suspicious on his social media profile. If you're the type of person who likes seeing her partner's social media activity, then you might find yourself falling into a rabbit hole of past posts about how his life used to be before you both got together. It's even very likely that you might get to find some old friends or past relationships of his.

Do you feel tempted to have a look at their profiles to see how they met? It's very tempting to compare yourself to his past partners. Though you have the freedom to go see their profiles, is it worth it? You have already noted how detrimental it can be to compare yourself to others and how that can increase your insecurity. Don't take the first step!

But what if you feel your boyfriend has been using social media for a very long period of time, more than usual and you start feeling suspicious. Well, if you really feel like it's bothering you very much, then talking to your boyfriend is a very good idea. Ask him if there's something new on social media that he's been enjoying lately. Without criticizing, tell him how you feel about his constant use of social media. Don't assume that your boyfriend is spending time online with someone else. And even if that's the case, you can tell him how you feel left aside from the relationship due to his being with the other person.

As long as it's not detrimental to the relationship, you should let your boyfriend has his online life if he wishes to do so. How he conducts himself on social media will show you how he really feels about the relationship. Your own use of social media may have raised eyebrows too for some time without you even noticing. Finding a balance between real life and online life will help you and your partner live more peacefully and have the quality time you wish to have.

Social Media as a Barrier to Communication

It takes a huge amount of time to get to know a person. Though social media can help you stay connected and communicate with people everywhere, it usually doesn't offer the same advantages as a face-to-face conversation. A conversation involves more than just words typed on a box, it involves tone of voice, gestures, posture and more. All of this helps the communication to be more engaging and more meaningful. It helps create a real bond.

The superficial style that is used on social media is linked to the fact that social media and other forms of internet communication were created with the intent of having quick, easy conversations rather than long, deep, and meaningful interactions. A relationship will always be nourished if it's maintained with daily communication. Don't just keep the conversation online. Engage fully in it by having some time off and discussing face-to-face.

The message and the intent of it can also get lost easily if communication is kept through social media. The lack of body expressions renders it cold. Therefore, it's easy to misinterpret what the other person is saying.

While messaging your significant other on social media can sometimes help the relationship, you shouldn't take it to an extreme. It might turn out that at the end of the working day you have nothing to tell your partner since you've been already telling him every single thing that's been happening to you during the day. And so, communication becomes stifled due to extreme familiarity.

Finally, the social skills necessary to keep a conversation are not the same as the skills used when engaging in an online conversation. By only maintaining online conversations, you might begin to lose the interpersonal skills that are vital to have a healthy relationship.

So, what can you do if you feel you're actually the one suing too much social media? One good way to start is being honest with yourself and examine how much time you spend on social media. Also, what you use it for. Do you use it to keep up to date with the latest news? Consider how vital and important they really are. Most of them might not even have any relation with you, your family, or your community at all. Do you like keeping your existing relationships online? Try to hang out with the people you care offline as much as possible. It might be hard if they are really far away from where you're living, but granted, you also have some relationships offline that are very close and likely available to meet.

Don't use social media when in important meetings. That's something obvious that you might already know by now. But this also applies to gatherings with friends and family. Don't just sit there with your phone. Try to be engaged in the conversation and use your social skills to strike and maintain the conversation that you would otherwise do online. Be respectful of other people's time by giving them the attention they deserve.

Talk to your partner about what constitutes inappropriate use of social media. You might want to establish some basic rules about the time and place where social media is to be used. You might want to limit the number of friends or the pages you and your partner are following. Talk about the people you feel shouldn't be followed on social media and tell the reason why.

Consider your partner's right to privacy in all of this. Your partner is a separate individual that has the ability to make his own intelligent decisions. Learn to trust in him by not asking for passwords if he refuses to do so. On the other hand, if you are the one who refuses to give a password, he must respect your decision.

Chapter 6: Keeping Love Alive or Turning It Back On

As time passes by, you and your partner might go through many difficult moments. The fact that you are still together proves that you both learned to navigate the difficult waters of commitment. But now, after so long, you feel you have fallen into a rut. You feel the relationship is pretty monotonous. It's not that you have unresolved issues, it's just that the routine has finally set in.

So, what can you do to keep the flame of love alive? How can you help your partner be excited about the relationship again? Is there anything that you can learn to turn love back on?

Like the First Time

Do you still recall how the relationship used to be in the past? Do you have fond memories of when you began dating? Then use that to your favor. Treat your partner the same way you treated him when you began dating. You may still remember how many details were involved in a date.

You were kind and loving with him. Why don't you try to talk to him with that same energy and excitement you had when you first got together? You liked showering with presents and letters. Why don't you bring back all of those special actions again? You liked hanging out together alone or even with friends. Why not try to do the same again?

Letters and presents help your partner realize that you still care about the relationship and him after so much time. Don't think that they are too cheesy! They might be just what your partner needs. You don't need to make them so elaborate. You only need to have him in mind.

Going out on a date in itself is an exciting idea. You can plan a date at the same place you had your first date. If that's not possible, you can think of a restaurant, park, or any other place that your partner might enjoy. Planning something together will also help you be united. Teaming with some friends will make it even more exciting and funny.

Don't limit your ideas to just what you used to do. You can also try something new that you've been thinking about for a while. Even if it seems something that your partner might not like, why not inviting him to see if he's also interested in joining with you?

Affection Is Still Important

Stress is still an issue that many of us have to deal with on a daily basis. Affection can relieve that stress. Showing affection is still important as it was during the first days of the relationship.

Show consideration for your partner's good qualities. Notice how your partner displays his perseverance when going to work, his effort when helping in the home, his determination to commit to the relationship. His good qualities are what endeared him to you.

Strive to show how much you value his good qualities by telling him how you feel about them. Men also need to be told how valued they are in a relationship. You can have his good qualities in mind when congratulating him. The point is that you need to acknowledge these good qualities and be truly grateful for them. Be observant.

In the coming week, you can try to put effort into noticing what your partner does to add positively to the relationship. Even things that you may take for granted. After much time, there's the risk of you taking your partner for granted or the other way around. You can easily start to focus, not on what he's doing, but on what he's not. Never underestimate how words of appreciation can have an effect on your partner. If you don't start feeling appreciation for your partner, it's easier for him to feel drawn to someone who does.

Take the Initiative

You should also be willing to take the first step towards keeping love alive. You may think that your partner also has to show some initiative since he's also part of the relationship. But your partner might be thinking the same!

Take the initiative by communicating how you really care about the relationship and your partner. Do nice things for him. Your partner might react in a very pleasant way. But even if at first, he may not seem to react in the way you expected, don't give up. It might take a little bit more effort or consistency for him to see that you really want their love to turn back on.

One issue that refrains many people from taking the initiative is infidelity. If this has happened to you, you know how difficult it is to regain trust. You may have felt his unfaithfulness was blown to the relationship. But there are steps you can take if you feel you want to give the relationship a second chance.

Chapter 7: How to Use Forgiveness for Your Benefit

If you were told to number the reasons why couples break up, what would be at the top of your list? Would unfaithfulness be the number one reason you think people split up?

Unfaithfulness on the part of one member of the relationship can hurt a lot. You may feel betrayed and insecure. Now that he has been unfaithful, you start wondering if you did something wrong in the relationship or failed to do something to stop it. While these thoughts may come naturally to an anxious mind, the truth of the matter is that we all examine ourselves after knowing the person we loved the most has betrayed us.

Though many people decide to end the relationship, this is not the case with everyone. Some decide to stay together and give the relationship a second chance. If you're one of them, how can you regain trust in your partner? If you still love him, how can you feel better by forgiving him?

Why It Is Difficult to Forgive

You might feel hurt after realizing your partner's unfaithfulness. The pain you feel is enough for you to think that your partner did an unforgivable thing. But you also know deep within that you love him and that you want to forgive him. You want to give your relationship a second chance.

You can blurt out the words "I forgive you", but do you really feel it? Do you feel like resentment can't be taken away from your heart? You need to understand that forgiving means "to let go". You are not required to forget what happened, you just choose to let go of it for your own benefit and that of the relationship.

Not to be skipped are the health risks that can stem from the lack of a forgiving attitude. Some experts even link high blood pressure, depression, and other illnesses if someone keeps holding on to resentment.

Have in Mind the Benefits of Forgiving

Since forgiving means to let go, it will mean peace for you and the relationship. Since you're letting it go, you shouldn't bring it up every time you and your partner have an argument. Remember, forgiving doesn't mean you're minimizing what happened.

When you finally let go of the matter, you allow for love to grow again in the place of resentment since resentment itself is a barrier for communication and love. This doesn't mean, though, that you shouldn't talk about the incident.

Talk About What Happened

At first, it might be very difficult for you and your partner to talk about what happened. Your partner might not even want to think about what happened. He would like to forget and lock it away. But it's necessary for you to talk about the incident and what led to it.

As the wronged part of the relationship, you may have a lot of questions. You'll be asking the reason why and how it happened, your mind will surely be inundated with more questions as days and weeks go by. The conversation that follows might be heated but if that's the case, you should both apologize to each other. The issue might become worse if at first, doesn't want to talk about while you are eager to search for answers. Don't pressure him to speak out, be patient. His unwillingness to answer at first might make you suspicious, but there's nothing to be afraid of.

As time goes by, you'll notice that the discussions you have with your partner will make the relationship stronger. You'll see what led to him being unfaithful and what you now can do to strengthen the relationship. The honest, open, and frank conversation will draw you closer together.

Change What Led to the Infidelity

After talking to your partner for some time now, you might realize what led to his unfaithfulness. There's no way to change the past, but you can help your partner change the routine or habits that pushed him toward unfaithfulness. What is involved in this?

If your partner cheated on you with someone at his work, then you could recommend your partner to break off all contact with her. He might not be in the position to change jobs, but he can do whatever it's needed within his circumstances to avoid taking the same steps that led him to commit unfaithfulness with his colleague. Changing work schedules and even telephone numbers might work to stop the contact if the colleague tries to reach out to him. Will all of this be worth it?

After such a blow, regaining trust will prove to be a difficult task. While there's not a minimum set time for the relationship to heal, you can choose to let go of resentment, forgive your partner, help him to change and give love a second chance.

Chapter 8: Strategies to Improve a Relationship

A romantic relationship is made up of two people. This means that both have agreed to stay together. Commitment motivates them to stick together even during difficult times. In all, you might still wonder what you can do to improve your relationship. Whether you're happy in a relationship and just wanting to add more excitement to it or want to heal your relationship after a setback, you can find comfort in the strategies that you'll find to improve a relationship.

Improving Yourself

To have an honest look at yourself, you can ask: "Am I the same person I was before getting into this relationship? Do I talk to my partner as much as it is used to? Do I still treat him/her with the same kindness? Has the routine set in?"

If after considering these questions you still feel like there's nothing else to improve, then you might be surprised about where you can get even more advice on how to improve yourself: your partner.

Sit down with your partner and ask him: "How can I be a better girlfriend to you?" Don't interrupt. Listen attentively. Resist the urge to disagree with him because of something that seems false. Remember you're asking for the input of someone who knows you a lot and what's important here is that you have to focus on what you can improve.

Determination and perseverance will be key. Sometime might have to pass until you see the improvements. On the other hand, if your partner tells you that there's nothing you need to do to be an even better girlfriend, take it as a compliment. What he's really telling you is that you're all he's been waiting for! But since we all make mistakes from time to time; chances are your partner will have something to point out.

Improving the Relationship

Now that you are together in a relationship, you'll have to begin thinking with the best interests of the other in mind. Learn what commitment means by openly communicating your thoughts, feelings, and opinions. Try to find a balance between what your partner and you want. Think about your decision and whether they'll have a building or detrimental effect on the relationship.

Be realistic about what you expect from your partner. Your partner might have a harder time committing and so he might not always choose what seems right at the moment. Support him by sticking with him even during times of doubt. Your partner will be forever grateful that you never diminished his choices and supported him through thin and thick.

You can also examine your view of the relationship. While navigating difficult water, you will see how you and your partner will react and try to solve the problems that will inevitably arise in every relationship. After viewing how you deal with these issues, you will have to take an honest look at yourself and your partner and see if the relationship is still worth fighting.

Think About the Future

As you both keep getting to know each other, you will surely come to see each other's flaws. Improving yourself will take some time and it's obvious to say that it needs to be constant. If you feel like your efforts are not yielding any fruit, don't despair, sooner or later your partner will see that you want to improve the relationship.

Every little thing that you do to nourish and strengthen the relationship today will add and make it stronger in the future. Try to show affection to your partner. Be respectful of what he thinks of your actions. Be mindful of his needs. Communicate openly and frankly. Show your love with little acts that will make your day and his brighter. Let him be your closest confidant.

Chapter 9: Increasing Self-Confidence: Learning How to Love and Take Care of Yourself

Love is a basic human emotion that all of us feel and express in many different ways. There's love for the family, for friends and romantic love. Love is defined, not only by what you feel but also by what it motivates you to do. In other words, love is not passive.

Self-confidence is also linked to love. It's actually healthy to have a measure of love and respect for ourselves. But again, it's how you show that love to yourself that matters. Do you eat healthy and take care of your body? Do you know how to maintain friendships? Do you stay away from harmful thoughts and emotions? Do you relax from time to time?

One way to increase self-confidence is to get to know yourself better. This means you're aware of your qualities and strengths. You know what you're very good at and how your words can be of great help. You know what your friends, your partners and everyone close to you know who you are and what your potential is.

This also means that you're aware of your faults and mistakes. You know you should ask for forgiveness if you made a mistake and try to be honest when it happens. You don't try to excuse your behavior but take responsibility when it's been clearly demonstrated that the fault is yours. You understand that you need to improve on many skills that you are not very good at or simply don't have. You are modest and realize that perfectionism is a trap and that it's normal to be sad on occasions. You are not afraid of criticism but take it in stride. You love yourself enough to understand you can become a better version of yourself with the help of others.

This is not easy. Many people have been raised in loveless families. The actions they witnessed while they were growing up can hardly be described as loving. You might be insecure about what you have to offer in a relationship. Let time pass. These changes will by no means occur overnight. It's a constant process, as everything important in life takes a while. But in the end, you'll learn one of the most precious skills to live happy: loving yourself.

Love Needs to Be Shown

You don't need to wait until you learn to fully love yourself to show your love to others. Actually, while you're at it, you can also try to show your love for other people. This will boost your self-confidence. How so?

It's simple: you'll be happy showing your love, and people will be happy because you showed them love. Doing nice things for others can even be therapeutically. When you're doing good things for others, you're not focusing too much on yourself but on what other people need. When you see your action fill a need, you are rewarded with the happiness that comes from giving of your time and effort. You help people and they, in turn, are thankful.

You might be a little afraid to take the first step, but taking that first step will be a test of self-confidence. Don't be too afraid. Just do it. You never know how your actions might brighten someone's day. You never know how people can react to your good deeds.

So, what is involved in showing love? Many things, actually. Love moves you to act kindly with your parents and friends. It moves you to be patient with people who might have a problem with you. Love for yourself helps you avoid the trap of comparing yourself to others. Love for your partner makes you realize he also needs some space.

Loving your partner also means that you will have to refrain from behaviors that will make the relationship worse rather than improve it. Excessive jealousy is not allowed between loving partners. And love for yourself will make you understand that you can choose better if he ever decides to leave. Letting go of the past and past hurtful words are in themselves acts of love. You will not yell or scream at your partner just because you feel like you want to. Love will move you keep your emotions checked because it's healthy for you and the relationship.

Being happy for others' successes is also an act of love. You love your friends so much that you want them to be successful in whatever they do. You want to see them succeed and you know they want the same for you, too. Don't be happy about the mistakes of others or feel glad when others fail. Love doesn't behave that way. Vengeance is never mentioned because love doesn't wish bad upon others, not even if they did you wrong first.

In all, your relationship will be greatly benefited if you also go the extra mile in showing love. Always remember that when you're showing an act of love, you're also showing that you love yourself. You love yourself enough to know that you need and care about your partner. Your self-confidence will increase over time when you see how people react to your acts of love and your partner will be thankful, too. Seeing how they react to your love will make you happy, boost your self-confidence and motivate you to continue showing love. They might also begin showing love in return.

Don't be discouraged if your love is not reciprocated at first. And if other people's reactions are not what you expected, don't lose faith in them. We live in a loveless world and sometimes it is surprising, even suspicious to some when someone tries to show love to them. You need to continue on.

Taking Care of Yourself

A measure of love for ourselves will motivate us to take care of ourselves. Good habits are necessary for someone who really wants to become a better person. What can you do to take care of yourself?

Take Care of Your Health

You need to know that taking care of your body will go a long way. Eating nutritious food, exercising, and getting sufficient sleep will help you deal with stress and anxiety and it will help you deal with the stresses of a relationship. You will feel more refreshed and also you will your concentration will improve and even your mood might become easier to control.

Take Care of Your Mind

Be careful with what you allow your mind to dwell on. Don't allow bad memories sour the present. Learn to let go of the past by focusing on what you can do now. Be grateful for what you have: your friends, your job, your partner, and your talents. Strive to improve yourself daily and always try to give the best of yourself.

Develop Good Habits

Don't spend many hours in front of a TV or a smartphone. It's never too late to grab a book and learn more about what you like. Develop an interest in new skills like playing an instrument, relaxation, dancing and more. Call a friend or a relative. Try to reconnect with an old friend or get to know more people. If possible, don't continue working or concentrating on your job once your shift is finished. Don't get into much debt.

Take Care of Your Friends

Let's face it: life can sometimes be boring. Let friends help you have a good time. Show how much you care for them with your actions and words. Don't expect perfection from them. Keep in contact! You would be surprised to know how many friends are over just because they forget to keep in contact.

Don't Try to Change the Unchangeable

There'll be many things in life that will be impossible to change immediately. The place where you live, the family you were born into and your physical attributes. Rather than trying to change all of that, try to love and accept yourself. Remember, too, that certain circumstances might be very hard to change. Do you hate your job? You can always quit but you may realize how difficult is to find a new job. The decision is ultimately yours but, will you be ready to face uncertainty while you're trying to get a new job? Be grateful for what you have now and learn to appreciate it.

Learning to love yourself has no set time so be patient with yourself. It will pay great dividends. As your self-confidence increases, you'll be able to take on more adventures and risks and so you'll continue growing little by little. Don't give up, it's just the beginning.

Conclusion

Were you thrilled to see that you are not the only person dealing with the feeling of insecurity? "Why would that make anyone thrilled?" you might ask. Well, the answer is simple: you're not alone. Never feel like you have to walk this world all by yourself without someone to turn to. In this book, we have seen how you can make the best out of all the relationships that you have and how to avoid behaviors that might not help grow your relationships. Whether the person you turn to is a family member, a friend, or your partner, you'll be ready to leave your insecurities aside and be open to them.

Of course, being insecure in love has its challenges. Even your partner might not understand at times why you do certain things. But this doesn't mean that the obstacles are insurmountable. You can unlearn bad and harmful patterns of behavior and acquire new ones that will improve your relationship. Your partner will be very happy to see how much you changed. What is more, that change for the better shows how much you love yourself and him. Your love on display will certainly impress your partner.

You have seen how frank communication is necessary for a relationship to flourish and at the same time how you need to give your partner a measure of privacy. Find a balance between these two. Continue talking to your partner about your feelings, voice your opinions and thoughts. Don't forget that your partner also has a voice and so he will also convey his own ideas and opinions. When confronted with disagreements, treat him kindly and avoid assuming your partner has hidden motives. He understands that he also makes mistakes and is trying to improve like you are right now.

Learn to let go of the past. Focus on the present and on what lies ahead for the relationship. Realize that your partner is your greatest confidant. Cherish the moments you spend with him and you'll have a great treasure of memories to contemplate in the future.

Made in the USA
Monee, IL
10 December 2024

73222969R00272